IMAGES
of America

GREENVILLE

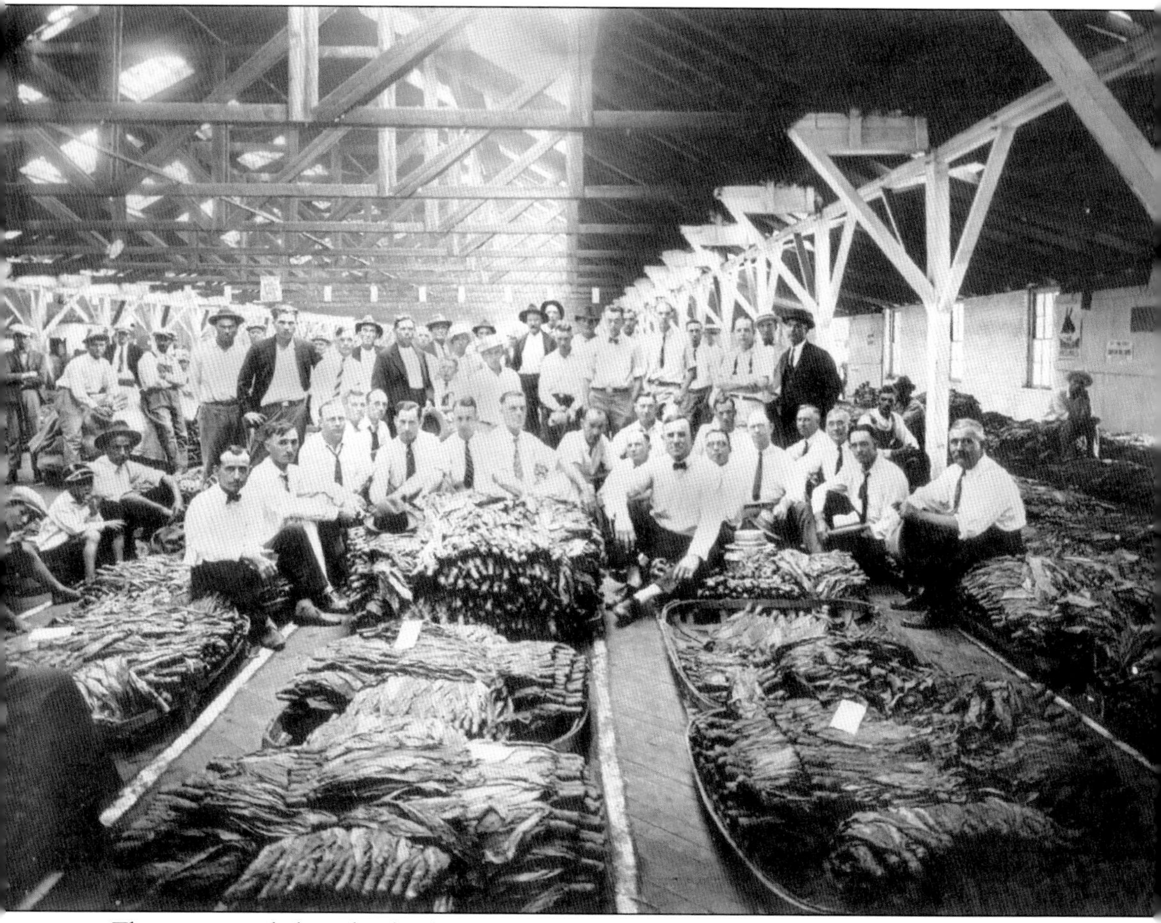

These men are believed to be the owners and buyers of the Smith & Sugg's Star Warehouse on October 26, 1931, at the largest sale of tobacco ever made at the time in the Greenville market. This is in contrast to the 1920 selling season when prices were less than half and averaged almost 21¢ per pound. Tobacco Town erupted in 1920 with 2,500 angry farmers arming themselves and ready to riot. Warehousemen were accused of conspiring with the buyers to steal tobacco, and the buyers were ordered to stop bidding for their own safety. Afterwards, there were numerous meetings and the tobacco growers devised ways of marketing their crops profitably. The price of tobacco remained low until after the Depression. (Courtesy of Charles Horne Collection.)

IMAGES
of America

GREENVILLE

Roger Kammerer and Candace Pearce

ARCADIA
PUBLISHING

ISBN 978-0-7385-1364-5

Published by Arcadia Publishing
Charleston, South Carolina

Printed in the United States of America

Library of Congress Catalog Card Number: 2001090010

For all general information contact Arcadia Publishing at:
Telephone 843-853-2070
Fax 843-853-0044
E-mail sales@arcadiapublishing.com
For customer service and orders:
Toll-Free 1-888-313-2665

Visit us on the Internet at www.arcadiapublishing.com

Contents

Acknowledgments		6
Introduction		7
1.	Olden Days	9
2.	Tar River Lore	25
3.	Churches and Schools	37
4.	Central Business District	51
5.	Tobacco Town	87
6.	People and Places	103

Acknowledgments

It is our pleasure to acknowledge with gratitude the many people without whom this book would not have been possible. For his support in facilitating the work on this volume, we thank Rick Smiley. He assisted with page layout and editing, offered computer expertise, and he and his wife, Jesse, graciously put up with us.

We remain indebted to the staff of J.Y. Joyner Library at East Carolina University, especially Martha Elmore and Mary Boccaccio of the East Carolina Manuscript Collection; Maury York, head of the Verona Joyner Langford North Carolina Collection; and Lynette Lundin of their photographic lab. Their knowledge and support was a tremendous help.

We thank Elizabeth Ross for her computer work and for letting us use pictures from her vast archive of local photographs. We also thank Stephen Masengill, head of the Photographic Division of North Carolina Archives for use of many rare photos of Greenville, including the steamboat collection of the late Fred Mallison. A number of individuals helped us tremendously in getting many rare and hard-to-find images, and we give special thanks to Lonnie Norcott, John F. Moye, and Alex Albright. We also extend our appreciation to Mrs. Dot Horne for letting us use the collection of old photos of Greenville owned by her late husband, Charles Horne.

We can't thank those people enough who let us delve into their family photos to pull a few choice ones. We would like to thank Jimmy Moye, Dr. John L. Wooten, Mrs. C.A. (Sarah Adams) White Jr., Mrs. Mattie Moye King Bridgers, Mrs. Louise Duncan, Julian Vainright, Mrs. Laura Bruce Hadley Nichols, Amos Evans, Goldis Starling Reel, Jimmy and Bonnie Evans, Ralph Heidenreich, Cecil and Libby Tarner, George Saad, and Dr. Charles Pace.

Though we wish we could have included more, we hope that these photographs will bring pleasure to you and your children, and that this volume will bring back many a pleasant thought of "our little town."

Our greatest reward has been getting to know all of you.

—Roger Kammerer and Candace Pearce

INTRODUCTION

Greenville, once called the "Queen City on the Tar," owes its expansive growth to the railroad, tobacco, and education. The founder of what was to become Greenville could hardly have envisioned what would become of the 100 acres he laid off into a fledgling village. The city of Greenville can trace its beginnings back to the creation of Pitt County in 1760 from neighboring Beaufort County. Because there was no county seat, Col. John Hardee, a leading citizen in the area, gave his home as the new county courthouse. The house, once located three miles east of Greenville in the country, is now within the city limits. This courthouse also served as a church and muster ground around which the small community known as "Log Town" developed.

By 1771, a Pitt County legislator by the name of Richard Evans decided to divide off his plantation in order to properly form the town. He chose a bluff on the south side of the Tar River, three miles west of Log Town. This town was named Martinsborough in honor of then-Royal Governor Josiah Martin and was the forerunner of present-day Greenville. Richard Evans died soon after and his widow, Susannah Evans, continued with the town. The newly chartered town was laid off into 100 half-acre lots by seven appointed commissioners authorized to sell the parcels by public auction. In 1774, the original charter was amended and Martinsborough became the county seat of Pitt County.

Martinsborough remained a very small river village until after the Revolution. On January 8, 1787, by act of the North Carolina General Assembly, Martinsborough became "Greensville" in honor of Gen. Nathanael Greene, Revolutionary War hero. This same act of assembly also chartered the Pitt Academy. The creation of this academy was the beginning of Greenville's long interest in education, and a history filled with numerous schools and academies under the auspices of many noted North Carolina educators. "Greensville," which later became simply Greenville, remained a small courthouse village with several stores and wharves.

During his Southern tour in 1791, President George Washington came through the area and noted in his diary that Greenville was an "indifferent place" of about 15 families and had a large tar and turpentine market. Greenville continued to grow very slowly but had numerous prominent citizens and even a jockey club.

In the 1830s a bridge was built over the Tar River, making way for steamboats and creating new prosperity. A number of factories established themselves in Greenville, manufacturing such products as carriages, cotton gins, and silk. The town began to fade in the 1840s when many of its prominent citizens left North Carolina during the mass exodus to the newly opened Southern and Western territories.

The Civil War overshadowed the town of Greenville. Its location on the Tar River made it a no man's land between Confederate and Union; the town was overrun in various skirmishes. Greenville boasted having several Confederate hospitals during the War under the control of the female citizens, since all the men were off fighting elsewhere. Reconstruction brought a carpetbagger type of government to both Pitt County and Greenville politics. Numerous killings and riots on the city streets only added misery to the poverty brought on by the war.

It wasn't until the late 1870s that Greenville began to come alive again. The town started to expand, new businesses flourished, and by 1890, with the coming of the train, Greenville opened up to the world. Soon after, tobacco reigned supreme as the cash crop and Greenville developed as the largest tobacco market in Eastern North Carolina. Greenville expanded its borders, built larger homes and businesses, and attracted new industry; its prosperity lasted many years. In 1907, the North Carolina Legislature established East Carolina Teachers Training School, now East Carolina University. With its opening in 1909, Greenville became the educational center of Eastern North Carolina. Greenville's beauty as a city was well-known for a long time as evidenced in 1919, when a newspaper in Atlanta, Georgia voted Greenville one of the most beautiful towns in the South.

Prosperous times soon gave way to the devastation of the Great Depression. Money was tight, businesses closed, and houses were neglected. It wasn't until the 1950s that Greenville Urban renewal plans of the 1960s tried to create a renaissance in Greenville and demolished many of Greenville's old buildings in hope of stimulating new development. Unfortunately, while many neglected buildings were razed, much of Greenville's past fell to the wrecking ball. Neighborhoods of beautiful homes were torn down for parking lots, and tree-lined streets were removed to enlarge them.

Greenville now boasts a population of over 50,000 and continues to grow, stretching out several miles from the old city center. The original downtown is in the midst of redevelopment again. Different historical and architectural groups are trying to save the heritage of Greenville's great past for future generations.

Photo Credits

ECMC—East Carolina Manuscript Collection, Special Collections, J.Y. Joyner Library, East Carolina University, Greenville, North Carolina.

UNC-Chapel Hill—North Carolina Collection, University of North Carolina at Chapel Hill.

Alex Albright—These photographs are from an original 35-millimeter film by John Warner. Reprints from the film are by Patrick Keough.

One

OLDEN DAYS

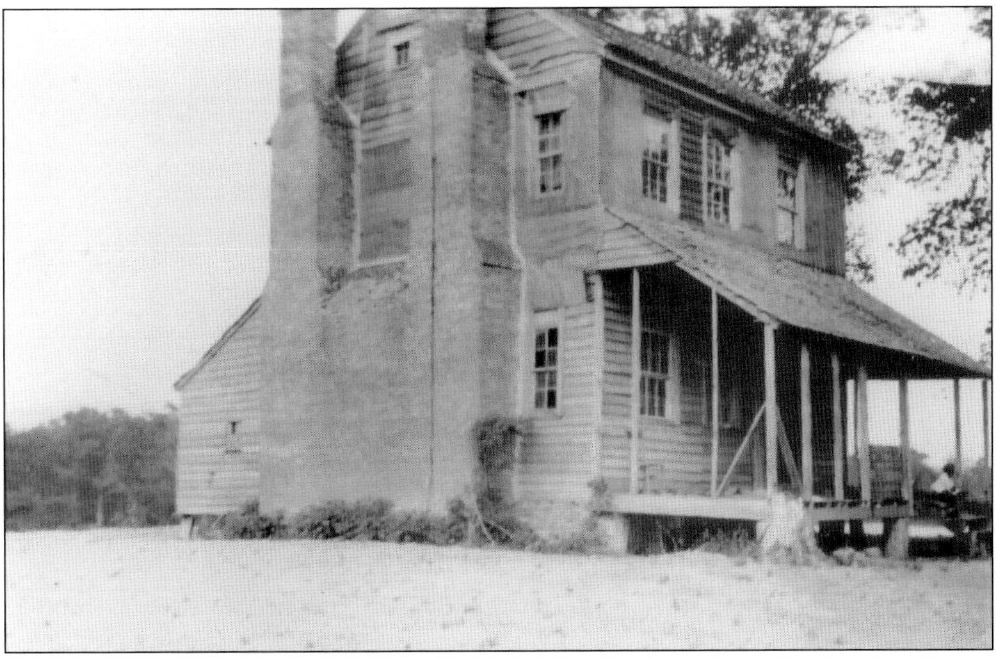

This house, pictured *c.* 1920, was owned by Col. John Hardee and was the first Pitt County Courthouse in 1760. Located on Highway 33 East across from the entrance to Brook Valley subdivision, it was used as a church and muster site in the community known as "Log Town." It was later used as a tenant house and school. The house was demolished in 1926; the sight is designated by a stone marker. (Courtesy of ECMC.)

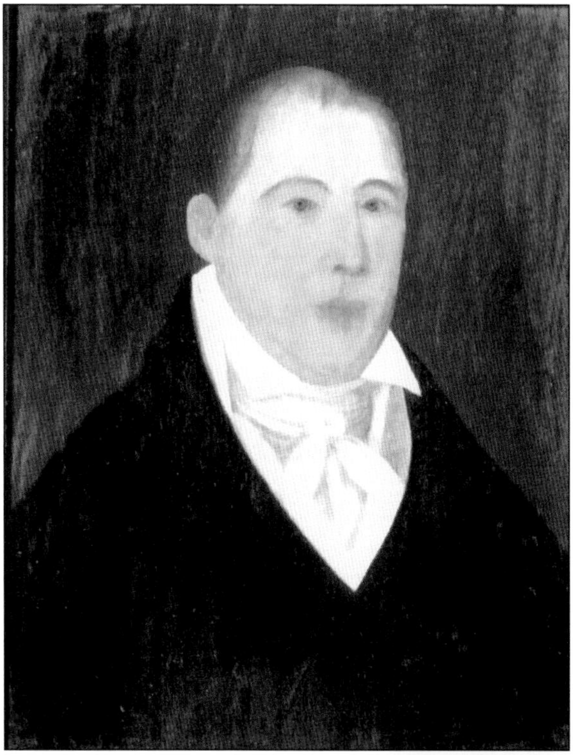

David Smith Jr. (died *c.* 1818), son of David Smith and Jemima Hardee, was an early Greenville resident. He married Elizabeth Smith in 1809. According to family legend, David Smith Jr. was killed when thrown from a horse. (Courtesy of Goldis Starling Reel.)

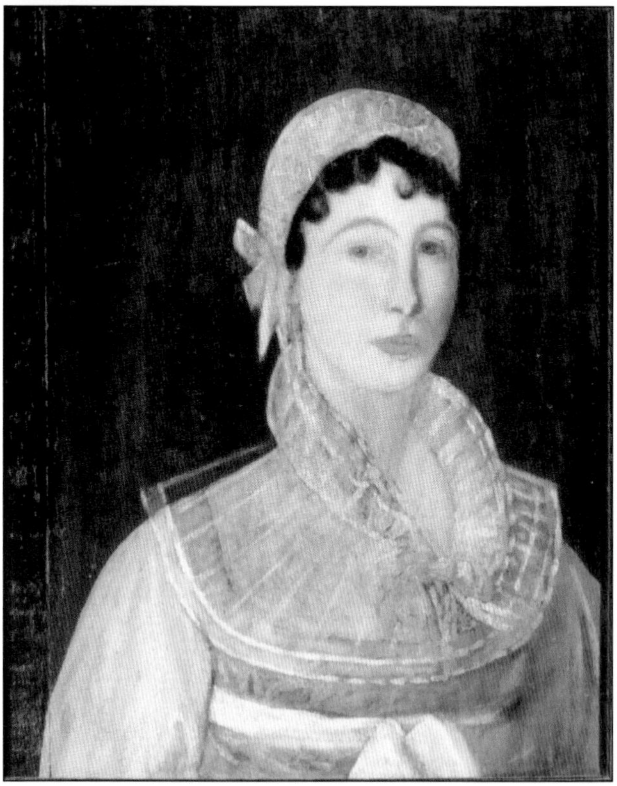

Mrs. Elizabeth (Smith) Smith, wife of David Smith Jr., was the daughter of Oliver Smith and Nancy Sheppard. She married James L. Mooring after her husband's death, c. 1818. These images were possibly wedding portraits done by a traveling artist. (Courtesy of Goldis Starling Reel.)

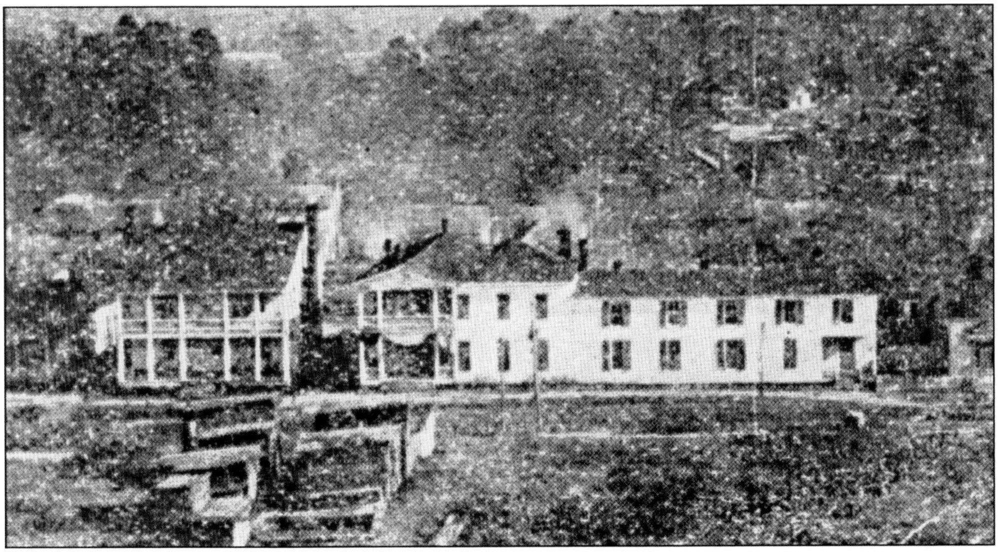

The Macon House Hotel, located on Cotanche Street between Second and Third Streets, was a landmark in Greenville for over 130 years and was the town's center of social and political life. Started about 1828 by Richard Evans, it changed hands many times and was called Clark's Hotel, Hoyt's Hotel, Union Hotel, and Hotel Macon. It was torn down in the redevelopment of the early 1960s. (Courtesy of North Carolina Archives.)

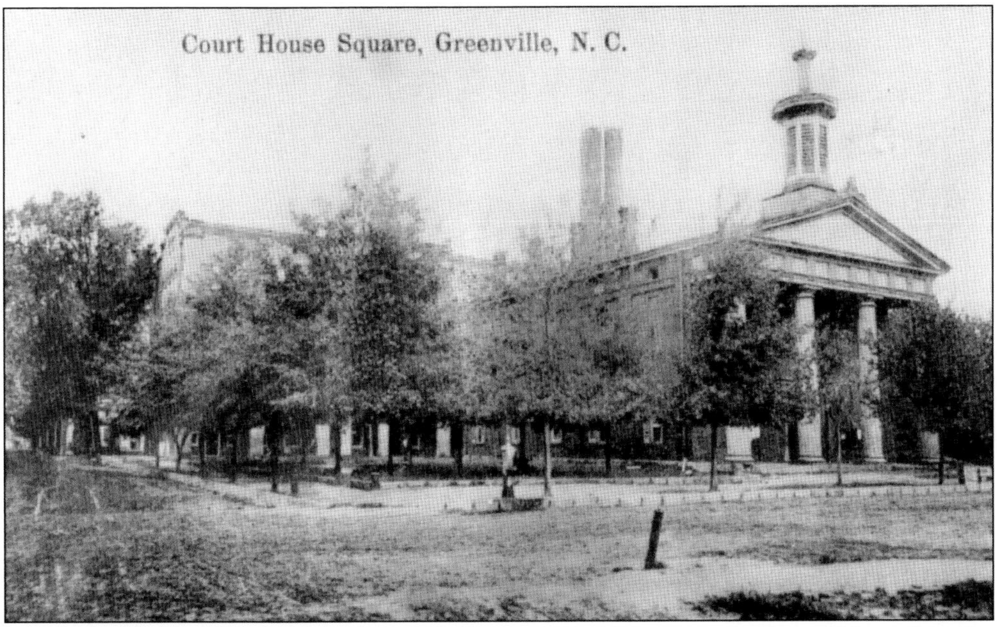

The old Pitt County Courthouse, then facing Evans Street, was started in 1860 and finally finished in 1877. On court days, witnesses and jurors stayed outside the courthouse until called to duty from a window by the bailiff. In 1901, government surveyors put a tablet on the side of the building showing that Greenville was 68 feet above sea level. This courthouse burned in the fire of 1910. (Courtesy of ECMC.)

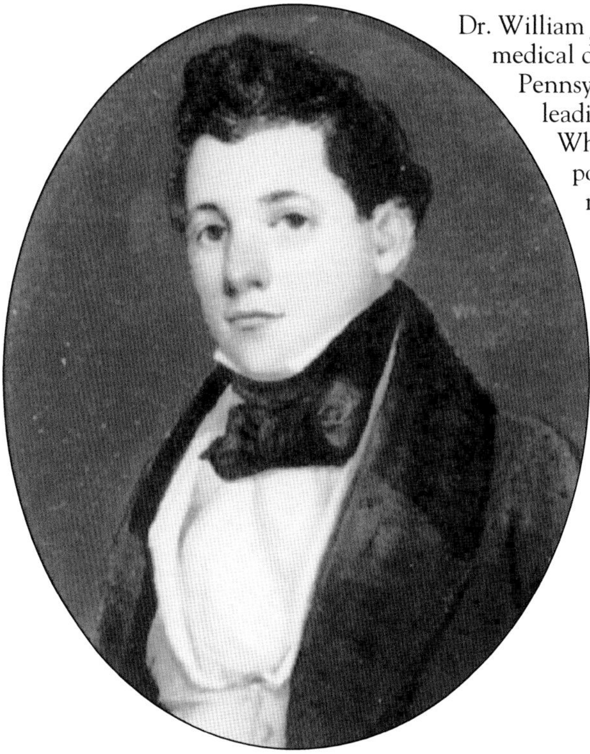

Dr. William James Blow (1818–1864) received his medical degree in 1840 from the University of Pennsylvania. He was said to have been the leading doctor in Greenville. An ardent Whig, he became embroiled in the political movements of the day which resulted in several duels. He was a Pitt County legislator and director of the State Insane Asylum. His wife, Dorcas S. Masters Blow, worked in the Confederate hospital in Greenville in 1862. (Courtesy of Mary Dorcas Carey.)

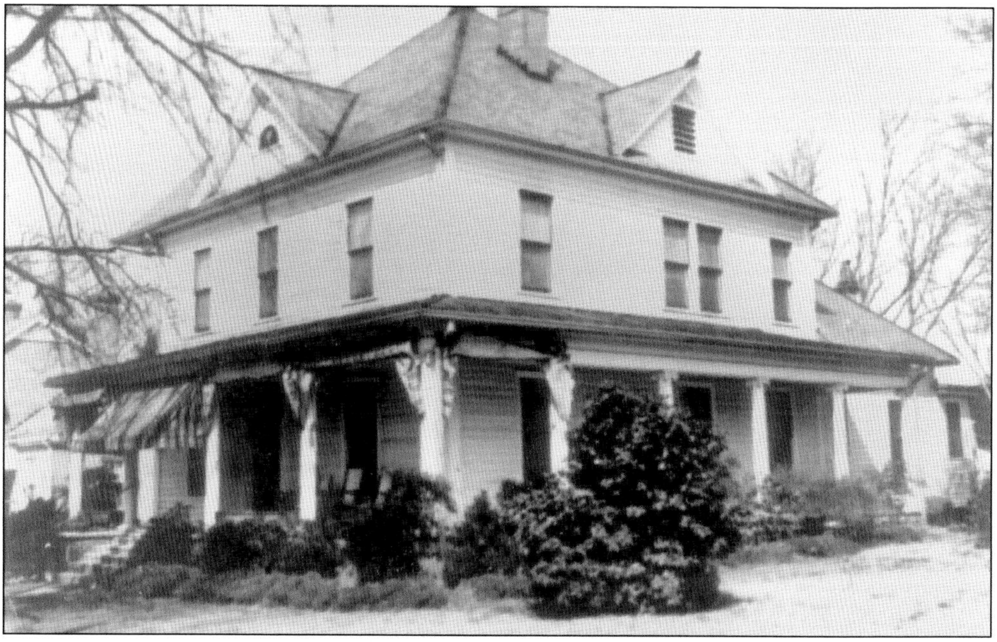

The Yellowley-Harrington House at 415 East Fourth Street, as it appeared in 1961, was the home of Col. Edward C. Yellowley, lawyer and victor in an infamous 1847 duel with Henry F. Harris. In Yellowley's day, the house sat on 180 acres, was a "story and a jump," and faced Third Street. The house was bought and renovated by the Harrington family before burning about 1977. (Courtesy of North Carolina Archives.)

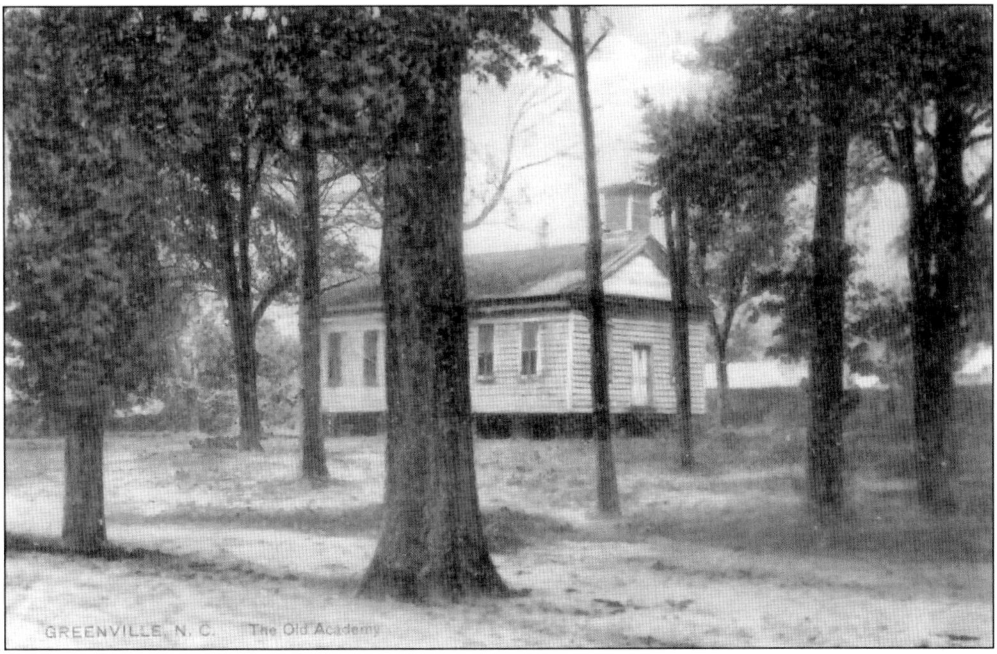

The Greenville Male Academy on Evans Street was built in 1849 on what is now the site of Sheppard Memorial Library and what was then the extreme southern edge of Greenville. Many noted teachers served as instructors here under the tutelage of Professor W.H. Ragsdale from 1891 to 1903. It was described as the "best school for boys the county had ever had." It was moved in August 1903 to the ravine on Fifth Street and used for storage. (Courtesy of ECMC.)

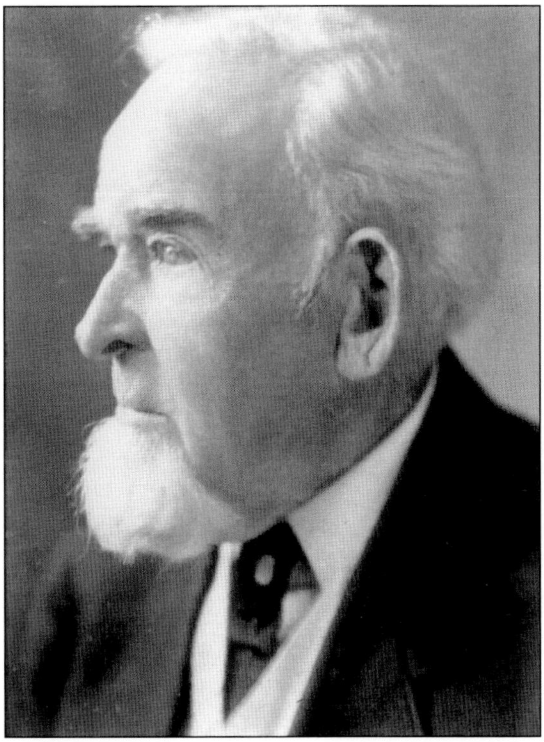

Thomas Crowder Davis (1830–1915), a native of New Bern, North Carolina, was the son of James Davis and Mary Mershon. He came to Greenville as a child and later moved to Wilson, North Carolina, where he was a merchant, clerk of Wilson County court, and postmaster. His "Recollections of Greenville in My Boyhood," published in the *Eastern Reflector* in 1901, gives the most detailed history found of the people and places in Greenville in the 1830s and 1840s. (Courtesy of Virginia Pou Doughton.)

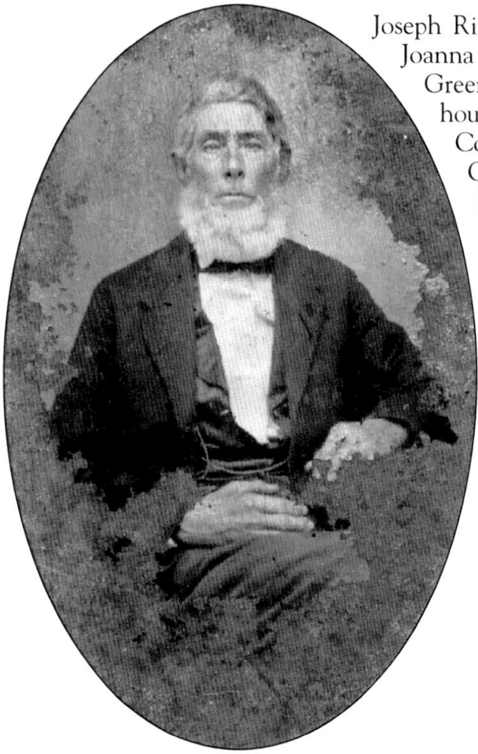

Joseph Ringgold (1804–1880) was the son of James and Joanna Ringgold. Joseph was a prominent planter near Greenville and was married three times. His large house and plantation sat on the hill where Minges Coliseum and Auditorium now sits on the East Carolina University campus. (Courtesy of Ross-Kammerer Photo Archive.)

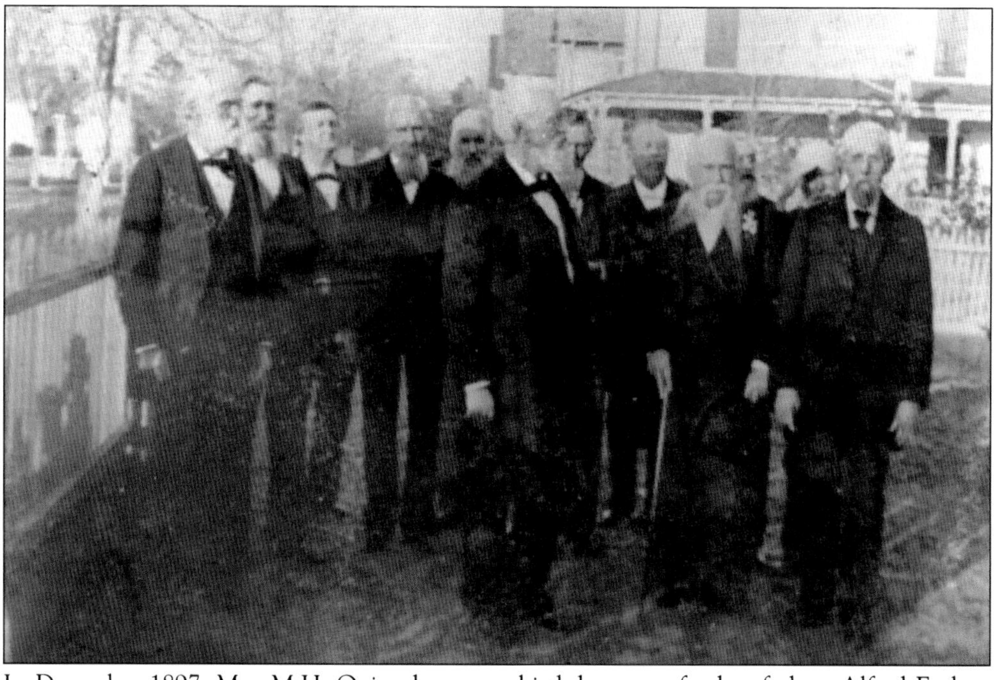

In December 1897, Mrs. M.H. Quinerly gave a birthday party for her father, Alfred Forbes, inviting only his friends over 65. This group includes Dr. C.J. O'Hagan, W.M.B. Brown. Capt. C.A. White, D.B. Evans, John Flanagan, J.B. Johnson, S.B. Wilson, J.J. Perkins, Allen Warren, H.A. Sutton, and B.C. Pearce. (Courtesy of ECMC.)

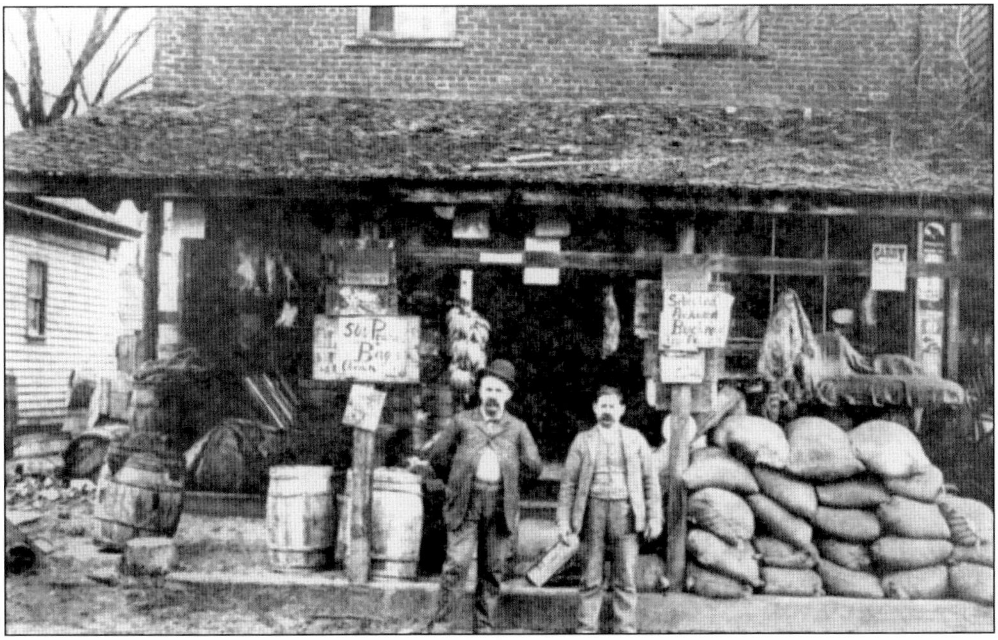

Samuel Shultz (right) and Tom Christman (left) stand in front of the Old Brick Store on Evans Street. Built in 1855 by George E.B. Singletary, it was the first brick store in Greenville. In the Civil War, it served as quarters for Confederate soldiers. In 1875, Samuel M. Shultz began a 20-year stay in the store and made it a famous landmark. It was purchased by the Greenville Banking and Trust Company and was remodeled in 1913 with a handsome classical-revival facade. (Courtesy of *The Bicentennial Book: A Greenville Album*.)

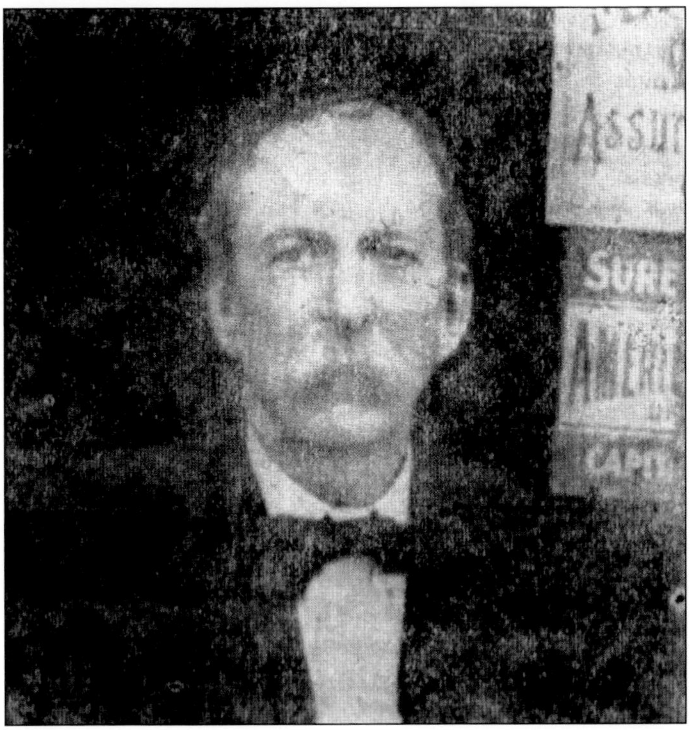

The first man in Pitt County to enlist in the Confederate Army during the Civil War was Charles D. Rountree (1841–1920). He was the son of Charles Rountree and Mary Rogers. "Justice Rountree," as he was known all over Pitt County, was a justice of the peace, a Mason, and a member and deacon of Memorial Baptist Church. He was one of the earliest farmers in the county to cultivate tobacco and one of the builders of the Star Warehouse. (Courtesy of Roger Kammerer.)

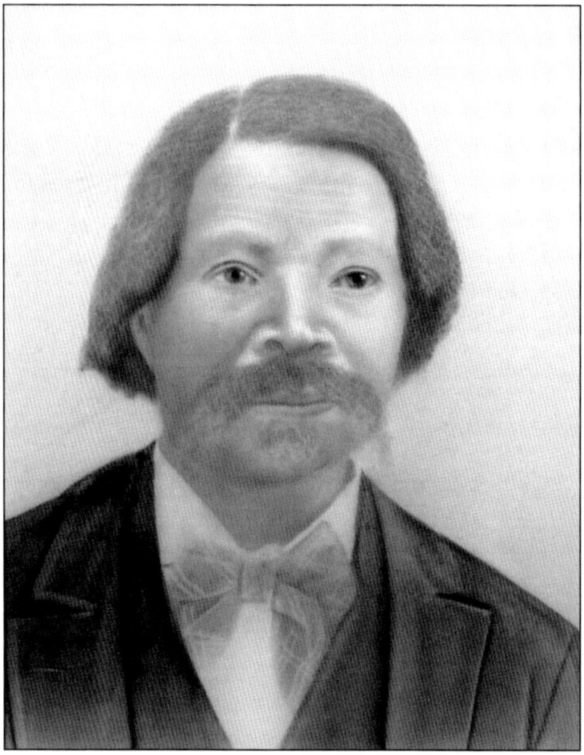

Wiley Peyton Norcott Sr., born in 1833, served as a county tax assessor and justice of the peace during the harsh years of Reconstruction in Greenville. He lived on Pitt Street and was a manager of a store in 1900. (Courtesy of Lonnie Norcott.)

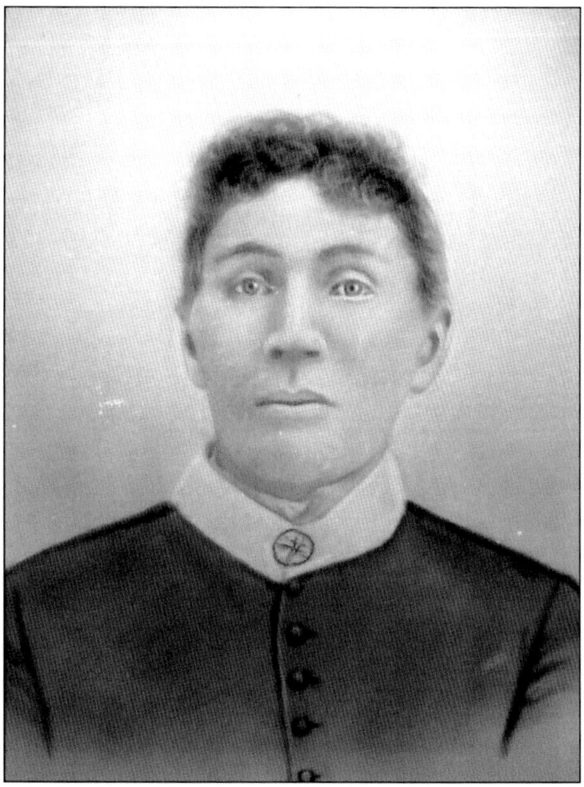

Olivia Brickell was the wife of Wiley Peyton Norcott. She was born in 1834 and had 15 children. (Courtesy of Lonnie Norcott.)

This is the only known image of the Whichard Schoolhouse, located at the corner of Pitt and Third Streets. The school was operated after the Civil War by Violetta H. Jordan Whichard (1835–1911), wife of David F. Whichard. The building was later used as a music school and a place to register voters. It is said the building was moved and became a wing of the Kennedy-Wooten house on West Third Street. (Courtesy of King's Sketches.)

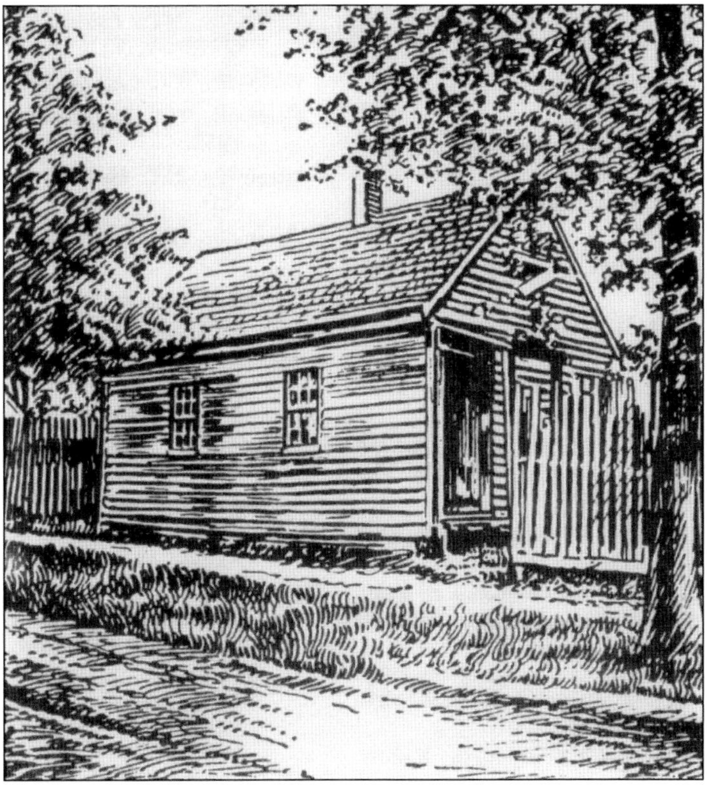

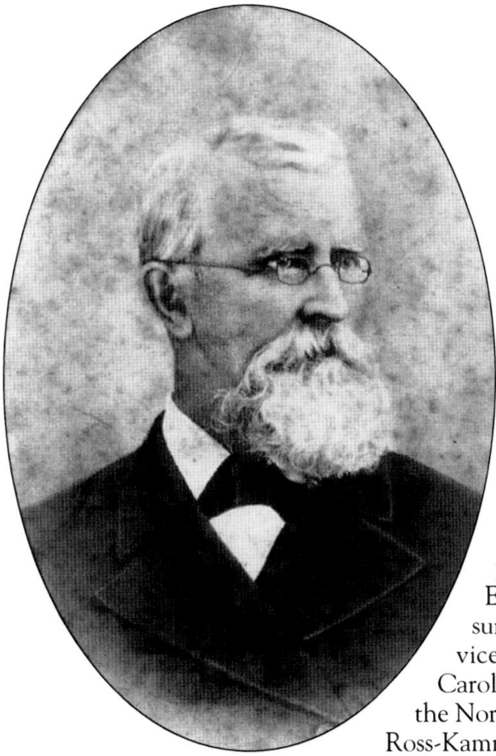

Dr. Charles J. O'Hagan (1821–1900) was born in Londonberry, Ireland, and came to Greenville as a teacher at the Greenville Academy. He then took up medicine, graduating from the Medical College of New York University, and returned to Greenville to practice. He gained a huge reputation across the Eastern United States. In 1862, he enlisted as a surgeon in the Confederacy. In his career, he was vice president of the AMA, president of the North Carolina Medical Society, and for years a member of the North Carolina State Board of Health. (Courtesy of Ross-Kammerer Photo Archive.)

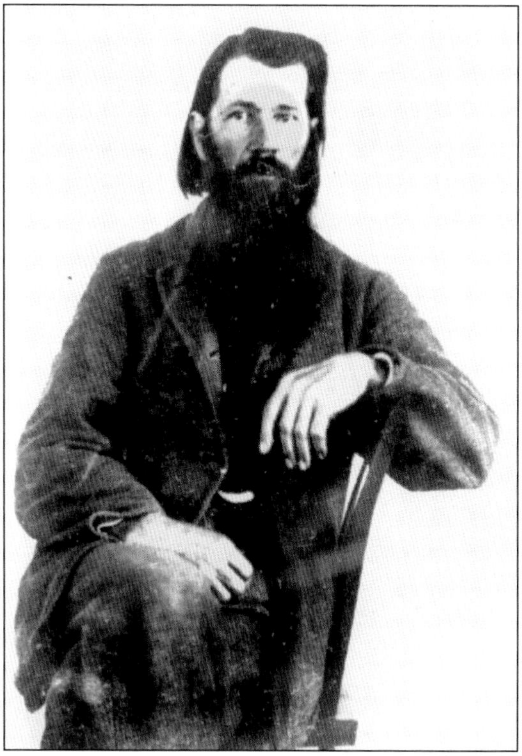

Oliver Perry Humber (1813–1891), a native of Goochland County, Virginia, came to Greenville in 1847 as a coach maker. He left Greenville several times before returning permanently in 1880. Married three times, he was an inventor, a mechanic, and a licensed preacher of the Methodist Episcopal Church. He had a foundry and machine shop beside his home on Fifth Street. (Courtesy of North Carolina Archives.)

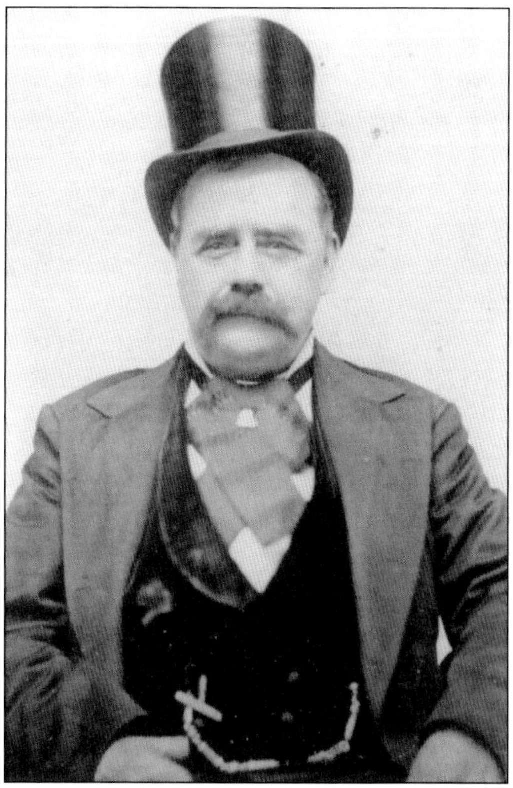

Dr. William Augustus Bernard (1827–1875) was the son of William Bernard and Ann Nobles. He was a popular doctor who married twice and later committed suicide. His second wife, Mary A.B. Smith Bernard (1831–1918), worked in the Confederate hospital in Greenville in 1862. (Courtesy of ECMC.)

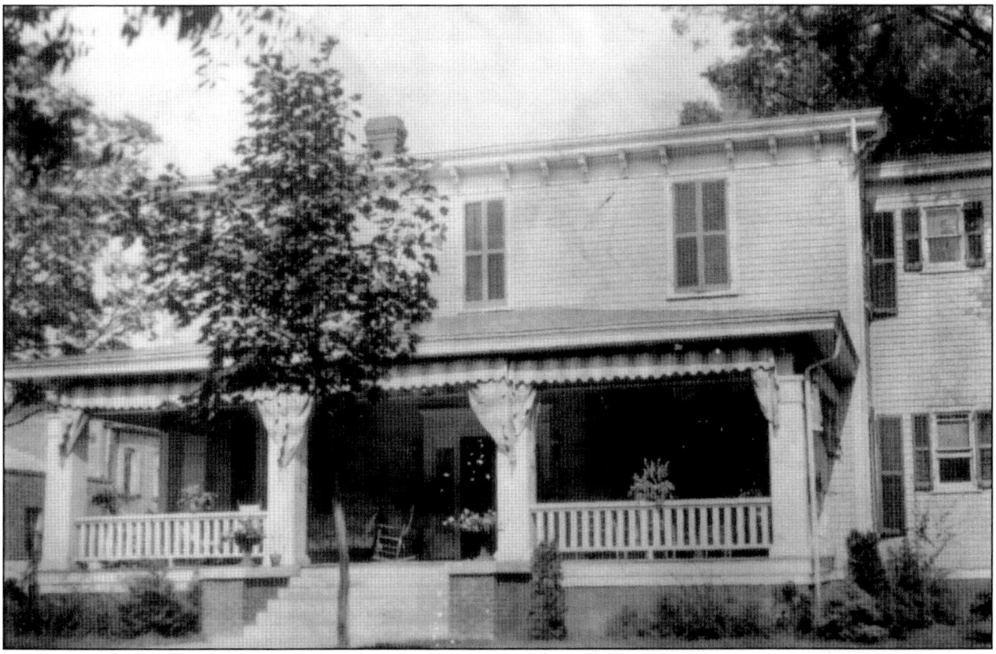

This house was built about 1870 on Evans Street by Alfred Forbes, one of Greenville's most prominent businessmen and landowners. Alfred Forbes (1829–1905) owned and developed property from Five Points to Tenth Street, which became known as "Forbestown." In 1904, a tree limb fell and crushed the porch. A new porch was added in 1918. The date when the house was demolished is unknown. (Courtesy of Jimmy Moye.)

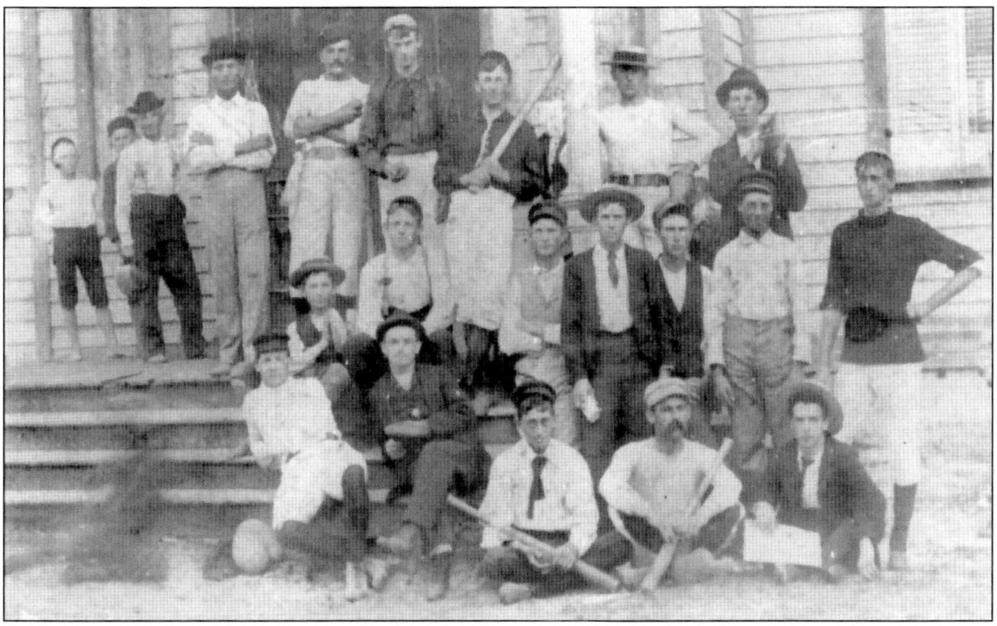

This photograph of the Greenville Baseball Team, c. 1895, is believed to have been taken on the porch of the old Greenville Academy. In 1885, the Greenville Baseball Team purchased its first uniforms consisting of garnet pants with light blue trimmings, light blue shirts with garnet shields and trimmings, and red and white caps. (Courtesy of North Carolina Archives.)

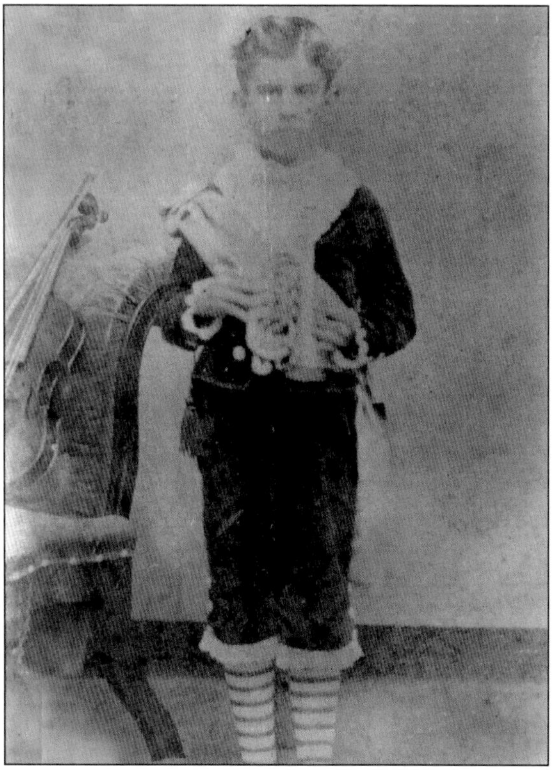

Osceola "Ola" Forbes (1868–1908) was a tobacconist, fertilizer salesman, bank clerk, Greenville mayor, and fireman. He was a prodigy on both the violin and the cornet. By age nine—his approximate age in this image—he was the leader of the Osceola Band, which was ranked among the best in the state. (Courtesy of Roger Kammerer.)

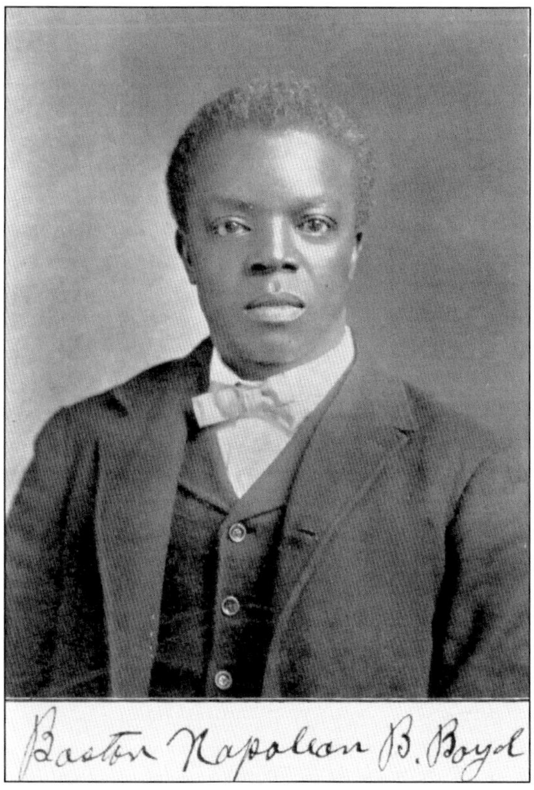

Boston Napoleon Bonaparte Boyd (1860–1932) was a native of Greenville who worked as a paper hanger, sign painter, and interior decorator. He served as a town councilman and superintendent of the black portion of Cherry Hill Cemetery, and he was the author of three religious books. Byrd was a large landowner who painted all his houses green. (Courtesy of Verona Joyner Langford North Carolina Collection, East Carolina University.)

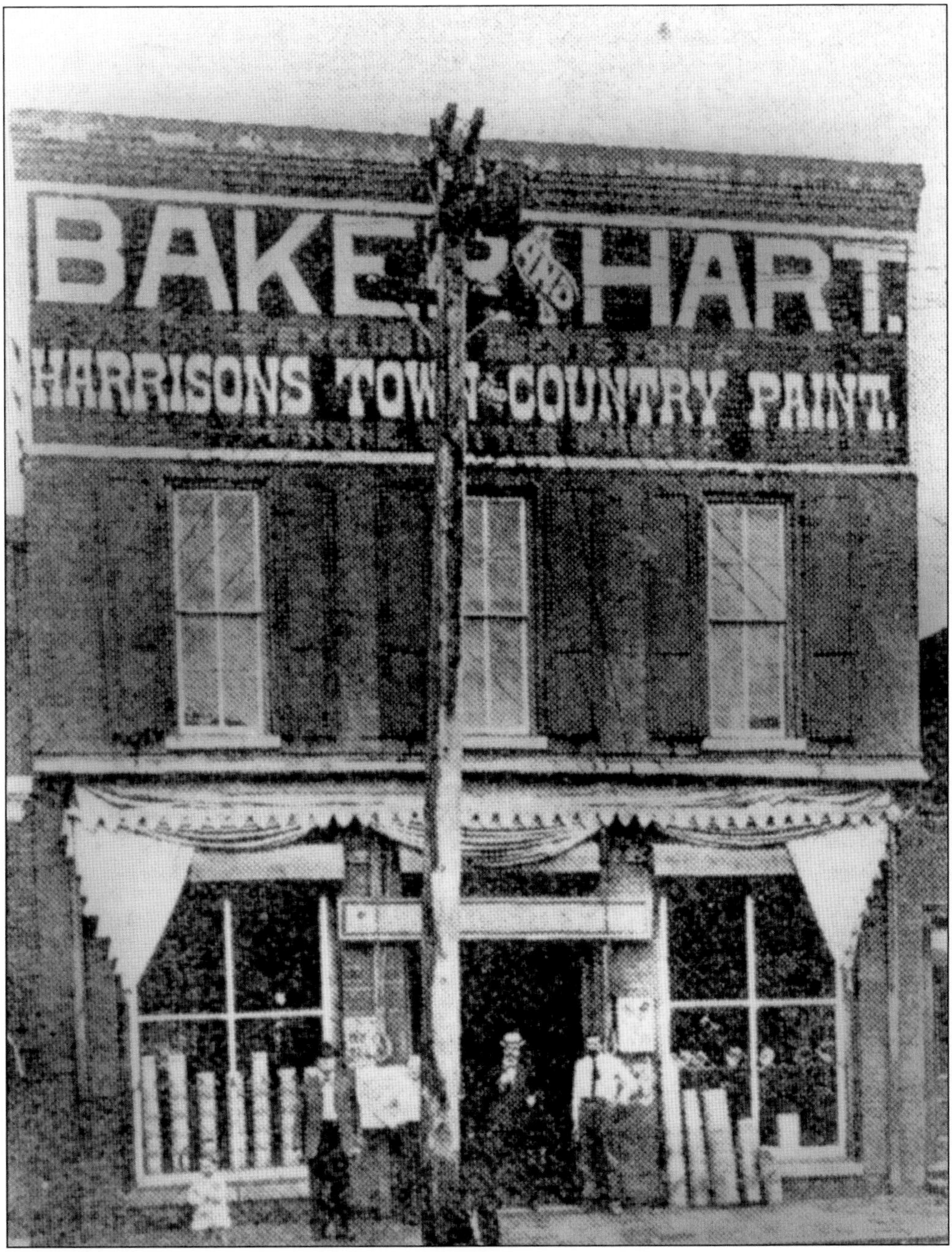

J.H. Hart and G.W. Baker were two young merchants who came to Greenville from Lewiston, North Carolina in 1896. Their first store burned the very next night after they opened, and they built a new store on Evans Street in just 12 days! They sold a large line of hardware, paints, and farming implements. In 1902, Baker and Hart moved into the the store pictured above, which was the old Alfred Forbes store built in 1880. They leased the second story to T.H. Bateman, who operated a tin shop. In 1905, they installed the first electric flashing sign in Greenville. In 1910, Baker died and Hart went into business with G.B.W. Hadley. After several ownership changes, the business became Globe Hardware in 1947. (Courtesy of NC Archives.)

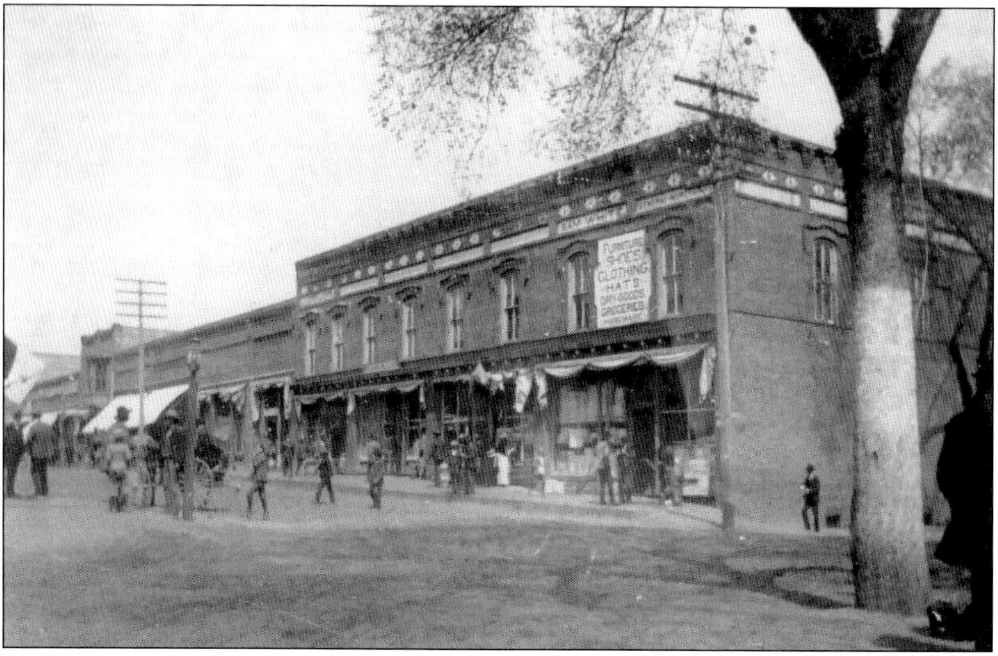

The Charles A. White Store, located at Five Points, was built in 1885 on the northeast corner of Fifth and Evans Streets. He installed in his store the first elevator in Greenville. Captain White sold the business to his son Samuel T. White in 1895. The building later became the Lautares Candy Palace and then, in 1938, Kares Restaurant. (Courtesy of ECMC.)

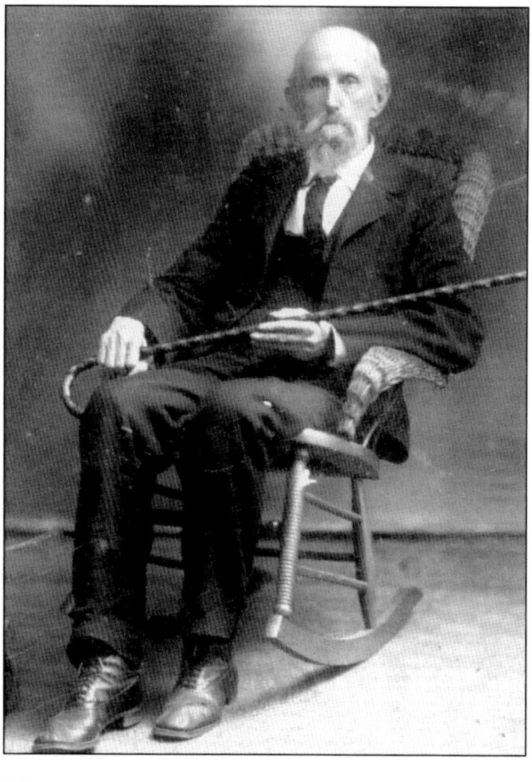

Capt. Charles A. White (1833–1914) was a Confederate veteran and a leading merchant. He moved to Greenville in about 1880 and opened a general merchandise and furniture store. He was a town councilman and an officer of the Tar River Transportation Company. (Courtesy of Mrs. C.A. (Sarah Adams) White Jr.)

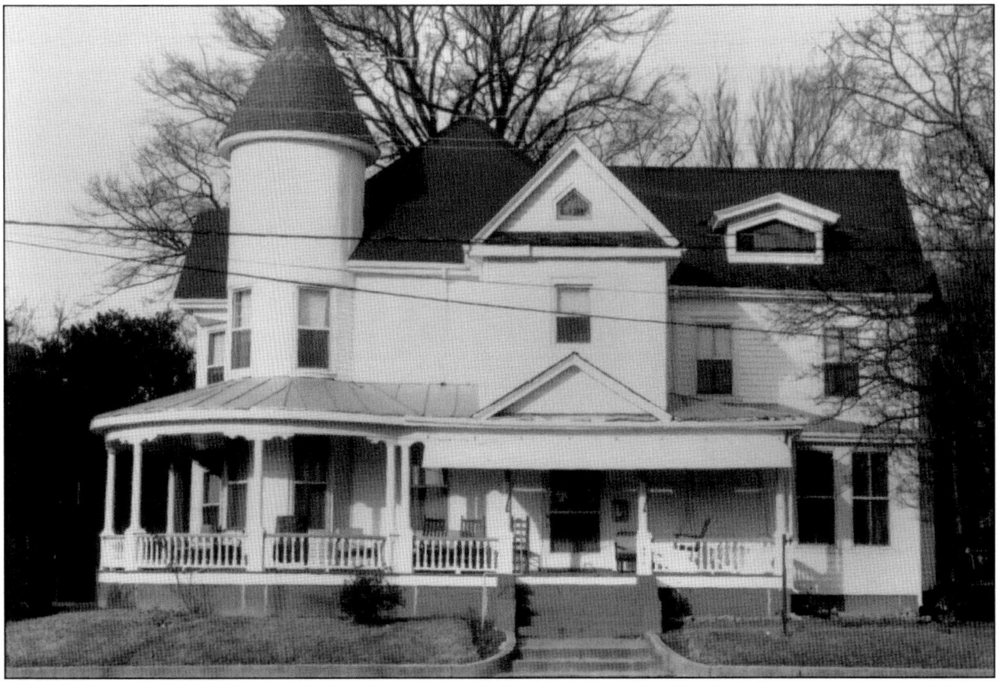

The O'Hagan-Laughinghouse House on Pitt Street was built in the mid-1850s for Dr. Charles J. O'Hagan (1821–1900). It was moved from Fifth Street to face Pitt Street before 1900. In 1903, the house was renovated into the 17-room Queen Anne style familiar to Greenville. In 1965, it became the Flynn Christian Fellowship Home. The house tragically burned on January 6, 1996. (Courtesy of North Carolina Archives.)

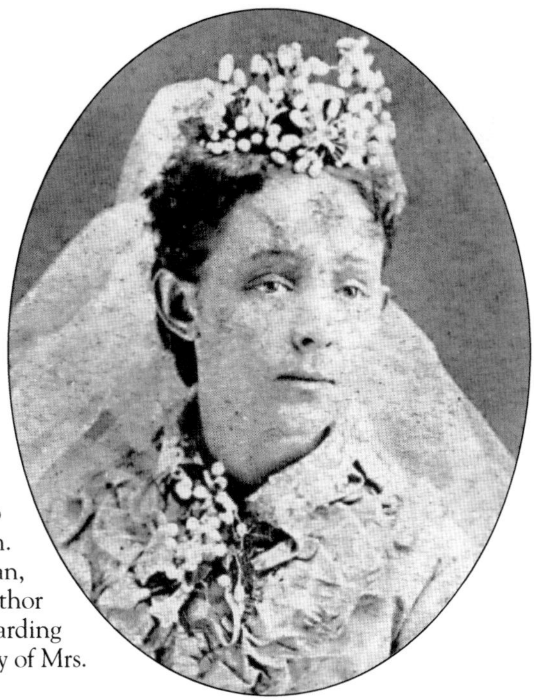

Ada Pearce Cherry (1855–1934) was the second wife of James Burton Cherry, a Greenville merchant. She was a well-known singer across the state. In 1872, she joined the Methodist Church where no service was too menial for her to perform. She rang the bell, made fires, played the organ, sang, and led the choir. She was the author of several published hymns and kept a boarding house at her home on Fifth Street. (Courtesy of Mrs. C.A. (Sarah Adams) White Jr.)

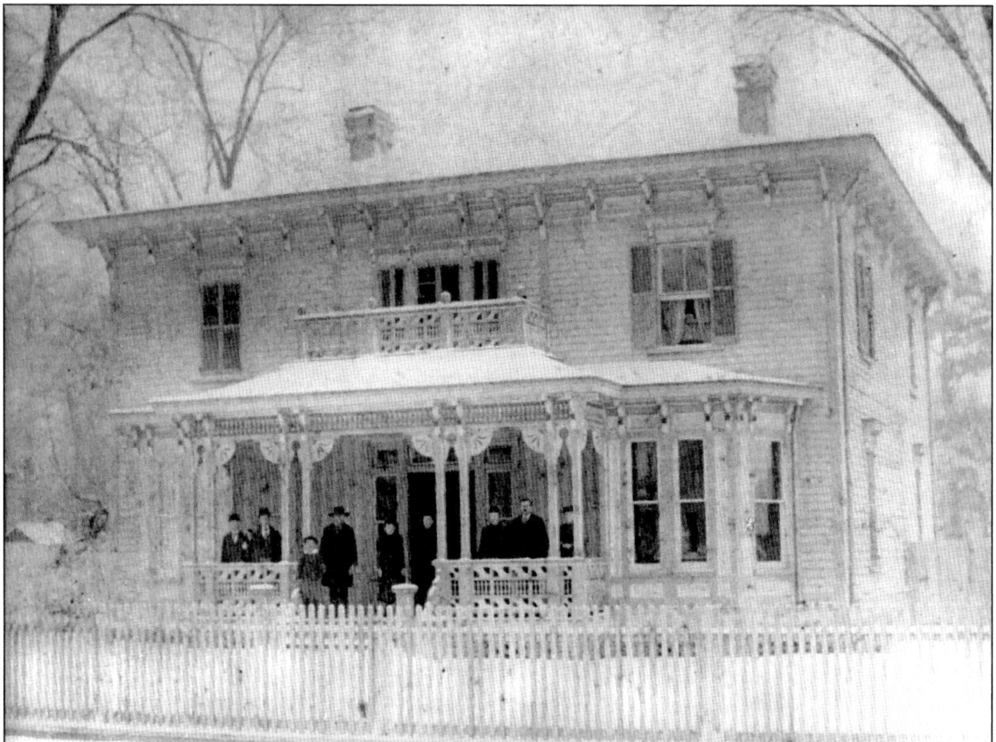

Built about 1880, the beautiful Capt. Charles A. White house was located on Dickinson Avenue and was later moved in 1925 to Seventh Street. In 1908, Captain White enclosed the front yard with a handsome iron fence. The house was demolished about 1969. (Courtesy of Mrs. C.A. [Sarah Adams] White Jr.)

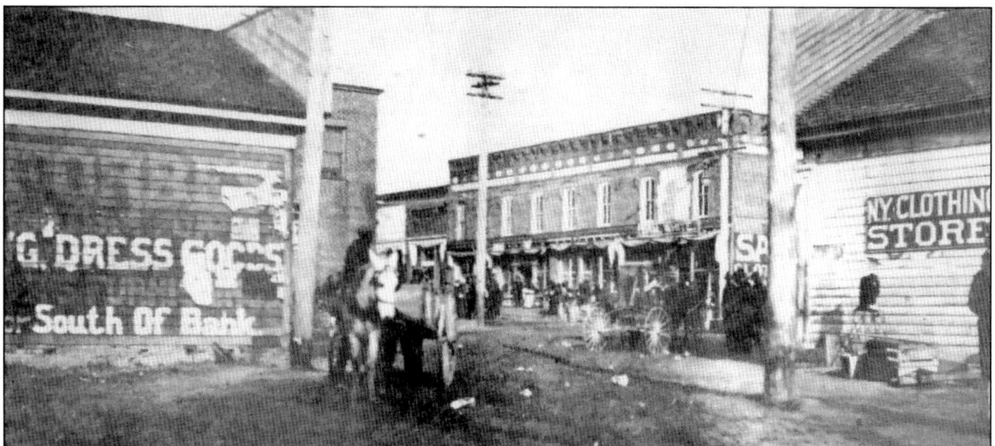

This is an early view of Five Points taken from Dickinson Avenue about 1906. In the center is Capt. C.A. White's store and on the right is C.T. Munford's old store. In 1903, D.C. James put up new street signs. He misspelled "Dickinson" Avenue as "Dickerson" Avenue, which led to much confusion on local maps for years. These streets were covered in mud until Evans Street and Dickinson Avenue were paved with brick in 1908. (Courtesy *The Bicentennial Book, A Greenville Album*.)

Two

Tar River Lore

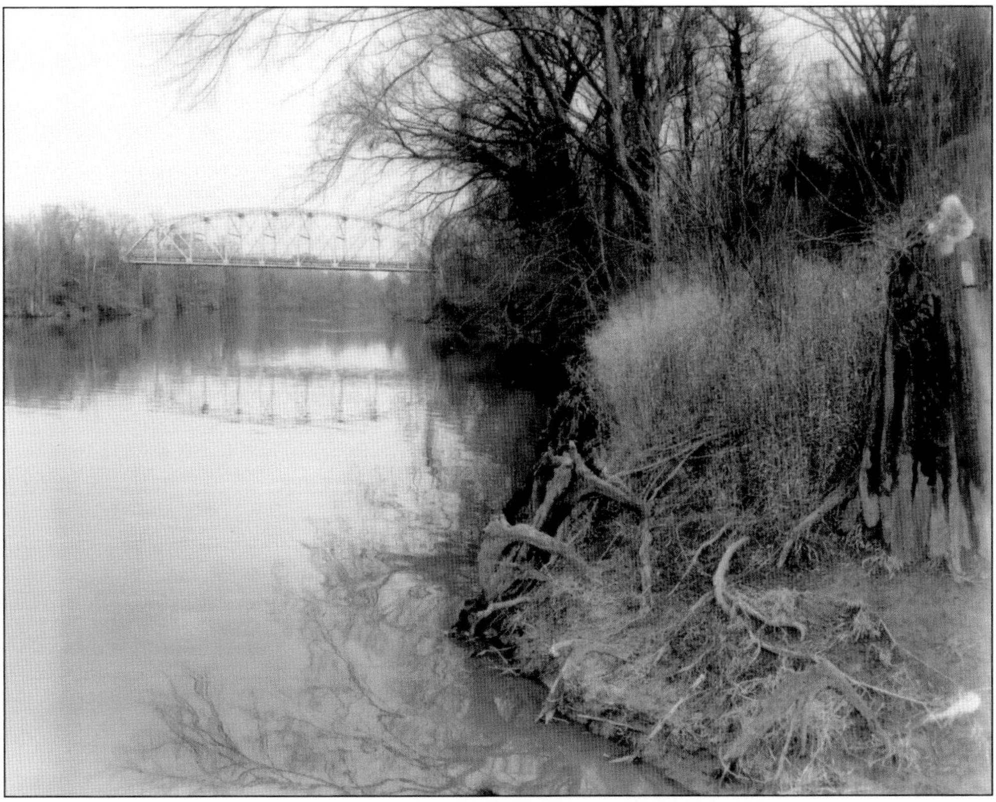

The Tar River, nicknamed the "Turpentine Run" and once Pitt County's greatest highway, winds its way from Roxboro to the Pamlico Sound. The river's story is filled with countless tales of Civil War battles, steamboats, floods, river locks, fishing, snakes, and ghosts. This river helped shape the development of a great portion of Eastern North Carolina. (Courtesy of ECMC.)

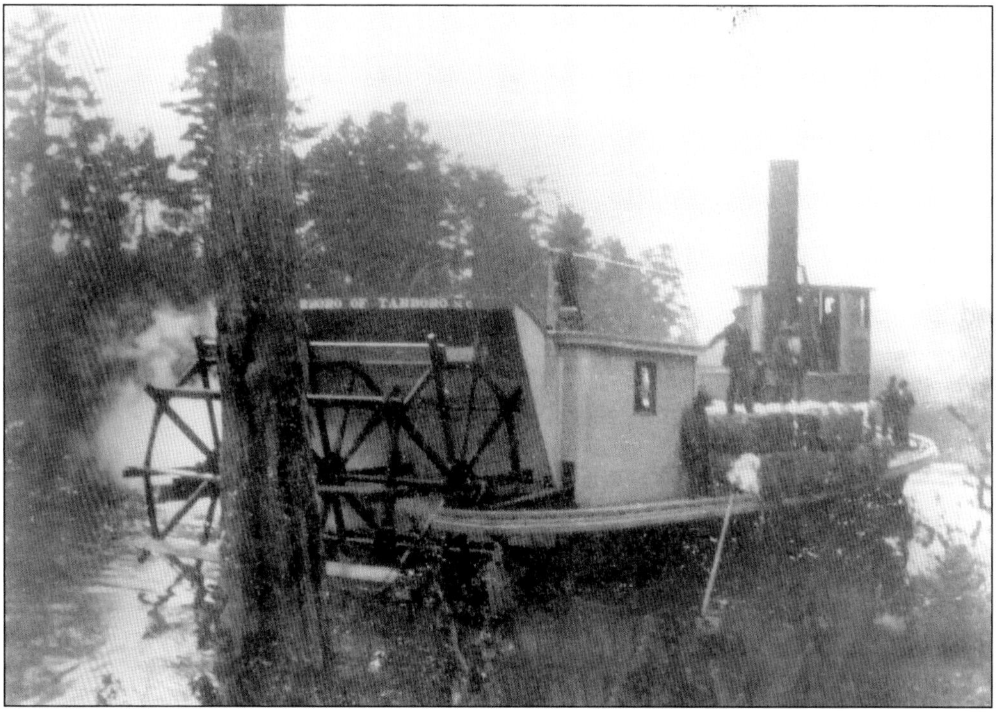

The steamboat *Tarboro*, shown here taking cotton down the Tar River about 1885, was built by A.W. Styron and launched in Washington, North Carolina on October 8, 1880. It was proclaimed to be "the lightest draft hull afloat." Even with its machinery and ballast, the boat drew only 8 inches of water! It was later sold to businessmen in Swansboro, North Carolina to run on the White Oak River. (Courtesy of North Carolina Archives.)

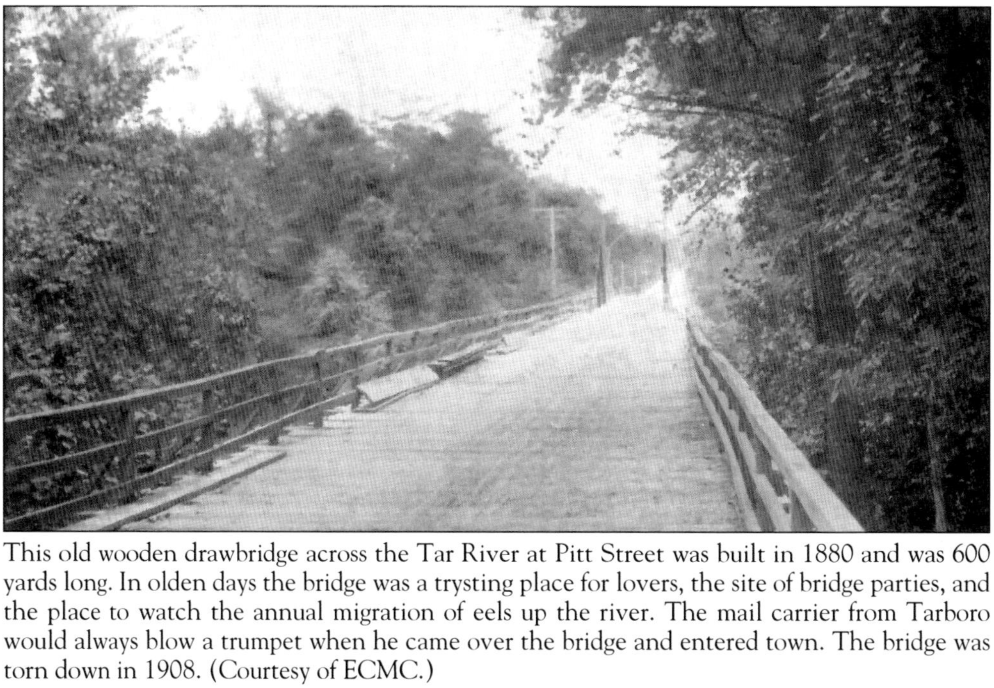

This old wooden drawbridge across the Tar River at Pitt Street was built in 1880 and was 600 yards long. In olden days the bridge was a trysting place for lovers, the site of bridge parties, and the place to watch the annual migration of eels up the river. The mail carrier from Tarboro would always blow a trumpet when he came over the bridge and entered town. The bridge was torn down in 1908. (Courtesy of ECMC.)

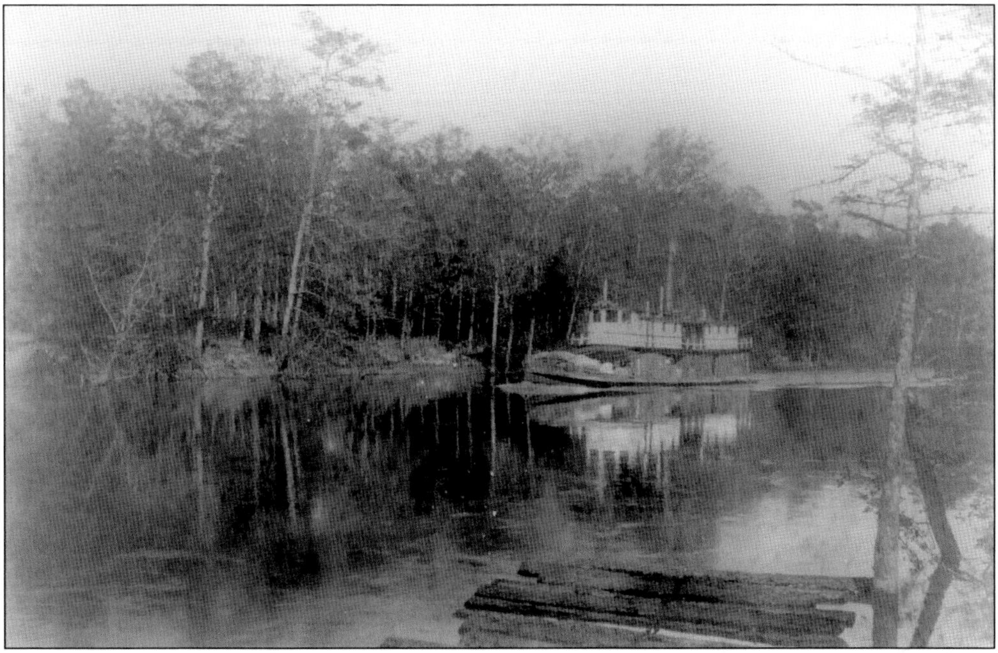

This bucolic view shows the steamboat *Greenville* loaded with goods coming up the Tar River. It is said that "river callers" or "hollers" would stand on the riverbank and call out "boats a-coming" so others could run down to see if a job could be had unloading the boat. (Courtesy of North Carolina Archives.)

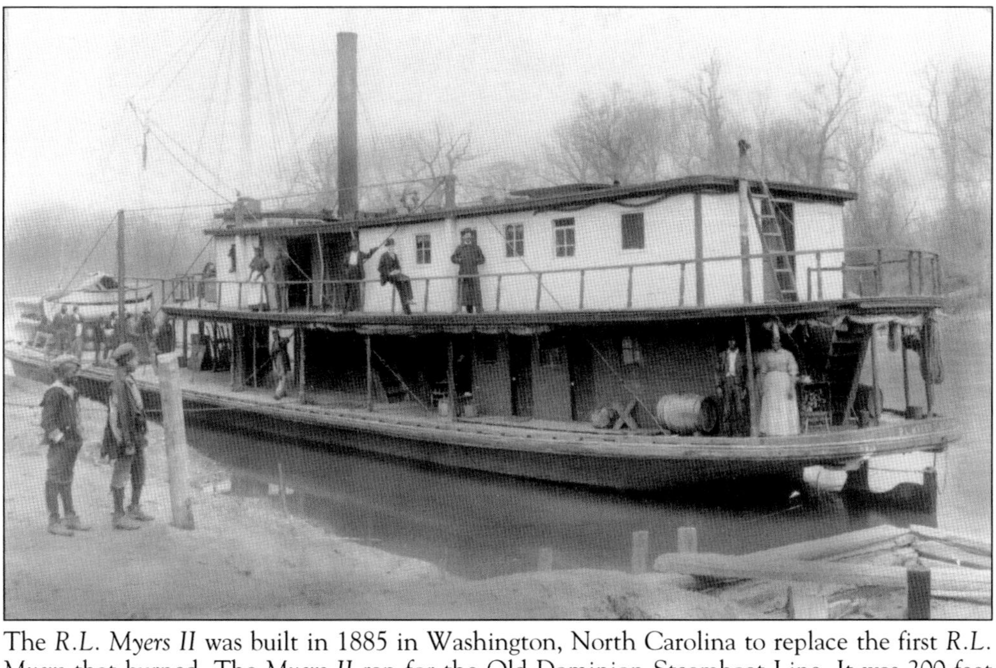

The *R.L. Myers II* was built in 1885 in Washington, North Carolina to replace the first *R.L. Myers* that burned. The *Myers II* ran for the Old Dominion Steamboat Line. It was 200 feet long and had 3 small saloons, a "Main," a "Ladies," and a "Colored." The *Myers II* was sold to the Norfolk & Southern Railroad in 1905. It ended its service on the Tar River in 1907 and was dismantled in 1908. (Courtesy of North Carolina Archives.)

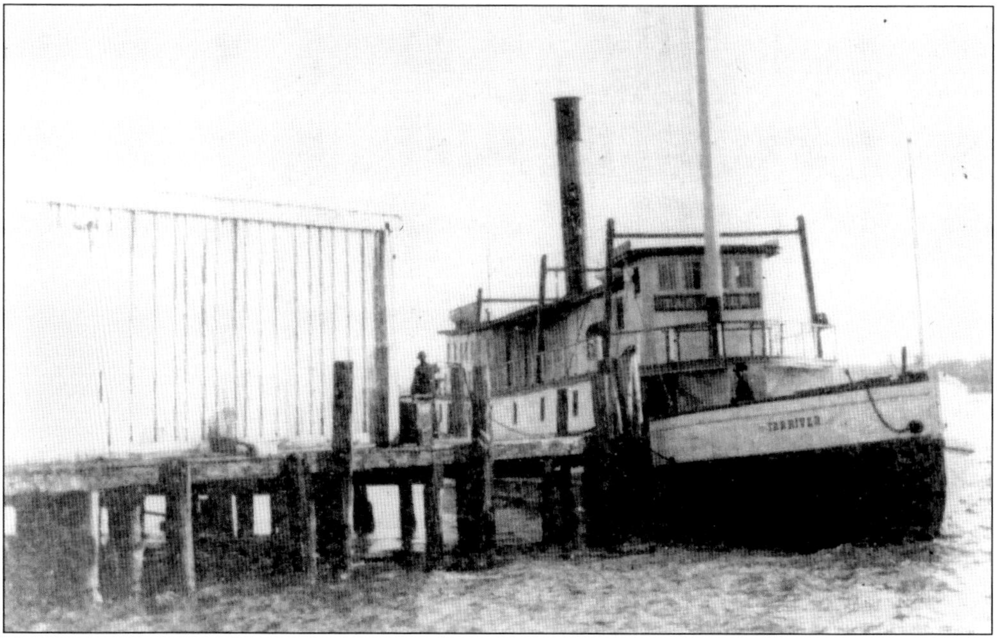

The steamboat *Tar River* was built in 1886 in Washington, North Carolina by the Old Dominion Steamboat Company to carry freight and passengers. Commanded by Capt. William A. Parvin, the *Tar River* was lighter and longer than the *R.L. Myers II* and was turned into a railroad barge in 1905. (Courtesy of North Carolina Archives.)

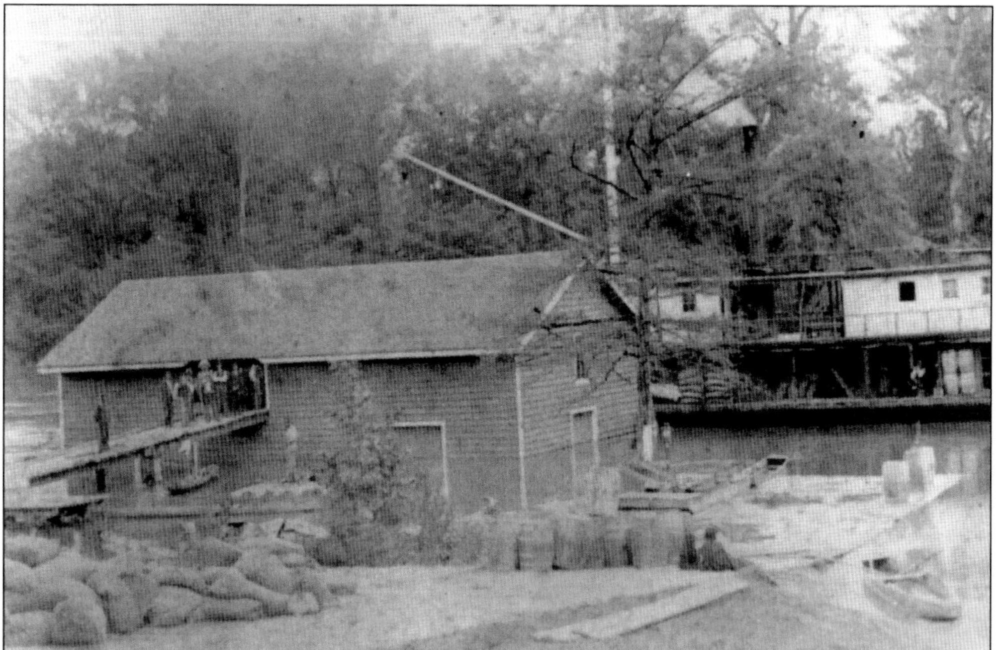

The *R.L. Myers II* sits at the Old Dominion Steamboat Company warehouse and wharf at Greenville during a flood. This two-story warehouse was built in 1892 to let the water run through the first floor, while still doing business on the second floor. In 1902, a flood even covered the second floor. (Courtesy of North Carolina Archives.)

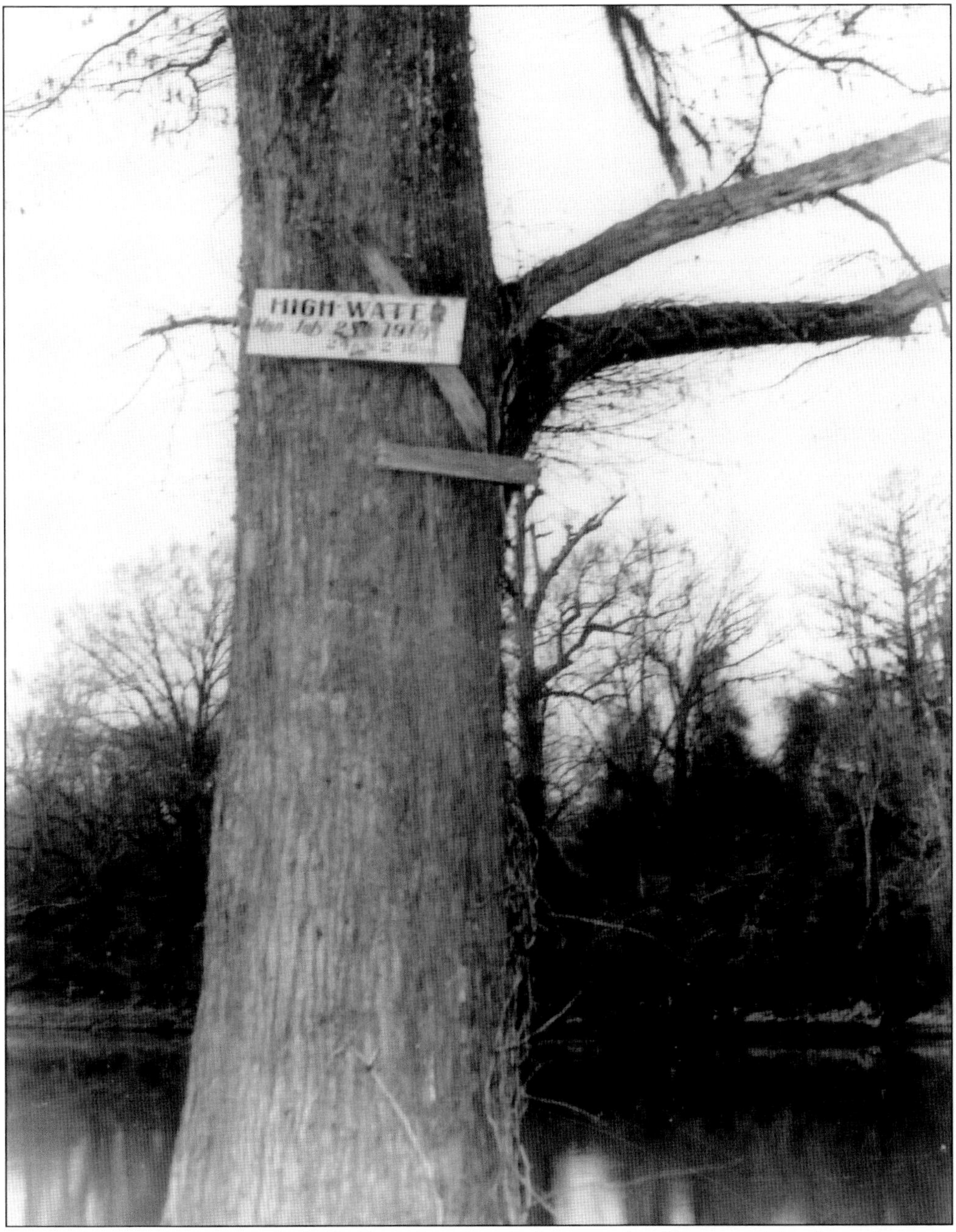

Located near what was called "Gallows Landing," this was the "Hanging Tree" on the river below First Street between Cotanche and Reade Streets. The 1919 high water mark of the Tar River is posted on this cypress, which stood on the riverbank. This tree, and an adjoining "twin," bore silent witness to the last public hanging in Greenville in 1899. The scaffold for the execution was placed between them. The spectacle was witnessed by a large crowd, including children. An older Greenville resident remembers the hanging from her childhood and recalled that the criminal's body was taken down from the scaffold and her mother took her to it and had her kick the body. In 1857, an old woman convicted of murder and two others were hanged in Greenville while 5,000 spectators looked on. (Courtesy of ECMC.)

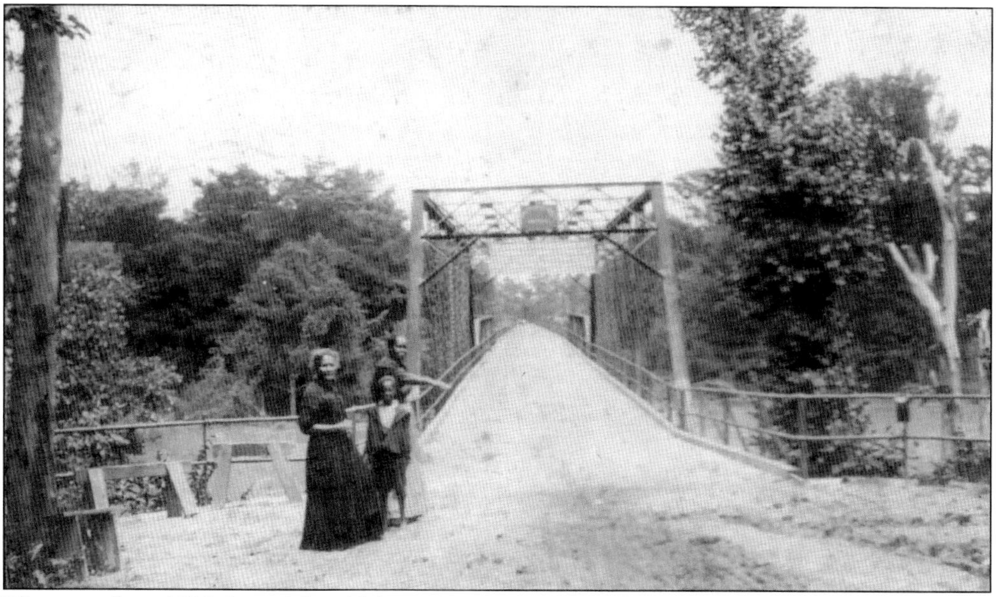

This view from 1923 shows Mrs. Alabama Norcott, Mrs. Sallie Norcott, and Marion C. Norcott standing in front of the old steel bridge on Pitt Street. William Norcott was keeper of the bridge in 1918. In the early 1900s, a Mrs. Lott had a black school on Pitt Street by the bridge. (Courtesy of Lonnie Norcott.)

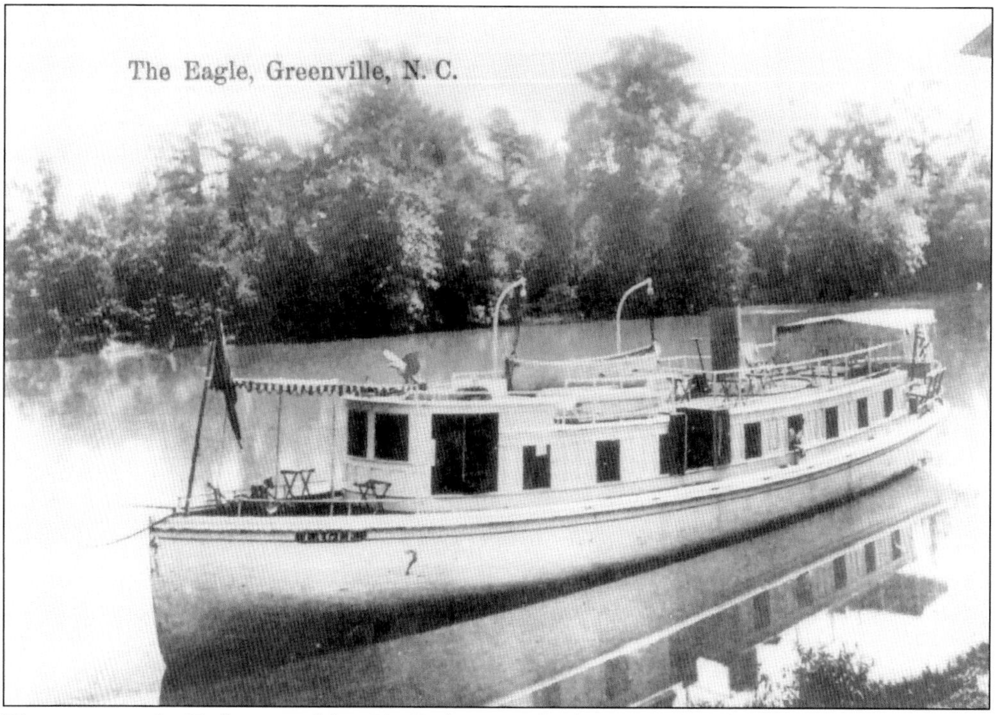

The steam yacht *Eagle*, owned by Ola Forbes, was built at Morehead City in 1907. It was 65 feet long and 13 1/2 feet wide. It was first used as a passenger boat from Norfolk, Virginia to the Jamestown Exposition in 1907. Forbes ran it as an excursion boat and sold it in 1909 to the U.S. government to be used in life-saving services. (Courtesy of North Carolina Archives.)

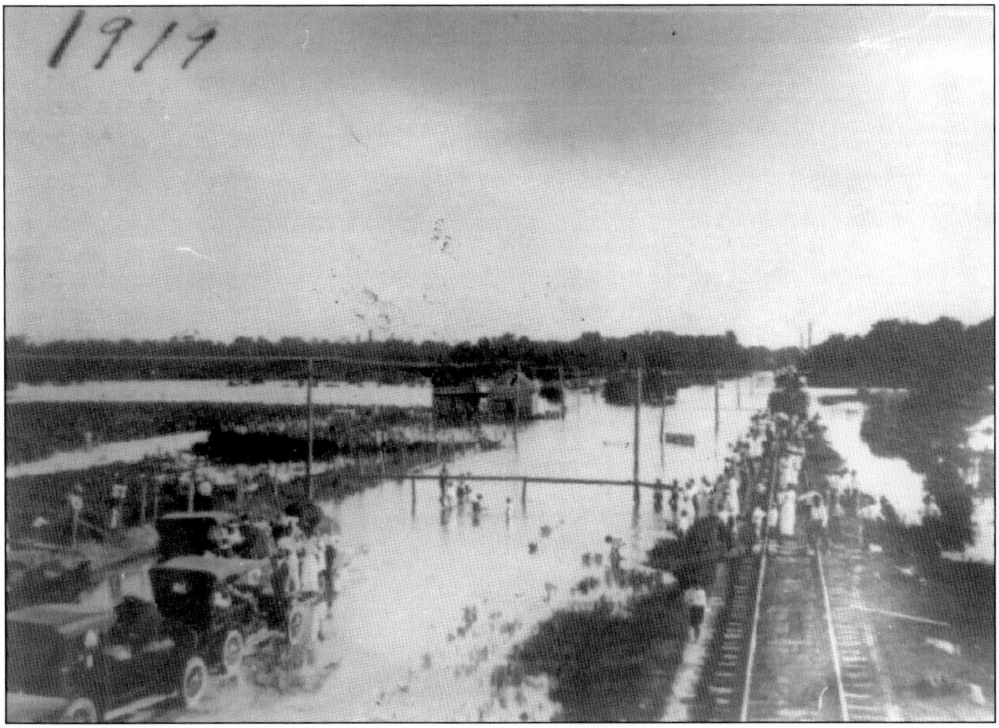

This view looks south toward the Greenville Power Plant from the Wilson Farm on the north side of the Tar River in July 1919. Called "freshets," other large floods happened in 1842, 1867, 1887, 1902, and 1904. Several of these floods were comparable to the floods of Hurricane Floyd on September 16, 1999. (Courtesy of Ross-Kammerer Photo Archive.)

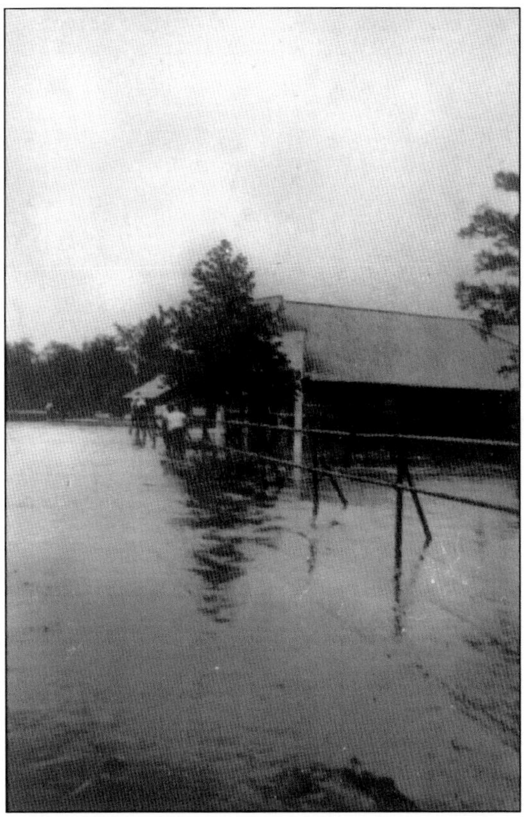

This dramatic photograph was taken on the north side of the bridge during the flood of 1919. It shows water rushing over the top of the bridge and flooding Stepp & Fleming's River Bridge Market. (Courtesy of Ross-Kammerer Photo Archive.)

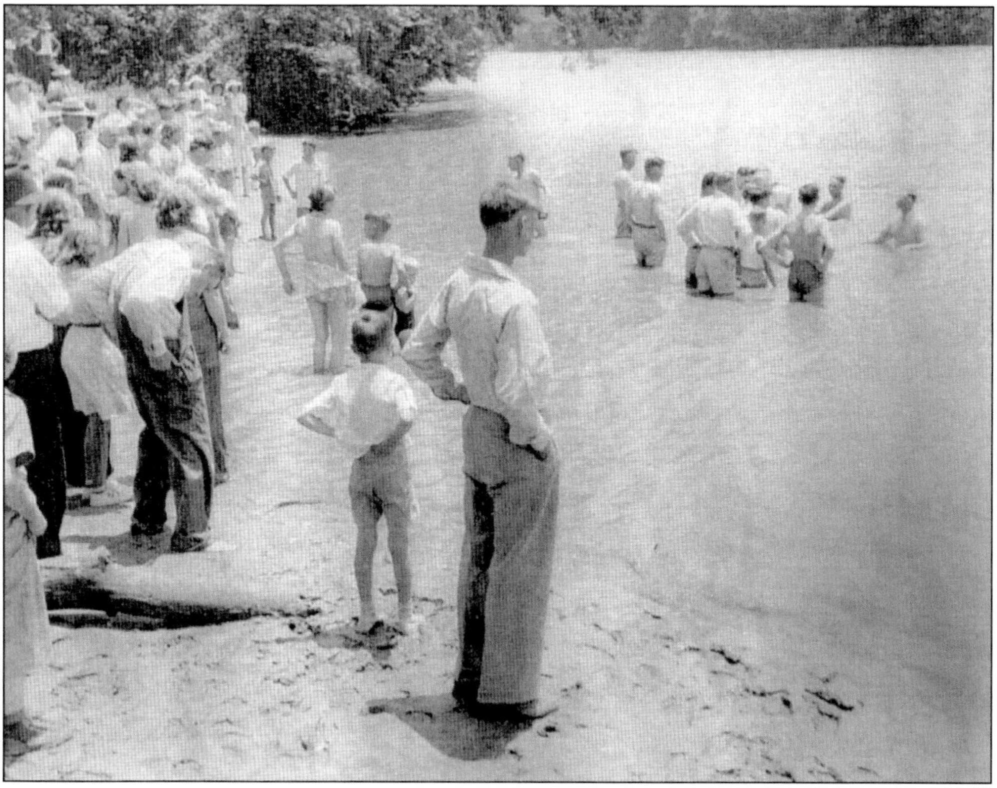

The Tar River was long used as a baptismal font by numerous denominations as illustrated by this late 1940s Jehovah's Witness baptism. The foot of Washington Street was called "Baptism Landing" and was also used as the ferry landing, a trash dump, a place for rowing parties, and the oyster boats' landing. (Courtesy of John F. Moye.)

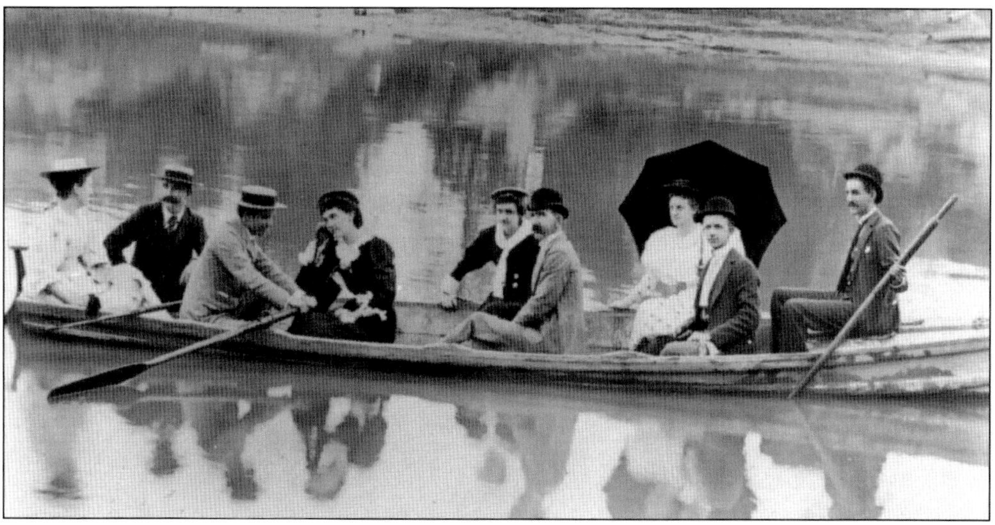

This turn-of-the-century view shows a boating party on the Tar River. These were days of moonlight cruises on steamboats, boating parties on gas launches, and rowing clubs up and down the river. There was a boat club chartered in Greenville as late as 1920. (Courtesy of ECMC.)

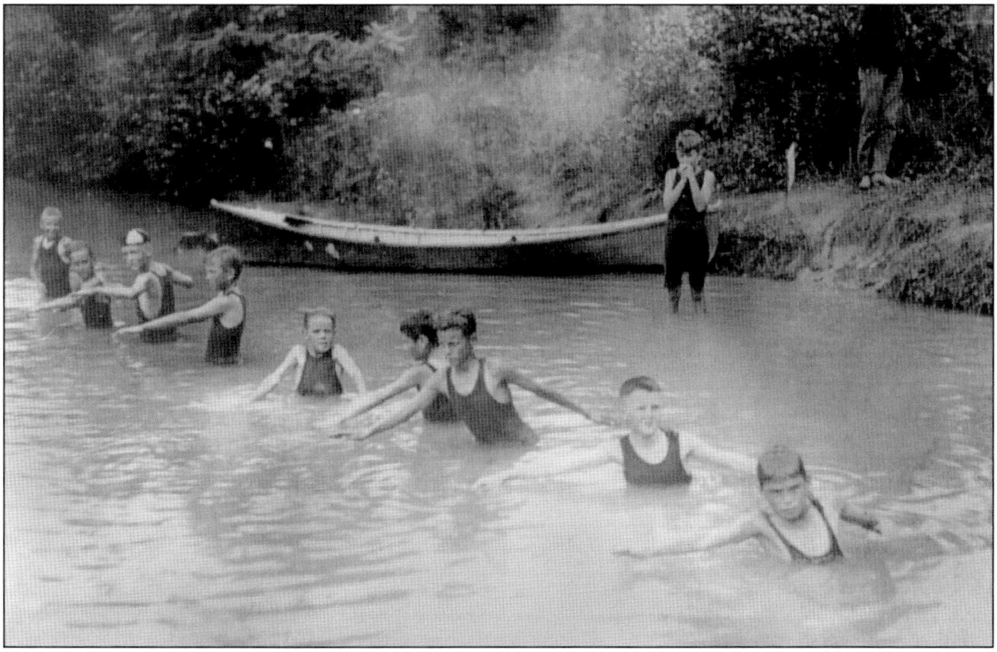

This is believed to be an early swimming class down on the river. In those days women complained that there was too much nudity along the waterfront with boys and young men swimming in view of people on the bridge. (Courtesy of ECMC.)

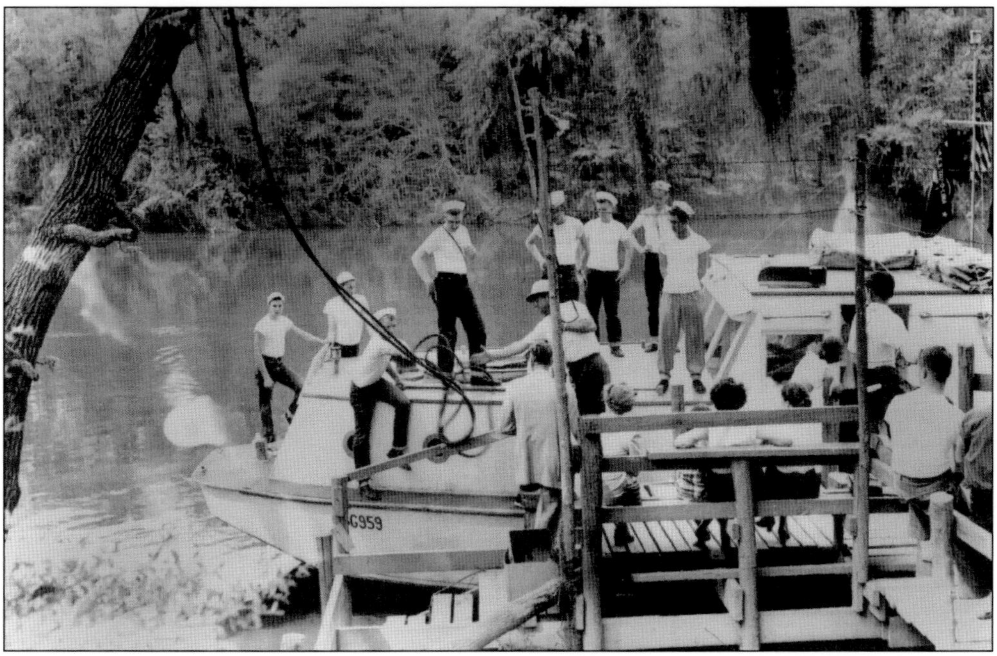

The Sea Scouts were reorganized in Greenville in April 1946 as a form of senior scouting. The boat, purchased in 1953 by the Sea Scouts, was originally built in Roanoke Rapids as a landing craft for the Navy. The Sea Scouts were under the guidance of Dr. James B. Hawes and Charles Whedbee, veteran Sea Scouters, acting as skipper and mate. The unit was reorganized again and became the Sea Explorer Scouts in 1950. (Courtesy of ECMC.)

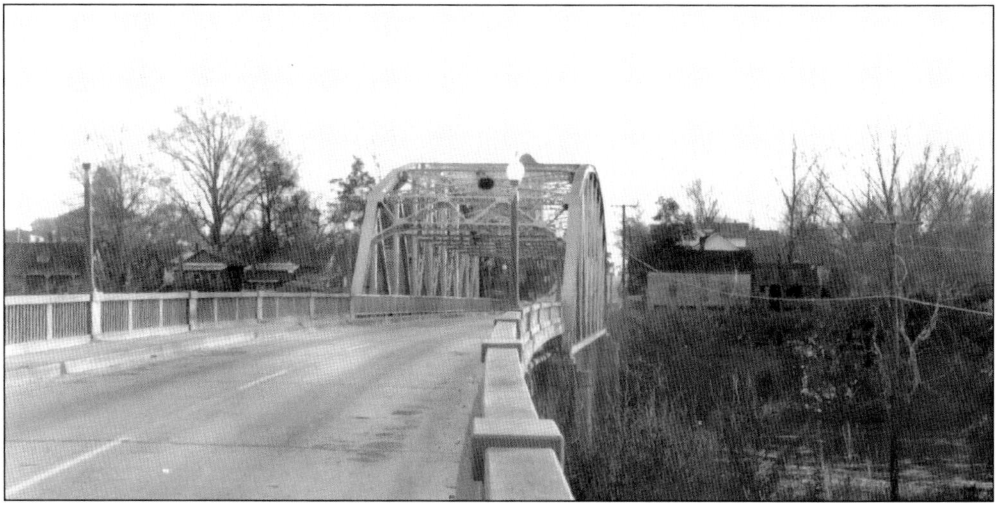

This view looking south shows the Greene Street bridge as it appeared in 1957. (Courtesy of ECMC.)

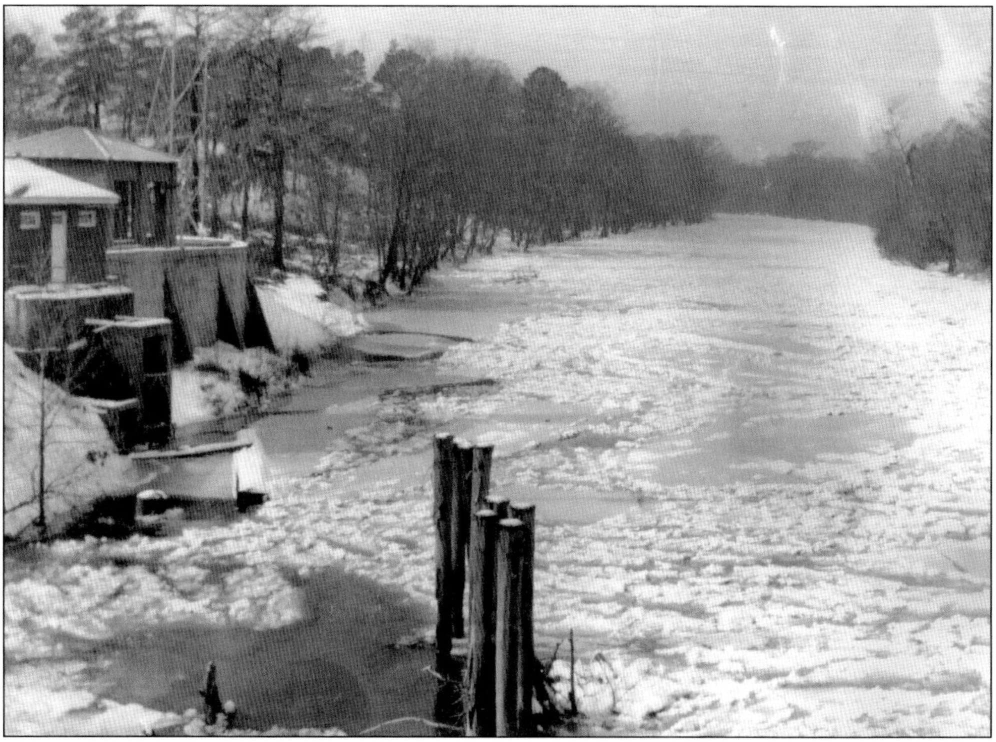

This photograph of the frozen Tar River, looking upriver from the railroad bridge, was taken by Paul Flye in 1936. The river also froze in 1857, 1886, 1893, 1917, 1920, and 1966. Ice would come down the river and create jams against the railroad bridge. It would freeze together and form a solid mass for miles upstream. Taking advantage of the situation, businessmen in olden days would cut ice and store it for sale in the ice warehouse near the wharf. (Courtesy of ECMC.)

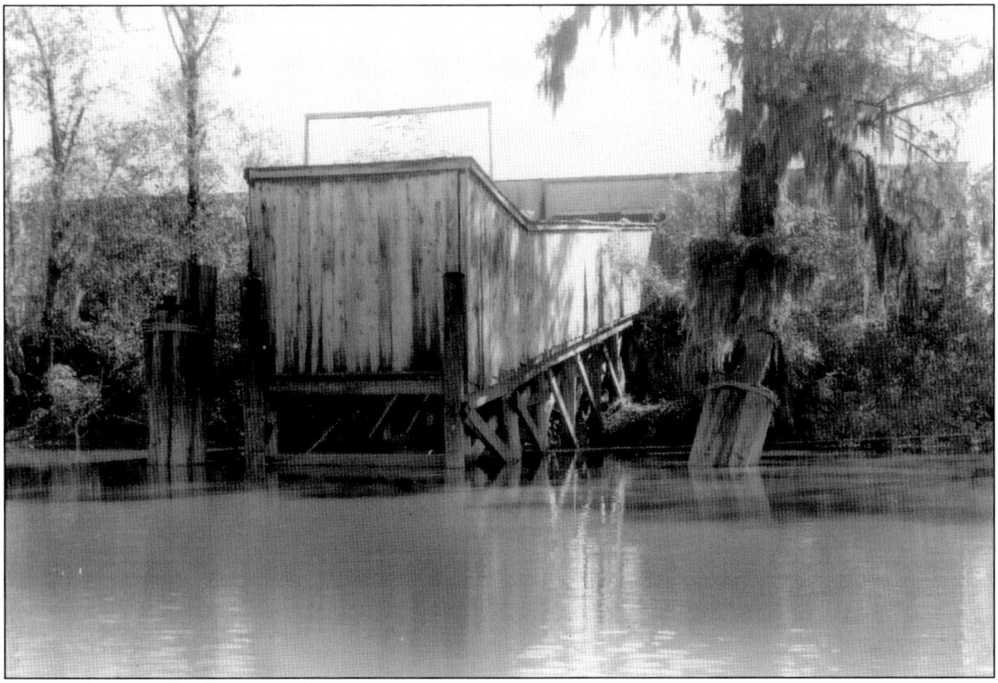

This scene from 1959 shows the covered runway leading from the Port Terminal dock on Hardee's Creek to the warehouse. It was once a busy avenue for cargo when freighters visited the port every other day from 1940 to 1942. The warehouse burned in 1969 and the site is now used as a boat landing by fishermen. (Courtesy of ECMC.)

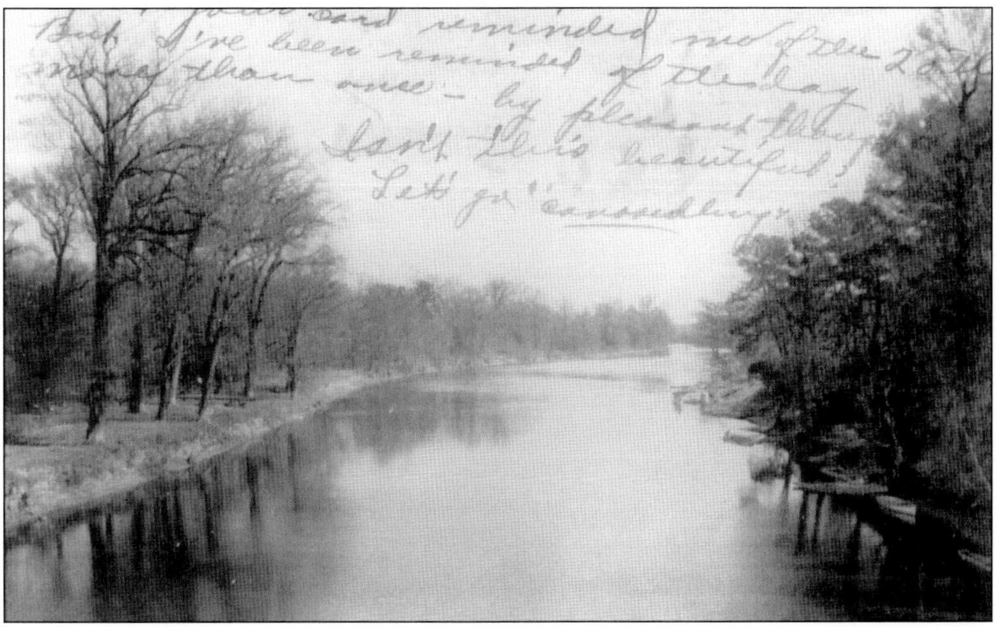

The beautiful Tar River has long played a part in Greenville's history. In 1791, Greenville was named by an Act of the General Assembly as an inspection point for tobacco on the Tar River. Old folks say, "if the Tar River is muddy in June, it will be muddy all summer." (Courtesy of ECMC.)

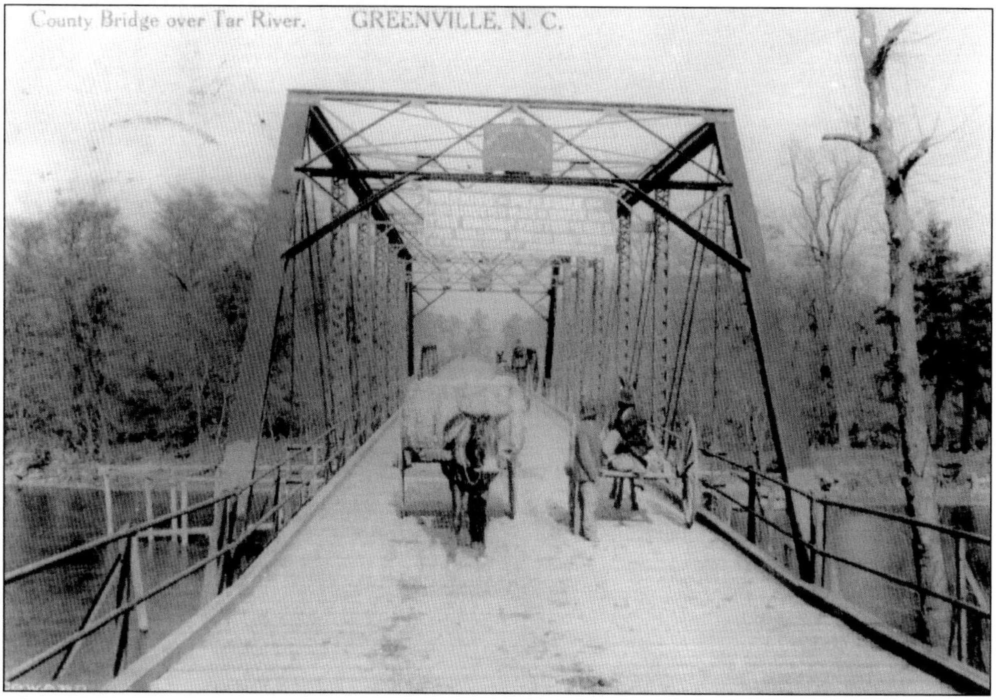

The New Steel County Bridge on Pitt Street was built in 1908. It cost $41,650.81 to build, was 18 feet wide, 1,556 feet long, and had a turn-table draw for boats. The speed warning sign hanging down over the bridge was regularly torn down and thrown into the river. It was picked up several times as far away as Grimesland and returned to its place on the bridge. The bridge was torn down in 1930. (Courtesy of ECMC.)

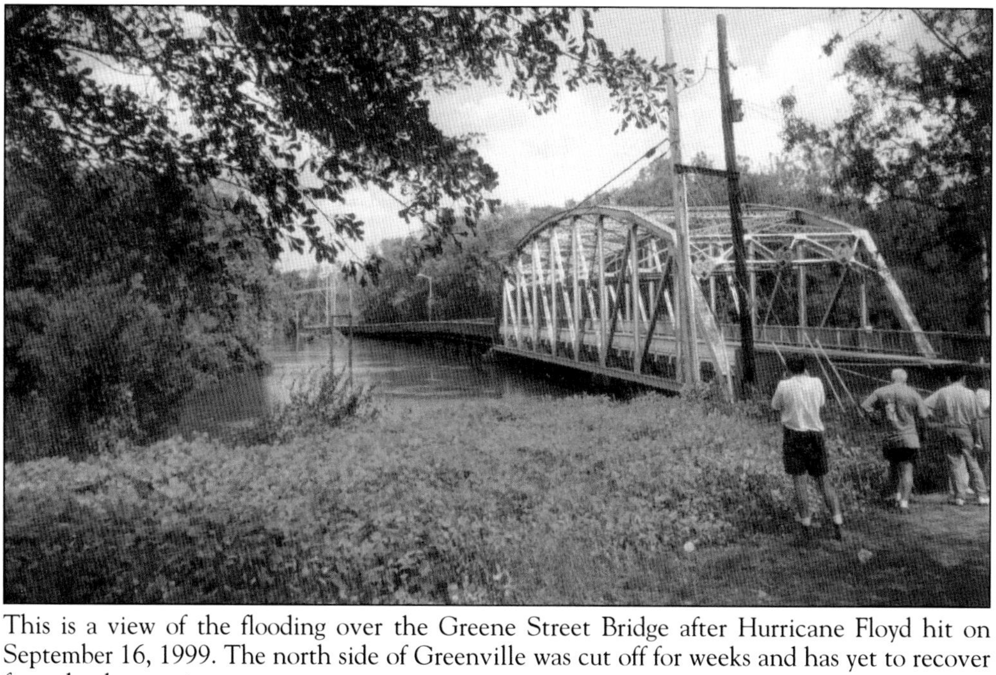

This is a view of the flooding over the Greene Street Bridge after Hurricane Floyd hit on September 16, 1999. The north side of Greenville was cut off for weeks and has yet to recover from the devastation.

Three

Churches and Schools

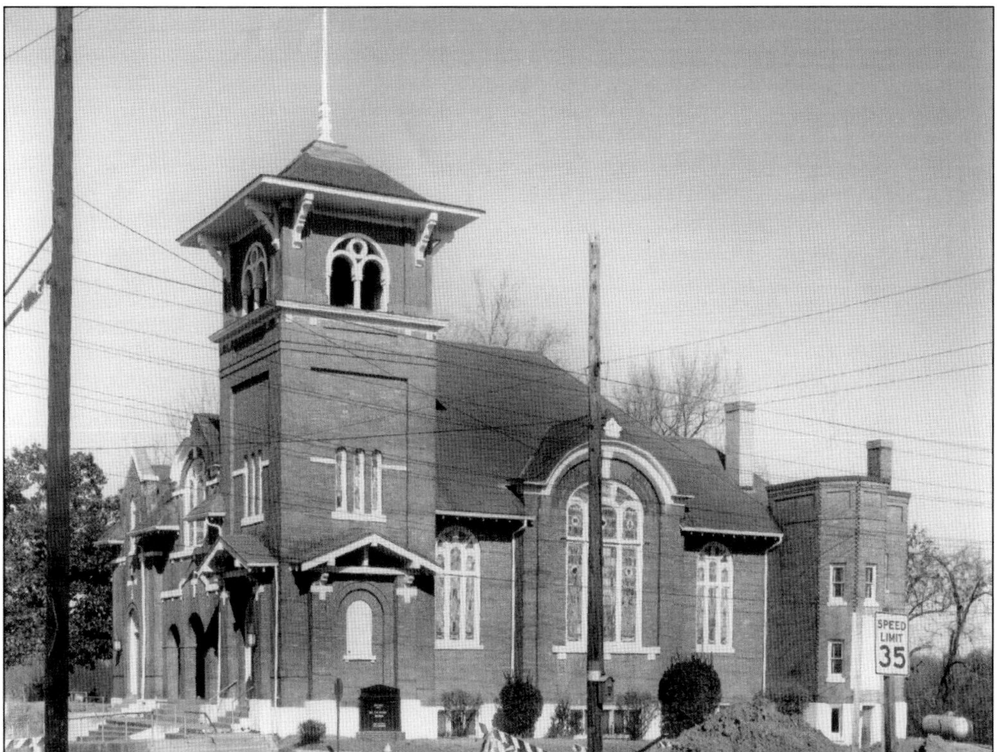

The once beautiful Sycamore Hill Baptist Church sat majestically on the northeast corner of First and Greene Streets. This church was built in 1916 after the old church burned. Because of the Shore Drive Development in the 1960s, the church was forced to be sold to the Redevelopment Commission. The congregation bought the former Eighth Street Christian Church and moved there on June 9, 1968. In February 1969, the vacant church was burned by an arsonist and Greenville lost forever another gem of its architectural history. The congregation now has a modern church on Hooker Road. (Courtesy of Lonnie Norcott.)

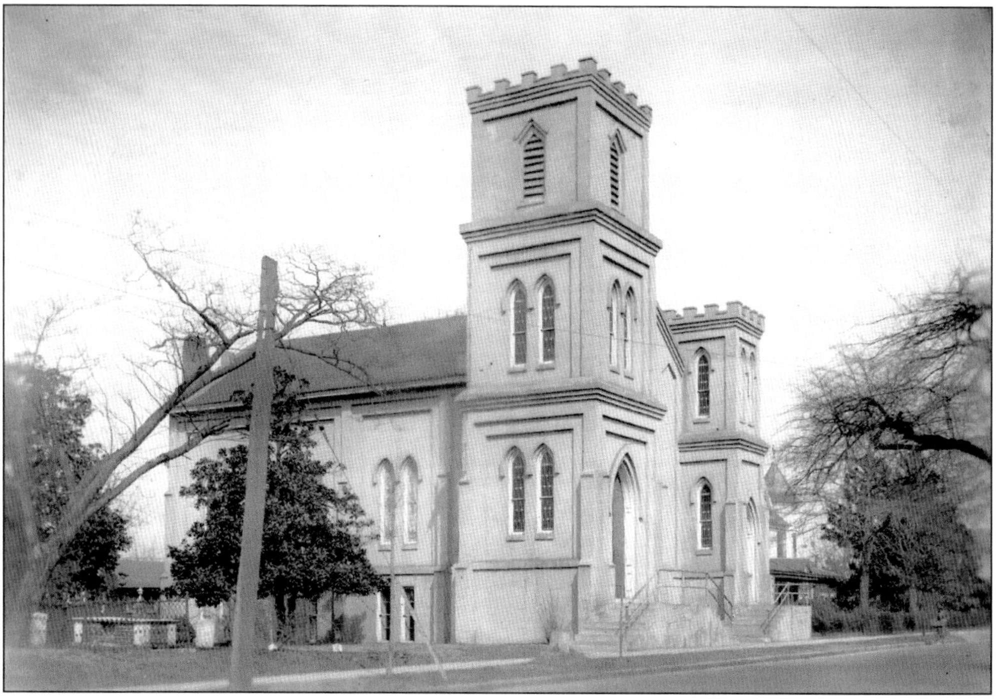

The Memorial Baptist Church, located on Greene Street, was completed in 1890. Designed by E.B. Cutts and started in 1883, the church held its first services in the basement in 1884. In 1948, a three-story educational building was added, which is now the Community Building and houses city offices. The church was torn down about 1973. The new church building is on Greenville Boulevard. (Courtesy of Charles Horne Collection.)

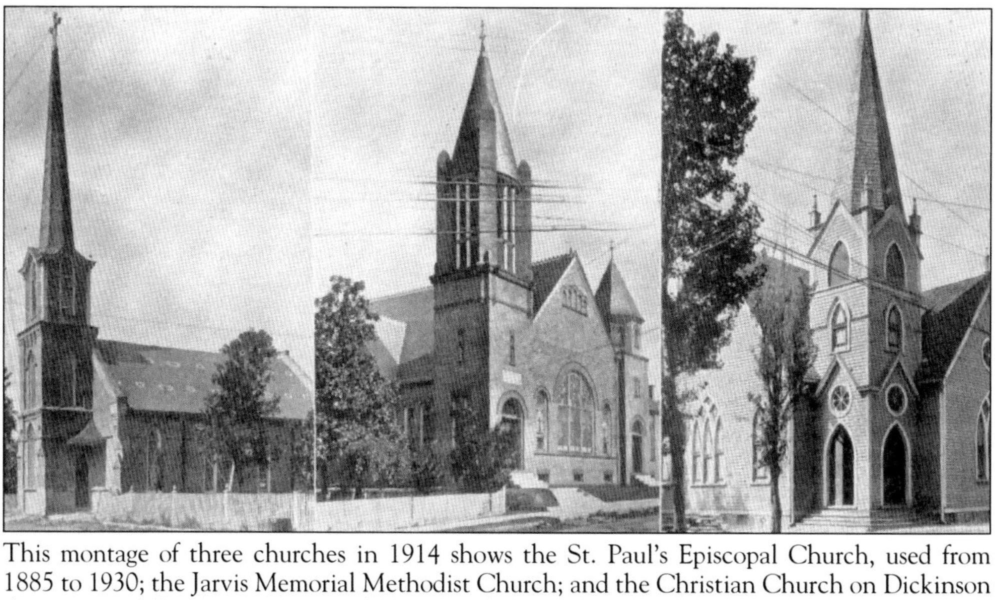

This montage of three churches in 1914 shows the St. Paul's Episcopal Church, used from 1885 to 1930; the Jarvis Memorial Methodist Church; and the Christian Church on Dickinson Avenue, used from 1901 to 1916. (Courtesy of "Illustrated City of Greenville" [pamphlet] Pitt County, 1914.)

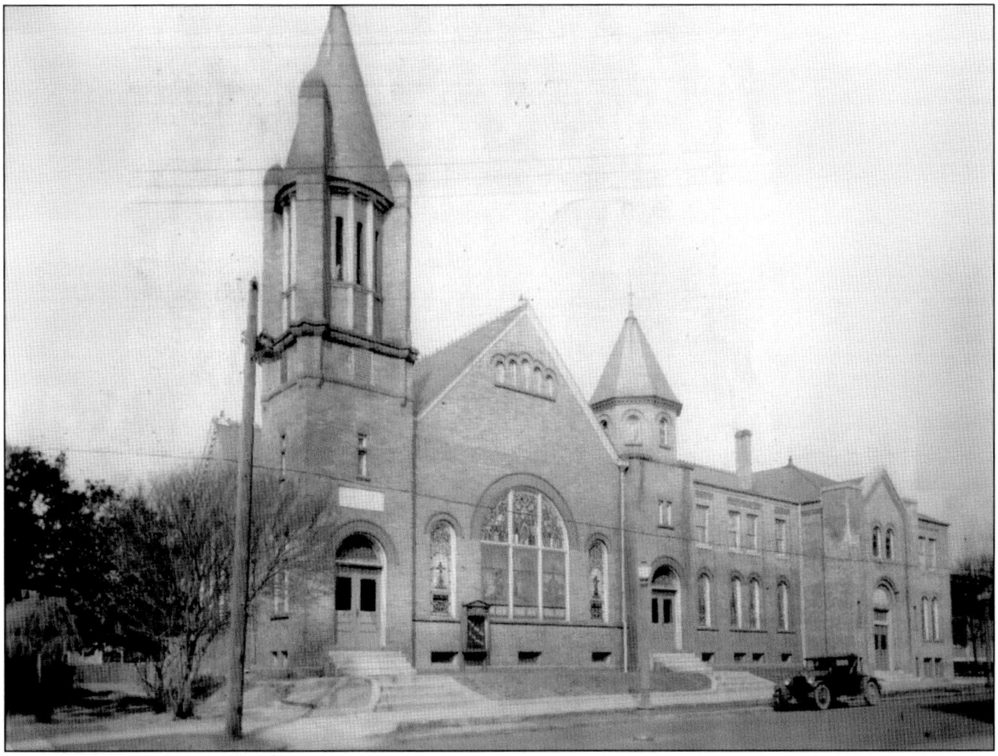

Jarvis Memorial Methodist Church, seen here about 1930, was built near the corner of Washington Street and Dickinson Avenue in 1908 to replace the old St Paul's Methodist Church on Greene and Second Streets. It was named in honor of one of its members, former Gov. Thomas Jordan Jarvis. (Courtesy of Charles Horne Collection.)

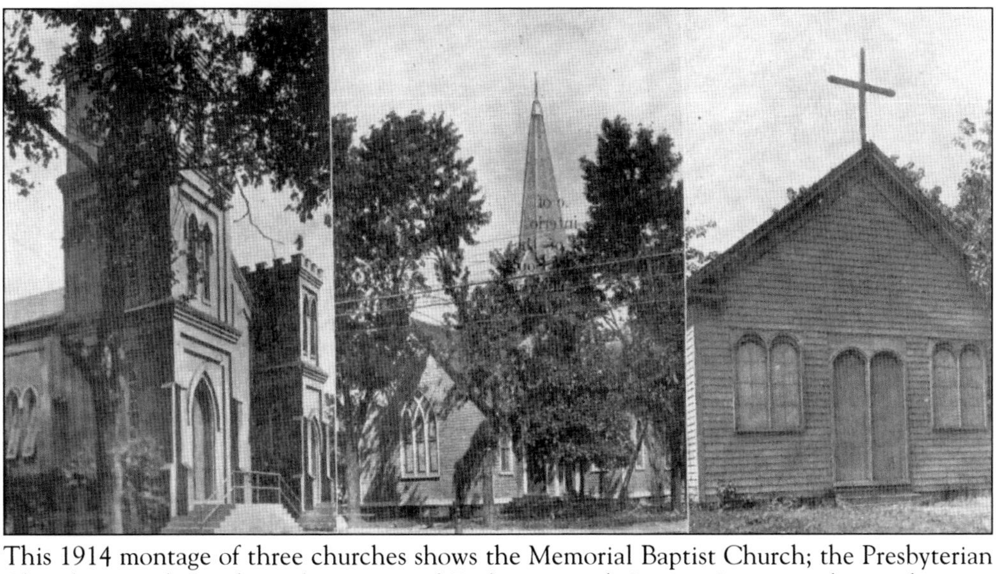

This 1914 montage of three churches shows the Memorial Baptist Church; the Presbyterian Church, once located on the corner of Dickinson and Greene Streets and torn down in the 1920s; and the Catholic Church. (Courtesy of the *Illustrated City of Greenville, Pitt County, 1914*.)

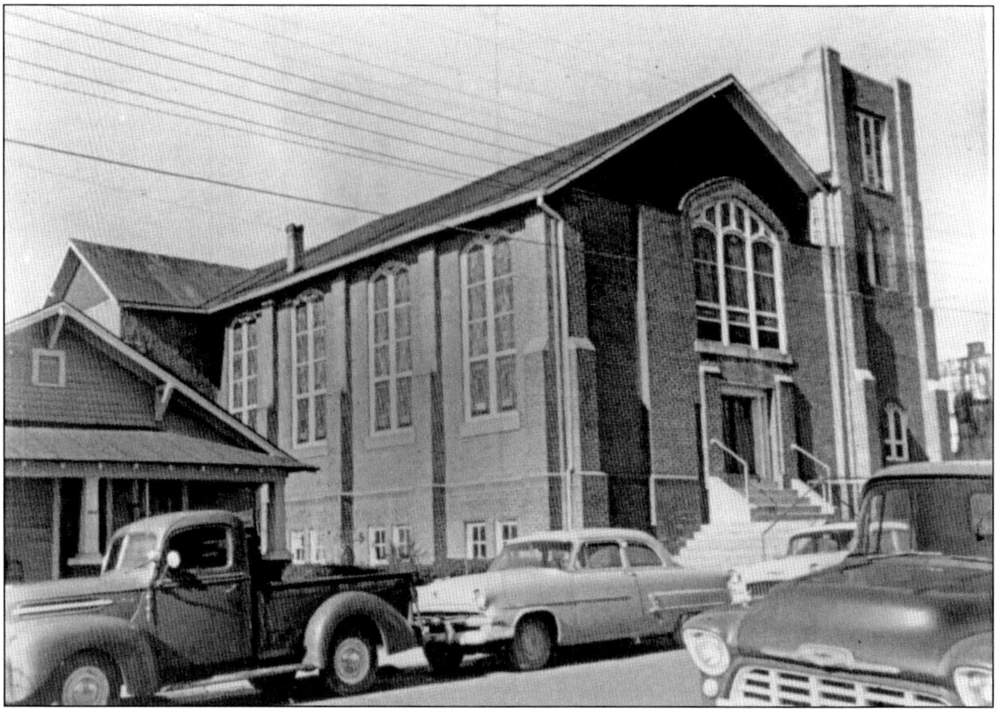

The York Memorial A.M.E. Zion Church had its groundbreaking in 1920 on Albemarle Avenue across from Askew's sawmill. The church was built in stages, the cornerstone being dated 1923. The church was beautifully renovated in 1957. Eventually, the congregation moved to Tyson Street and this building sat vacant for years. It was torn down in the 1980s. (Courtesy of Alex Albright.)

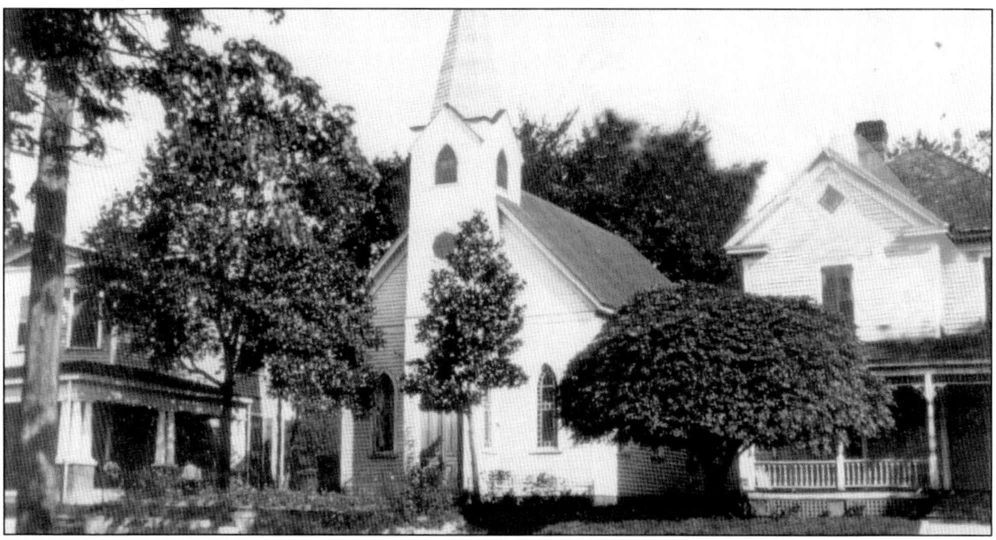

Through the efforts of Mrs. Delphia Moye, wife of E.A. Moye, a Universalist Church was built on Dickinson Avenue in 1905–1906. In 1906, the church was dedicated as the Delphia Moye Chapel. The congregation disbanded in the 1920s and by 1922 the Great Swamp Primitive Baptist Church met there. In 1931, the building was donated to the Salvation Army and was demolished by 1950. (Courtesy of UNC-Chapel Hill.)

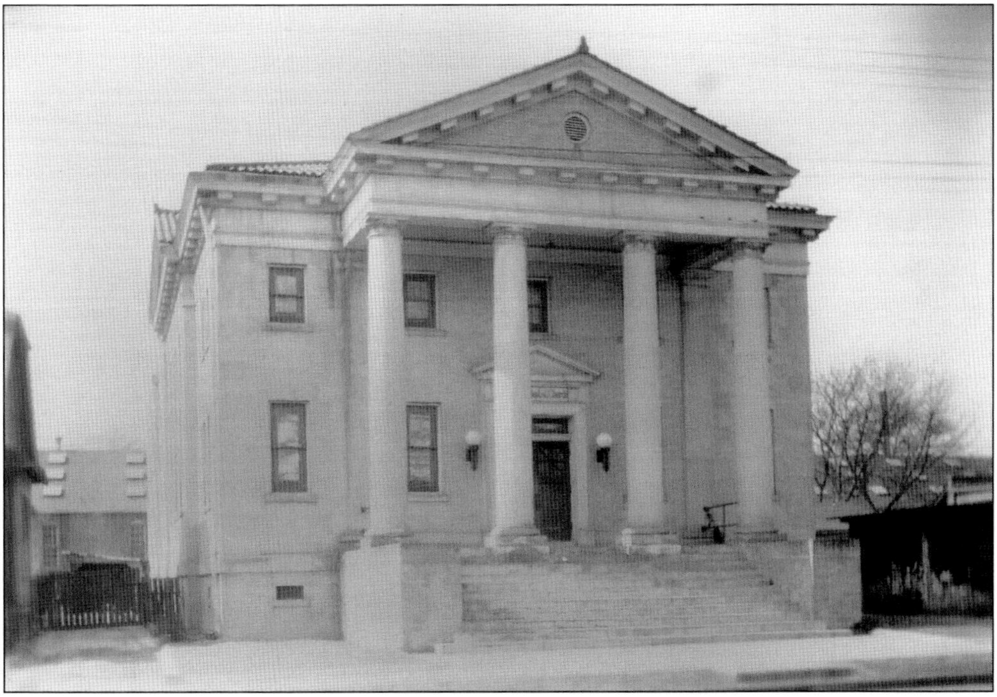

The Immanuel Baptist Church on Eighth Street was formed in 1915 by members of Memorial Baptist Church. The building was built in 1916–1917 and the first service was held on September 30, 1917. In 1967, the congregation moved to a new site on Elm Street. The church was then occupied by other congregations but stood vacant from 1986 until it was razed in 2001. (Courtesy of Charles Horne Collection.)

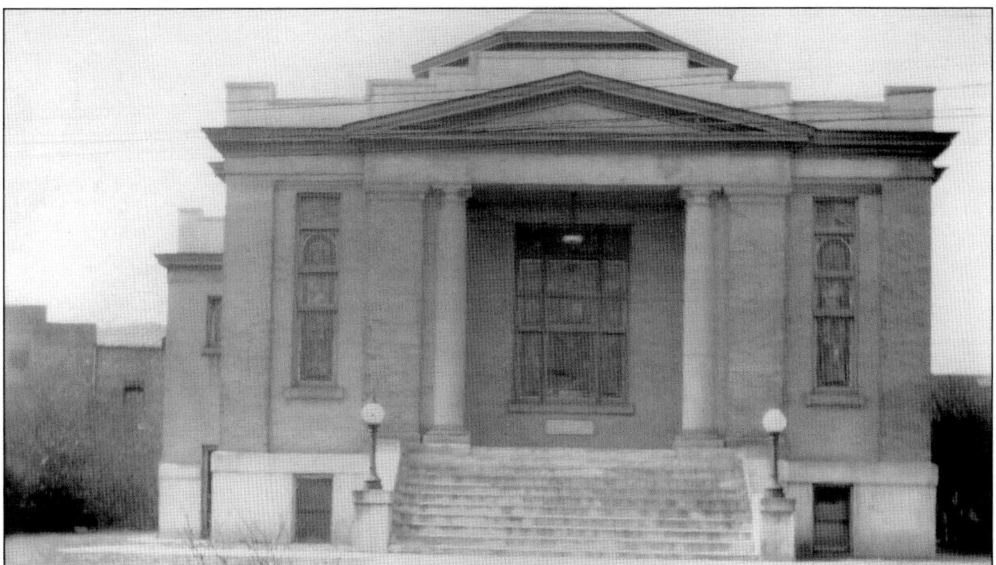

This 1932 photo shows the Eighth Street Christian Church on Eighth Street. It was built in 1916 to replace the old church on the corner of Dickinson Avenue and Pitt Street. In 1968, it became the new home of the Sycamore Hill Baptist Church. (Courtesy of Charles Horne Collection.)

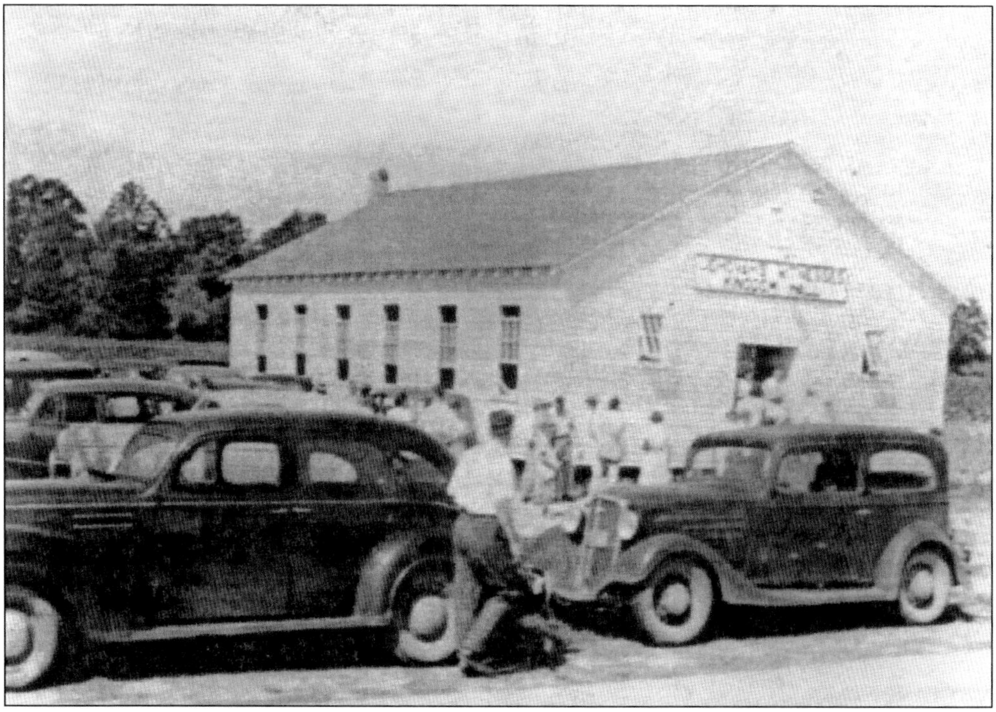

The first Jehovah's Witness Kingdom Hall was built in 1942 on land west of Greenville given by Clarence E. Manning. The hall was dedicated on June 14, 1942, and was enlarged and bricked in 1963. The congregation has grown steadily and now has four congregations in Greenville. (Courtesy of John F. Moye.)

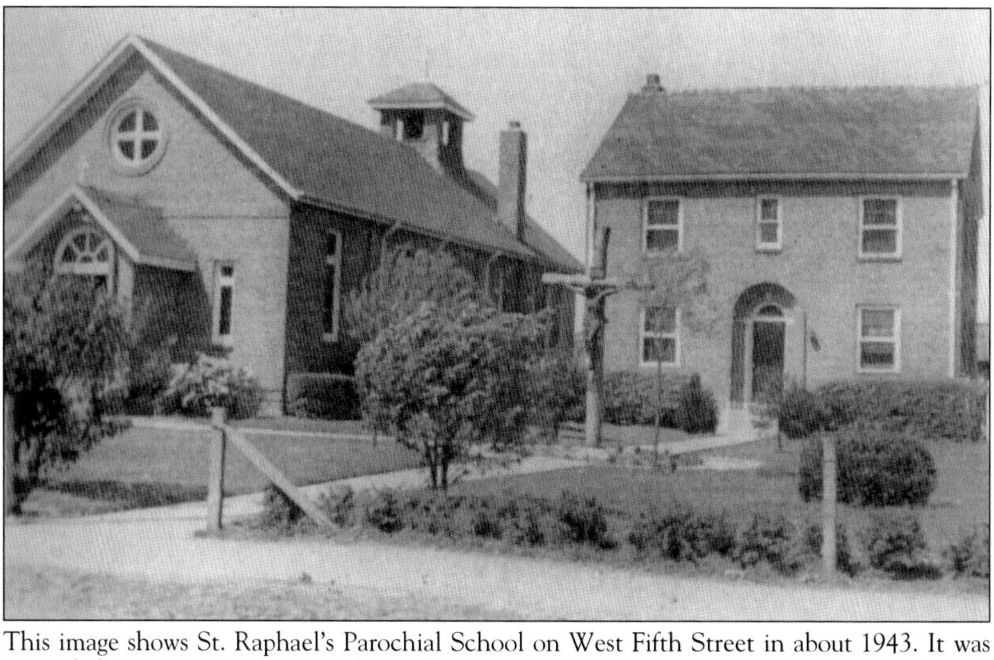

This image shows St. Raphael's Parochial School on West Fifth Street in about 1943. It was expanded in 1948 to a nursery and school, with a cafeteria-auditorium combination. (Courtesy of ECMC.)

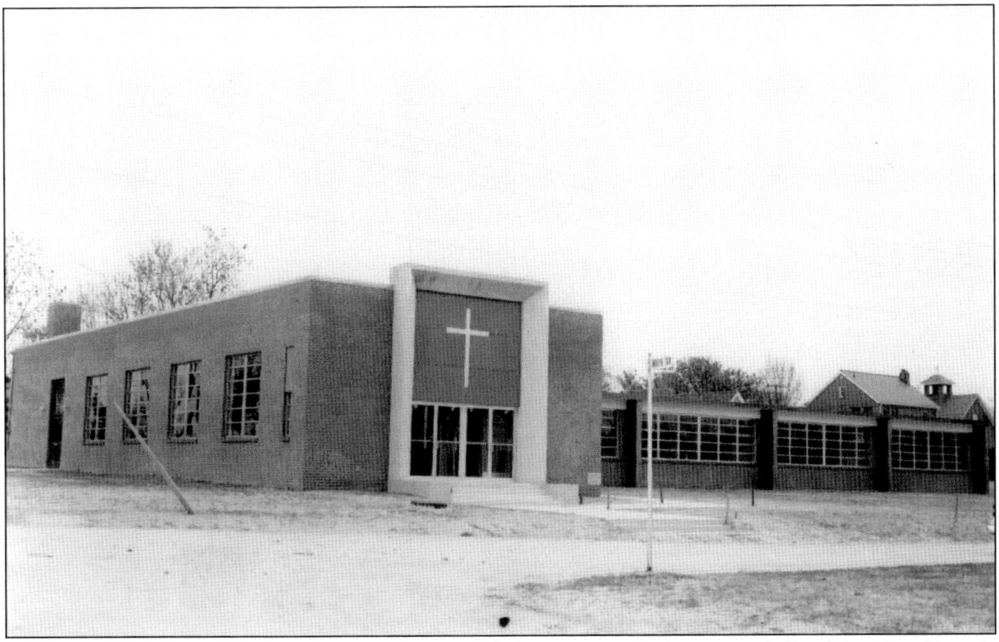
This 1956 photograph shows the dedication of the St. Peter's Convent-School on East Fourth Street. The school has expanded and the new St. Peter's Church and Parish Hall was dedicated beside it in 1991. (Courtesy of ECMC.)

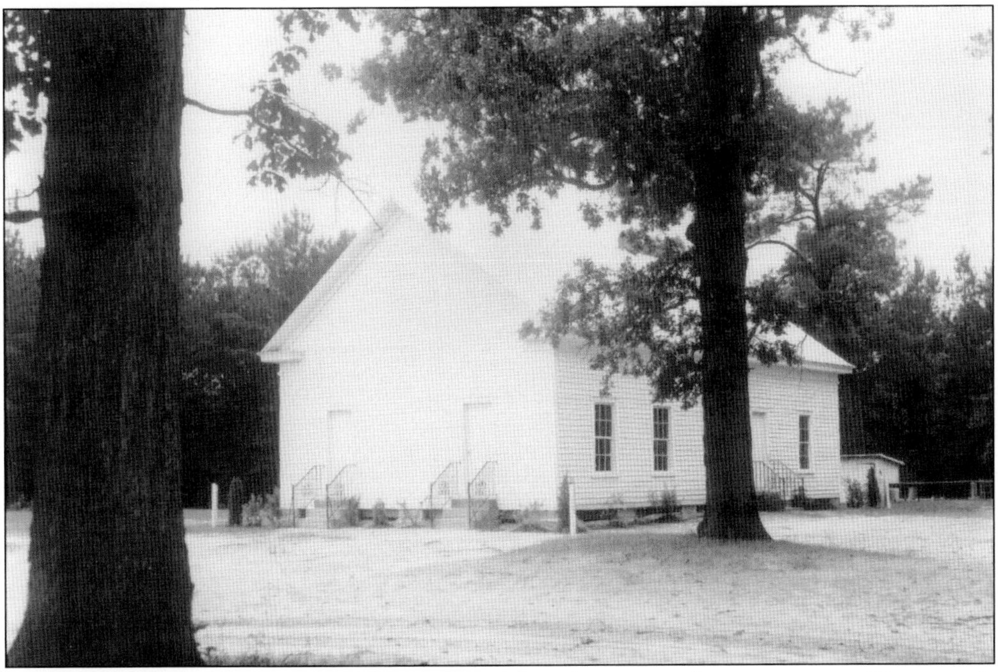
The Red Banks Primitive Baptist Church, located at what is now the intersection of Fourteenth Street and Firetower Road, was built in 1893. The congregation dates back to 1758, when the church was originally situated north of the river. During the Civil War, federal soldiers burned down the older church during a skirmish. In 2000, the church was given to the Pitt County Historical Society for preservation. (Courtesy of ECMC.)

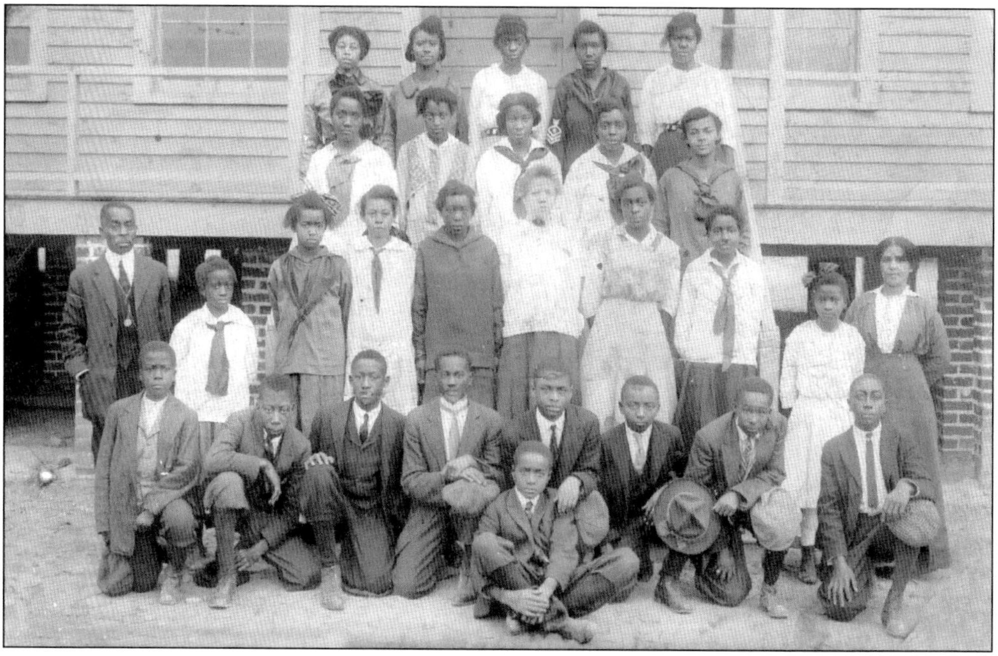

This picture from about 1904 shows the students of Greenville Colored Graded School. The school was built in 1903. To the left stands Prof. C.M. Eppes, the first principal. (Courtesy of Lonnie Norcott.)

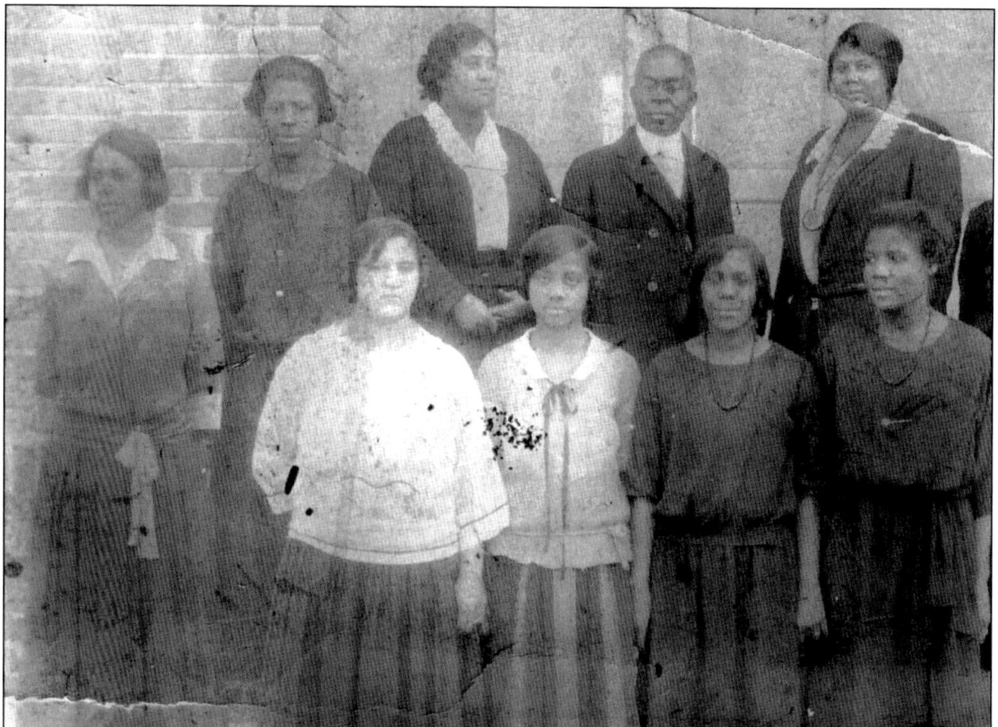

Prof. C.M. Eppes stands with his faculty at the Fleming Street School in the 1930s. (Courtesy of Lonnie Norcott.)

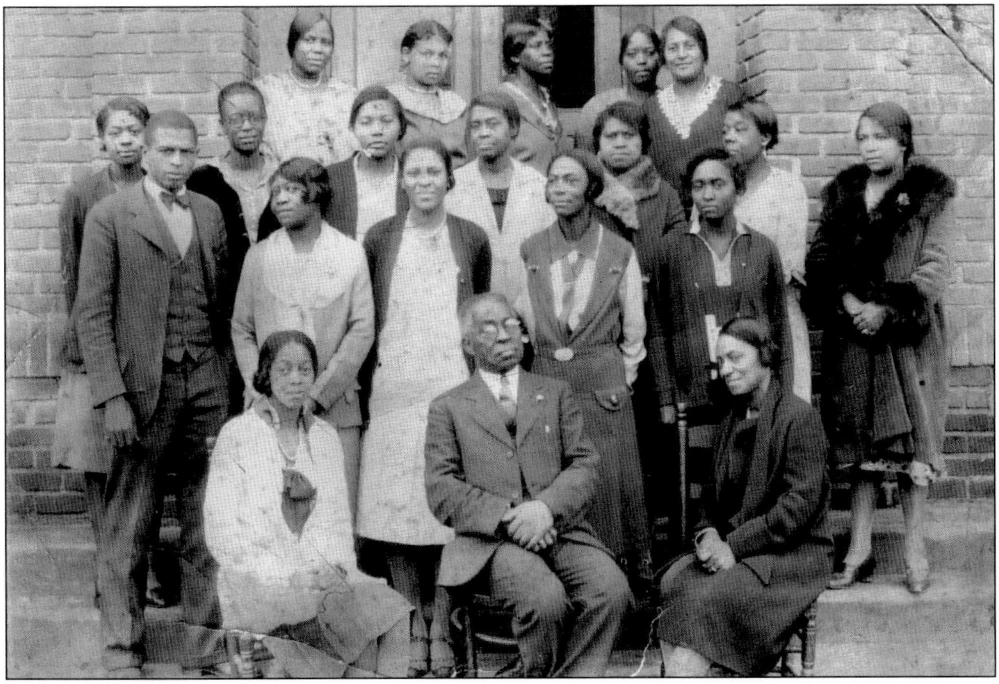

Prof. C.M. Eppes sits with his faculty at the Fleming Street School in the 1930s. The Fleming Street School was built in 1923 and burned in 1970. (Courtesy of Lonnie Norcott)

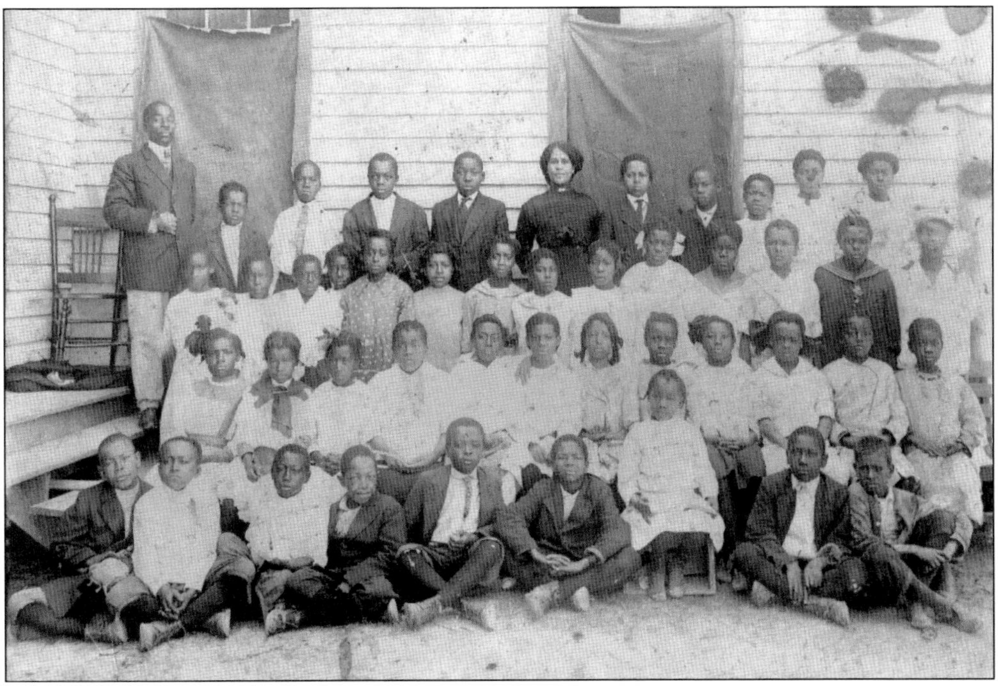

The Greenville Colored Graded School is shown as it appeared about 1905. This school was hit by a tornado in 1910 and Professor Eppes went for a ride when a wing of the school went airborne. The same tornado destroyed the Tar River Institute, a black theological school. (Courtesy of Lonnie Norcott.)

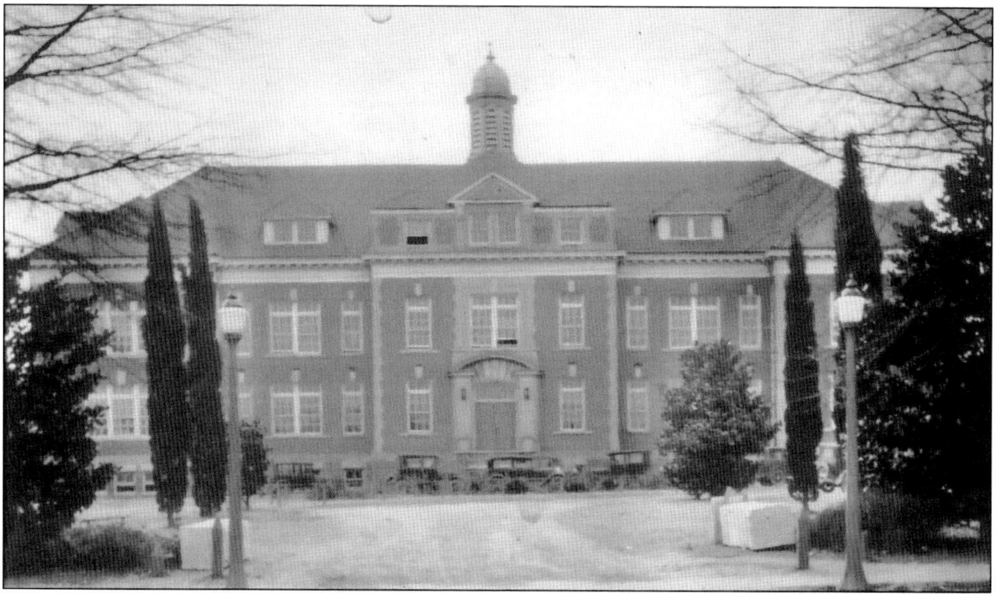

Austin Building, which once had a gold cupola, was the first building completed at East Carolina Teachers Training School in 1908–1909. It was named in honor of Herbert Austin, one of the 13 teachers who made up the first faculty when it opened in 1909. The building was demolished in 1968, and the Leo W. Jenkins Fine Arts Center now sits on the site. The university remembers it with a replica of the cupola located on the mall. (Courtesy of Charles Horne Collection.)

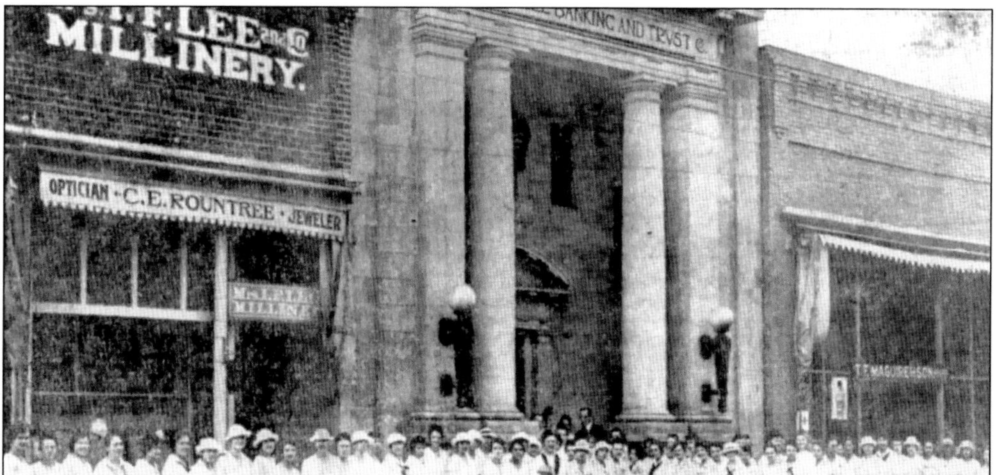

These ECTC girls are shown making a deposit in the Greenville Bank & Trust Company in 1918. During World War I, training school girls picked cotton and did other work normally done by men during their free time to pay for Liberty Bonds as part of the United War Work Campaign. Big wagon loads of girls, under the direction of faculty, would go out into the country to pick cotton carrying their lunches in paper bags. (Courtesy of Roger Kammerer.)

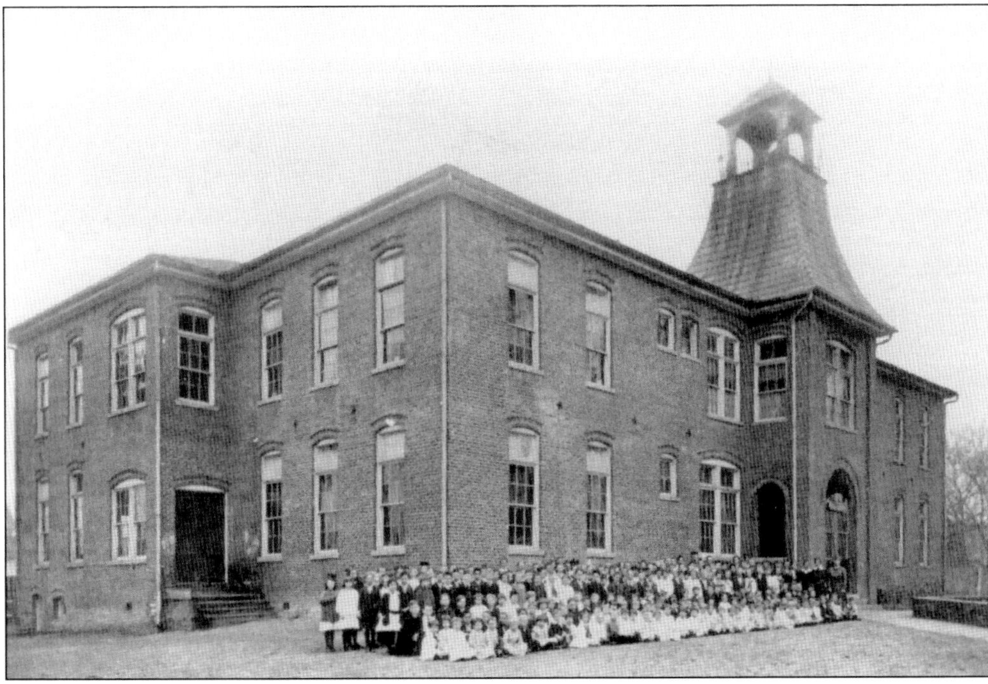

The Greenville Graded School was built in 1903 on Evans Street and is now the site of Sheppard Memorial Library. The school was built by Burwell Riddick, who had rebuilt Greenville twice after fires. This school had a library and chapel. It burned in January 1929. (Courtesy of North Carolina Archives.)

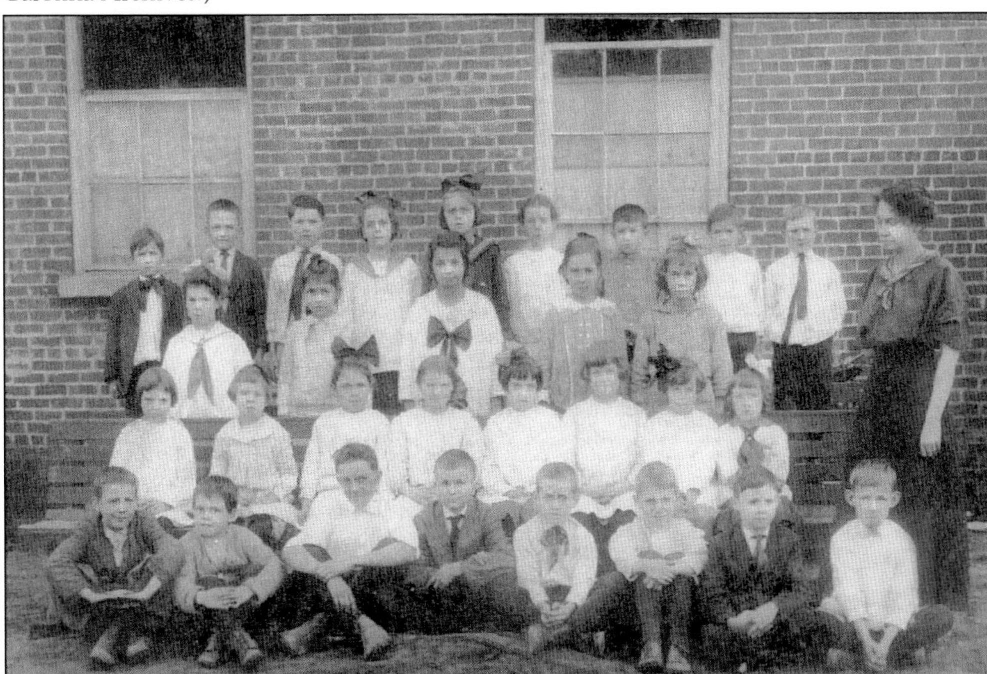

This is one of the classes at the Greenville Graded School (also called the Evans Street School) in about 1917. (Courtesy of Amos Evans.)

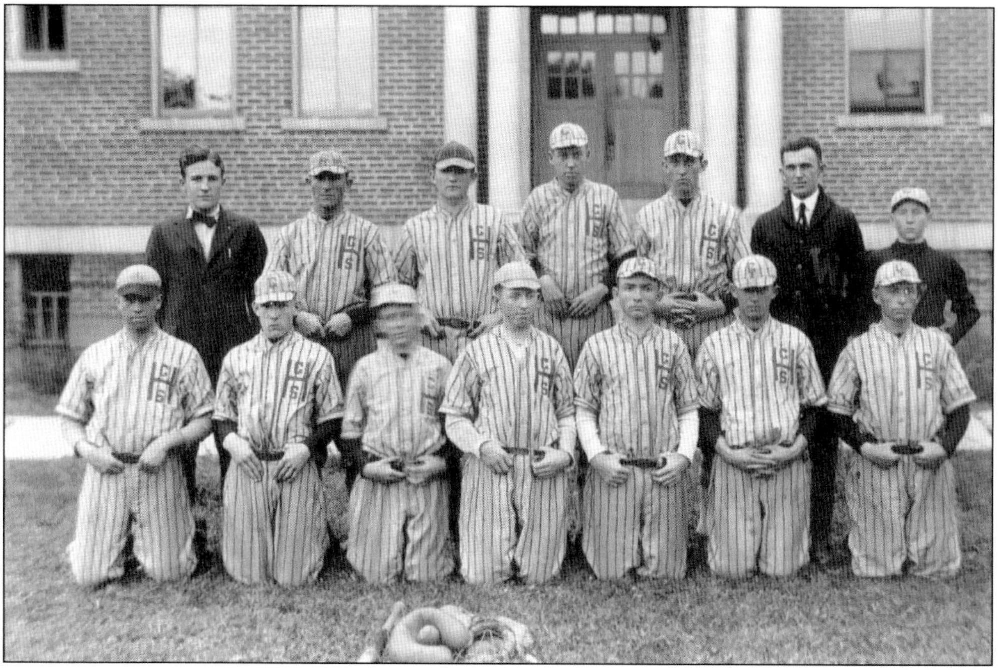

Greenville High School's baseball team in 1922 consisted of the following members, from left to right: (kneeling) Richard Williams, Wesley Harvey, Douglas West, Frank Harrington, Berry Jenkins, Robert Forbes, and Cecil Satterthwaite; (back row) Wyatt Brown, Jimmie Barber, Zeno Brown, Fernando Satterthwaite, C.B. West, Cecil Bilbro, H.H. Duncan, and Wyatt Brown (manager). (Courtesy of ECMC.)

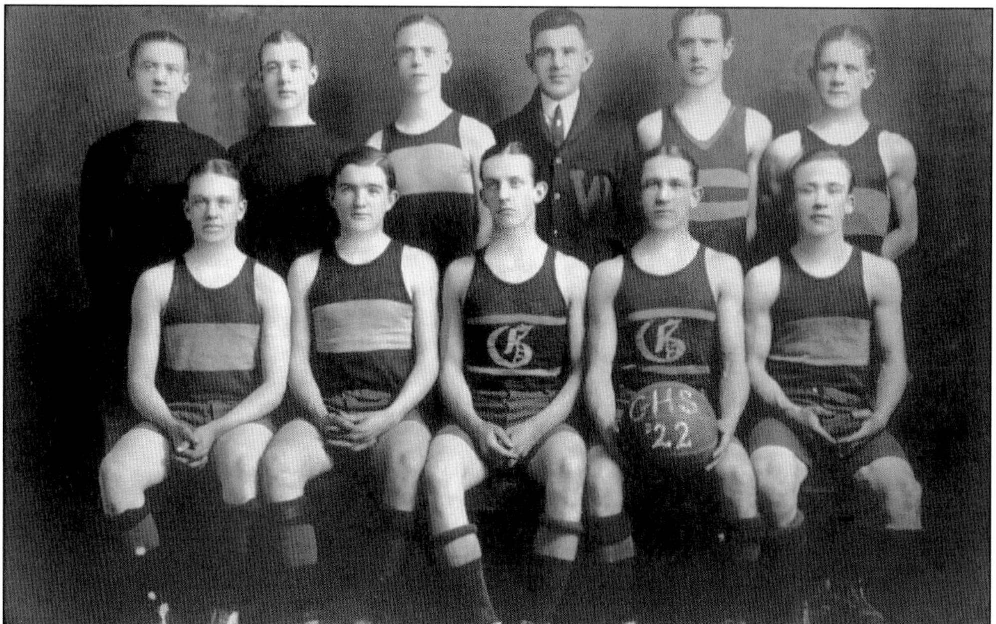

The Greenville High School basketball team is shown in 1922. Herman H. Duncan, a science teacher and baseball player, was the coach and is fourth from the left in the top row. (Courtesy of ECMC.)

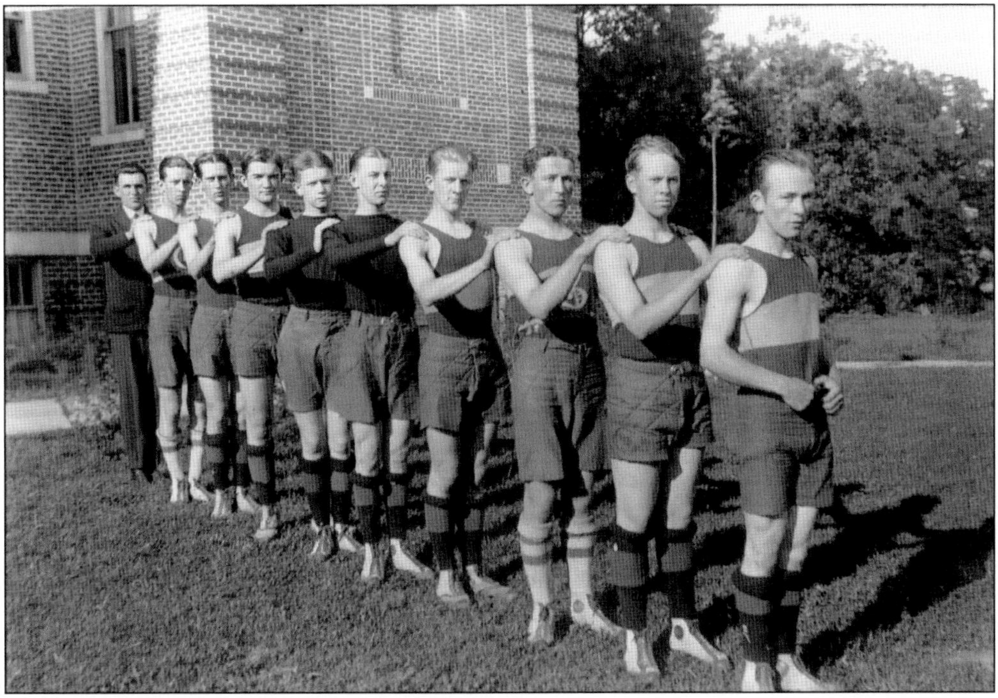

The 1922 Greenville High School basketball team members were (front to back) Tom Foley, Richard Williams, Jimmie Barber, Guilford Smith, Norman Winslow, Joe Moye, Zeno Brown, Roy Hardee, and C.B. West. Herman H. Duncan was coach and Roy Hardee was manager. (Courtesy of ECMC.)

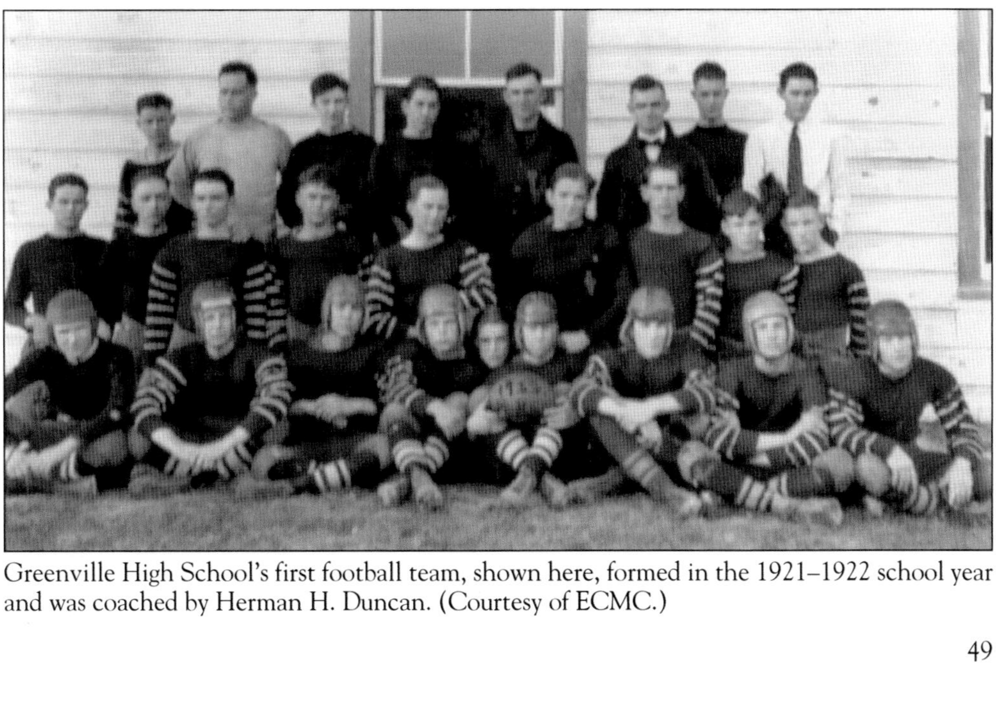

Greenville High School's first football team, shown here, formed in the 1921–1922 school year and was coached by Herman H. Duncan. (Courtesy of ECMC.)

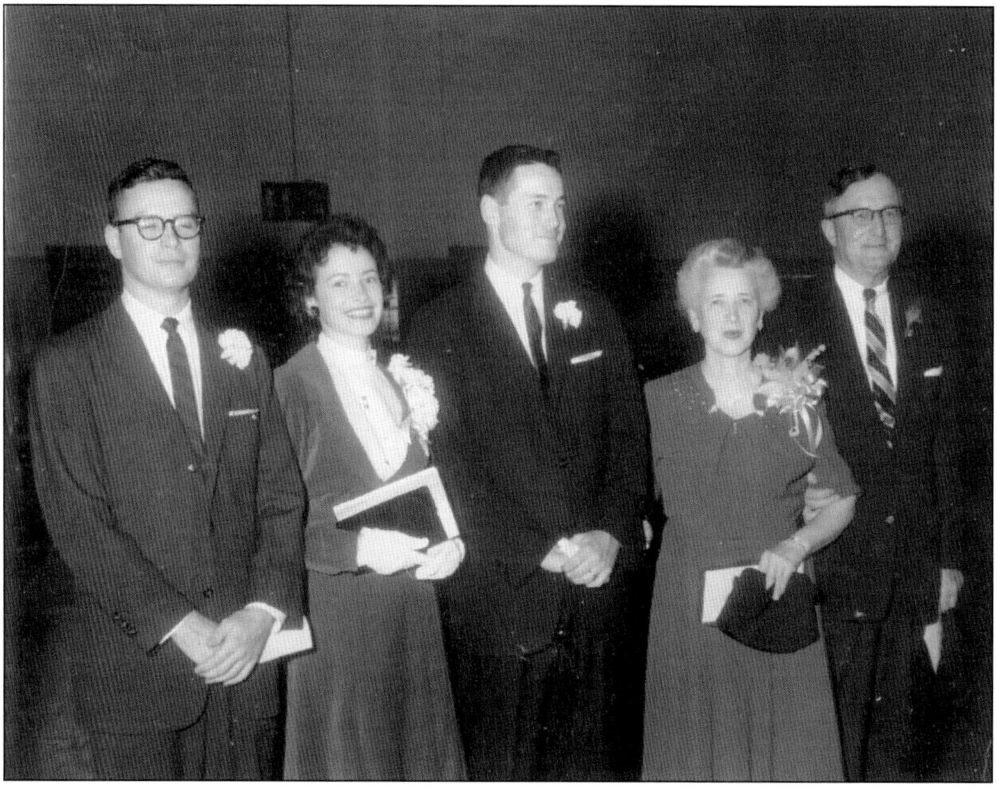

This 1957 photograph of Junius H. Rose and his family was taken at the dedication ceremony of Junius H. Rose High School. Junius H. Rose (1892–1972) was a veteran of World War I. He wanted to be a railroad man but went into education. He came to Greenville in 1919 as principal of the Greenville High School and served many years as superintendent of city schools. He was also the Civil Defense Chairman of Pitt County and a Boy Scout Leader. (Courtesy of Lonnie Norcott.)

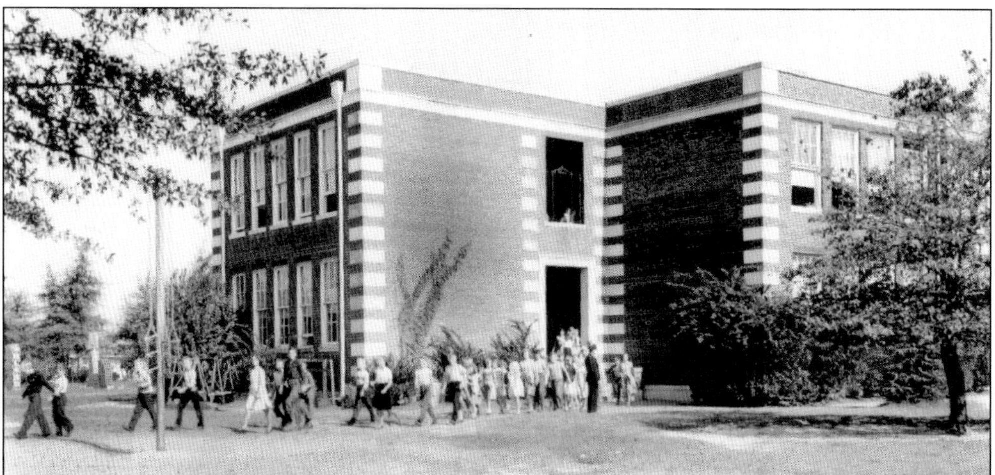

This 1950 picture shows a fire drill at Sadie Saulter School in West Greenville. During the Cold War, A-bomb (drop and cover) drills and other tests were a common part of school life. (Courtesy of ECMC.)

Four

CENTRAL BUSINESS DISTRICT

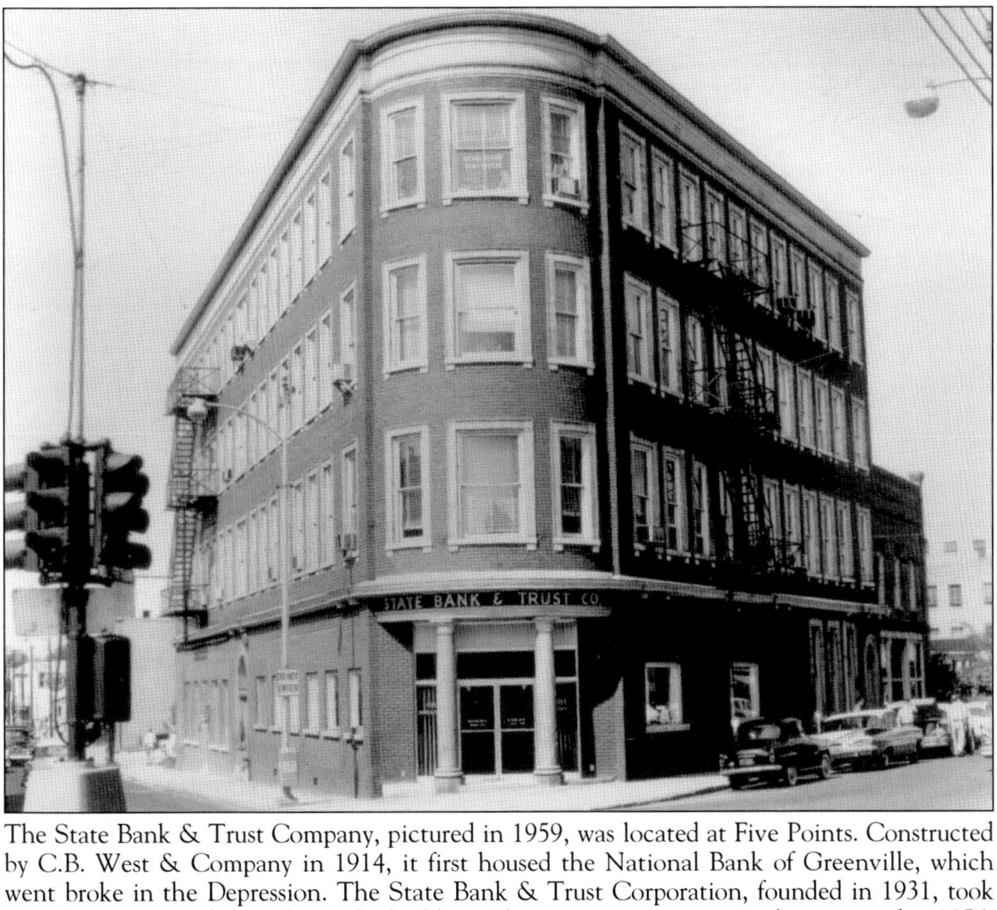

The State Bank & Trust Company, pictured in 1959, was located at Five Points. Constructed by C.B. West & Company in 1914, it first housed the National Bank of Greenville, which went broke in the Depression. The State Bank & Trust Corporation, founded in 1931, took over their assets and moved into the building. The property was extensively renovated in 1956. The bank occupied the first floor and part of the second floor. Five doctors and six insurance agencies occupied the rest of the building. It was demolished in 1975. (Courtesy of ECMC.)

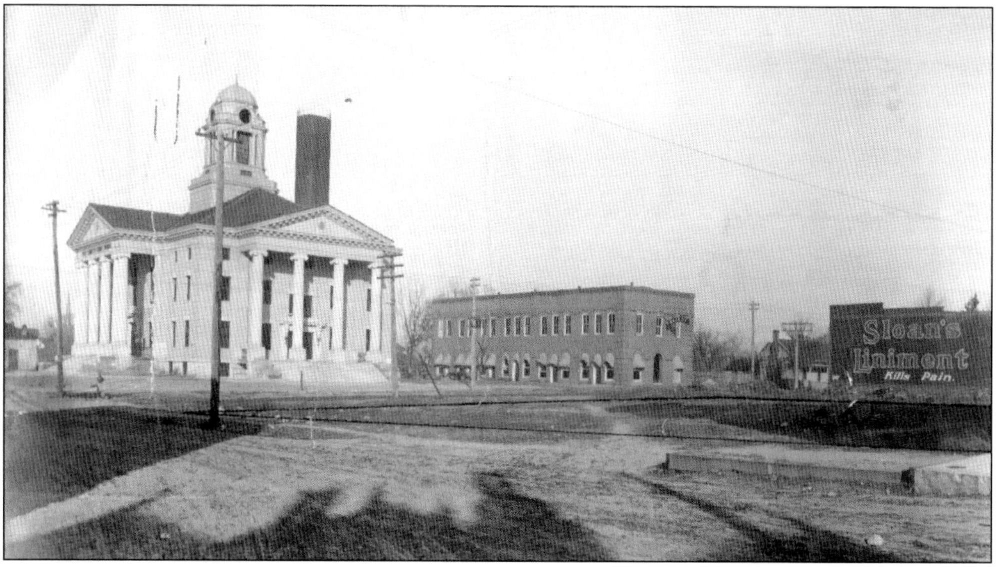

This view shows the Courthouse Square in 1911. In the center was the H.C. Edwards building, constructed in 1911, with a theater upstairs and offices below. The building on the right facing Evans Street was the Wiley P. Norcott barbershop and billiard hall, built in 1910. In 1918, the courthouse became an emergency hospital for victims of the Spanish Flu epidemic. (Courtesy of Cecil and Libby Turner.)

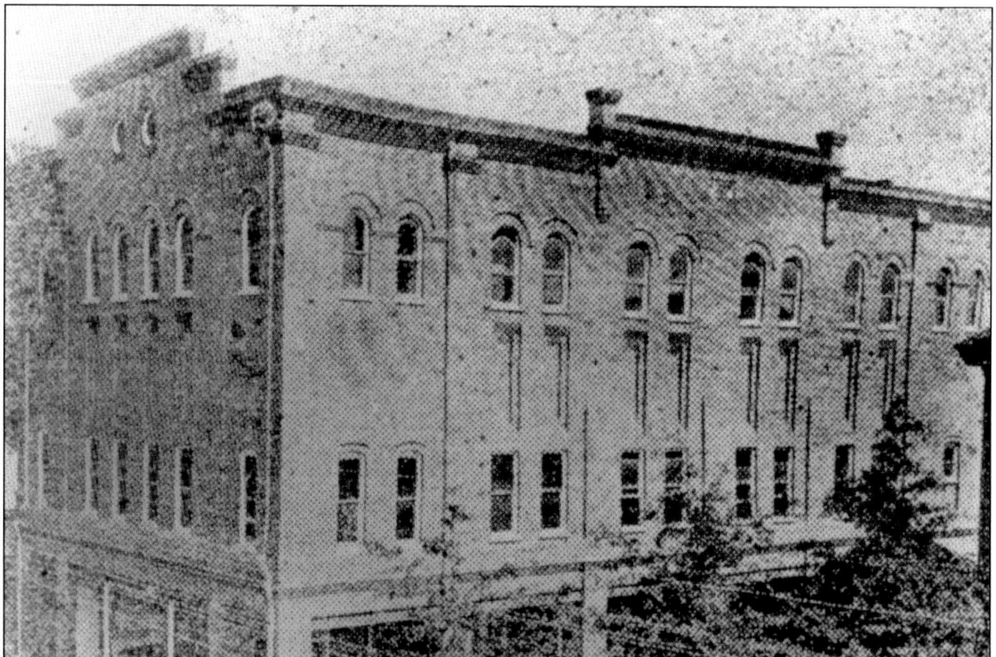

Facing Third Street next to the courthouse, the Masonic Temple was built in 1903. The first floor housed the board of education, law offices, the Greenville Public Library, and city offices. The next two floors were a modern opera house with stage and balcony. The top floor housed all of the Masonic groups in town. It burned on February 24, 1910, in a fire that destroyed much of downtown. (Courtesy of North Carolina Archives.)

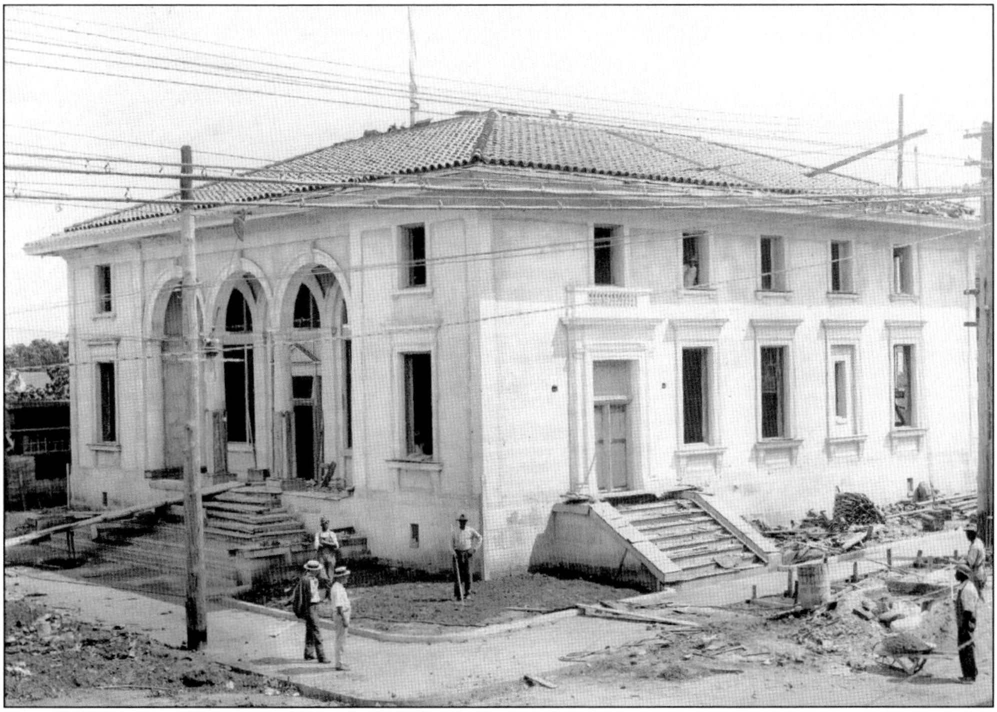

The old Greenville Post Office was located on the corner of Third and Evans Streets and appeared like this in 1914. It was begun in the fall of 1913 and completed in January 1915. The W.J. Brent Construction Company of Norfolk, Virginia constructed this building for the Treasury Department. It cost $50,475. In 1969, it became a federal office building. (Courtesy of Cecil and Libby Turner.)

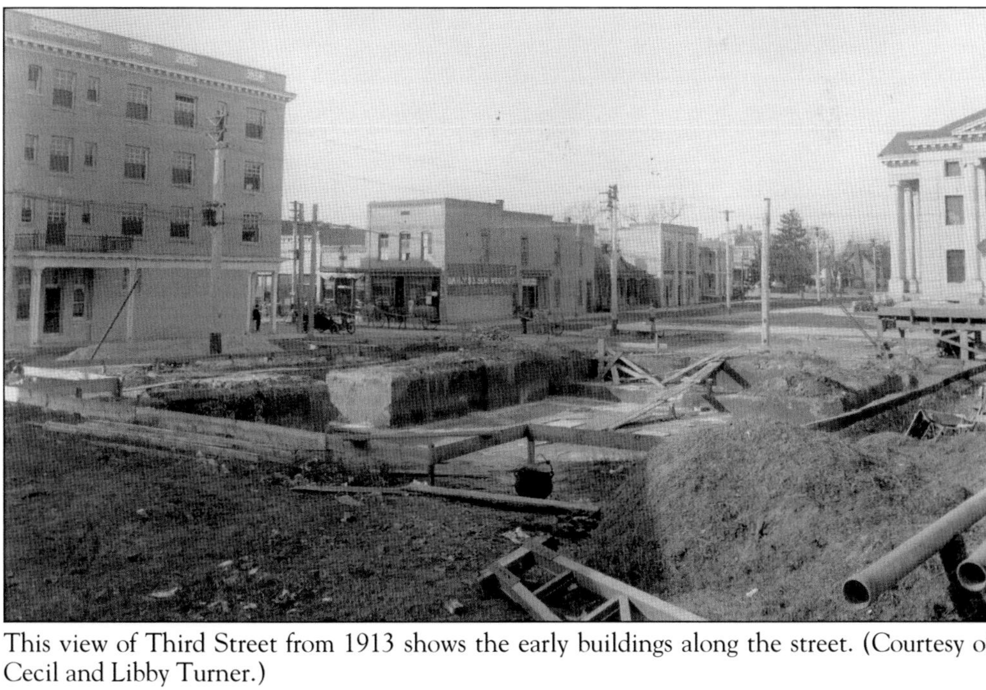

This view of Third Street from 1913 shows the early buildings along the street. (Courtesy of Cecil and Libby Turner.)

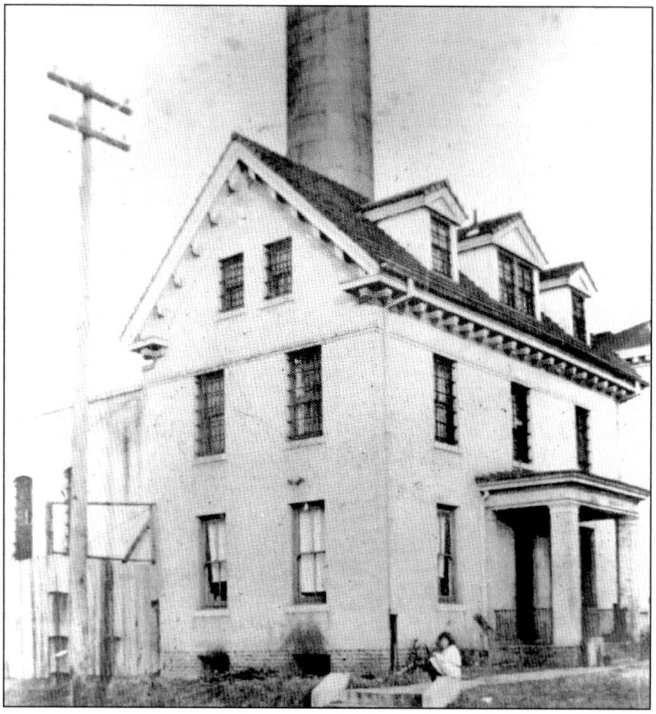

Located west of the courthouse, the Pitt County Jail was built in 1910 and torn down in 1965. The water standpipe behind the jail, used from 1905 to 1939, held the town's water supply. (Courtesy of ECMC.)

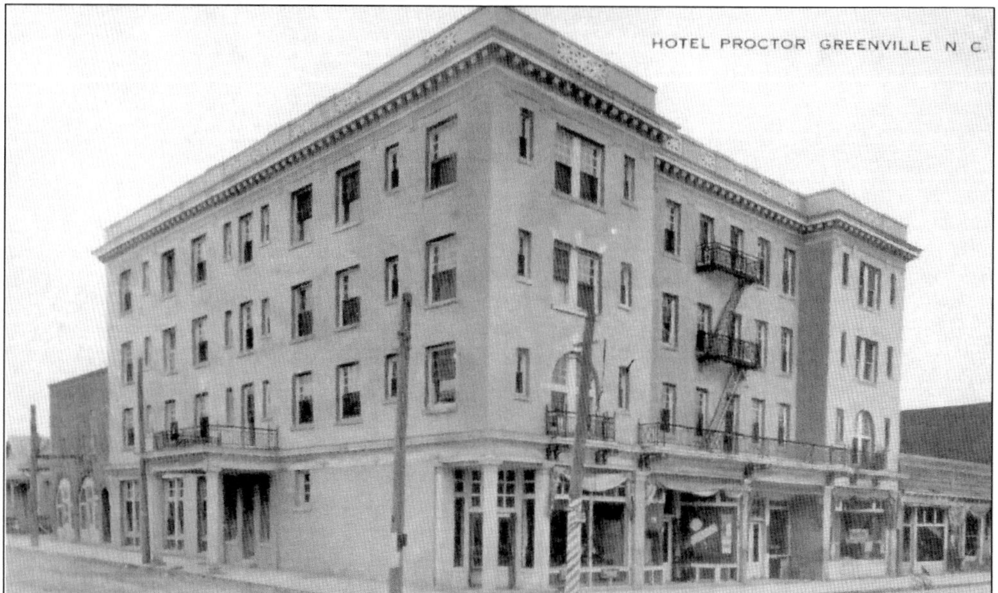

The Proctor Hotel was built in 1912–1913 on Evans Street by a company headed by J.O. and W.E. Proctor, businessmen from Grimesland. The 60-room hotel, which opened on June 20, 1913, featured a bridal suite located on the northwest corner with a view of the courthouse. The street level housed Batchelor Brothers clothing, the Proctor Hotel Dining Room and Barber Shop, and the Proctor Cigar and News Stand. It is interesting to note that Proctor Hotel towels were seen all over the Pacific in World War II. The building is now known as the Minges Building. (Courtesy of ECMC.)

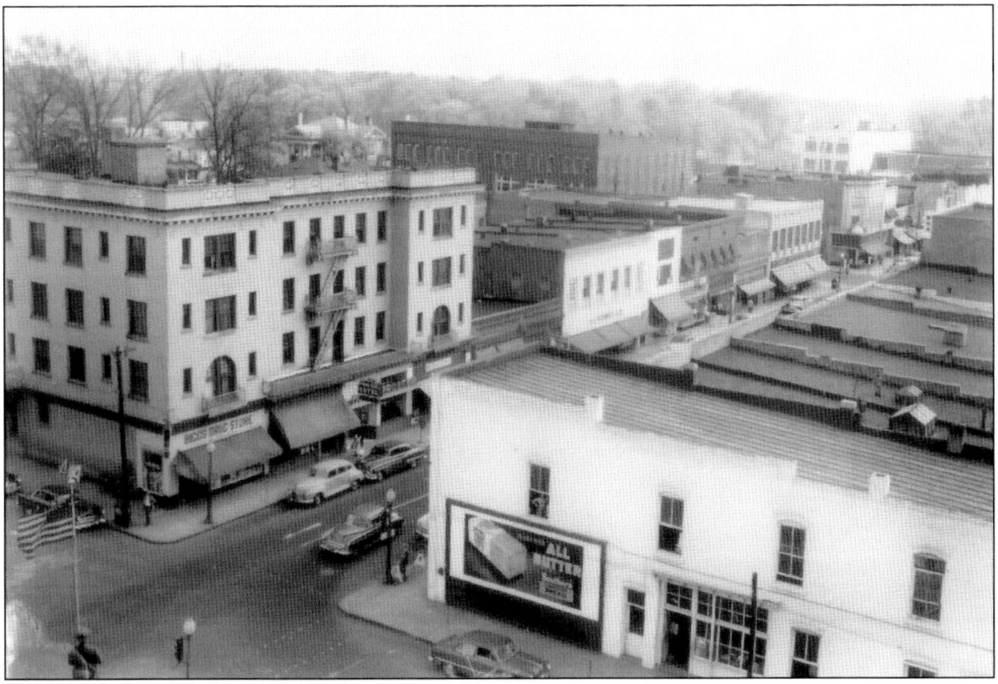

This view of downtown was taken from the roof of the courthouse in 1955. The city had survived the damage from the earthquake of 1886 and four major fires. A large storm in 1915 even covered the streets with eight inches of hail! (Courtesy of ECMC.)

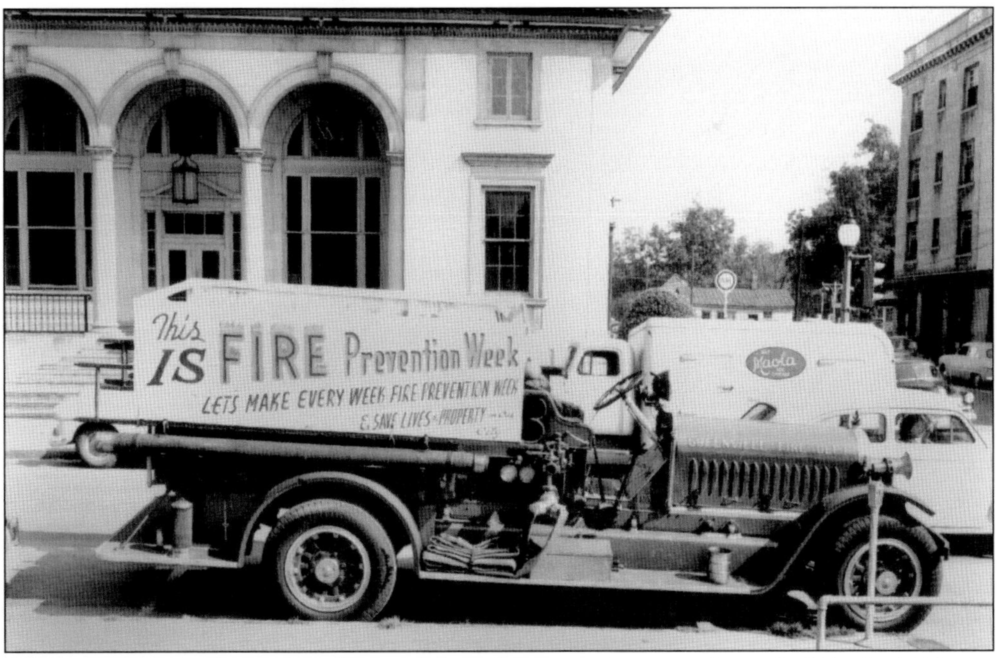

This Stutz Fire truck was bought in 1922 and answered every call until 1928. In 1923, the driver was killed when he lost control and wrecked the truck at Elizabeth and Fifth Streets. The truck's last call was on October 20, 1956, at the Dixie Tobacco Warehouse fire; it was later sold by Greenville in the 1960s. (Courtesy of ECMC.)

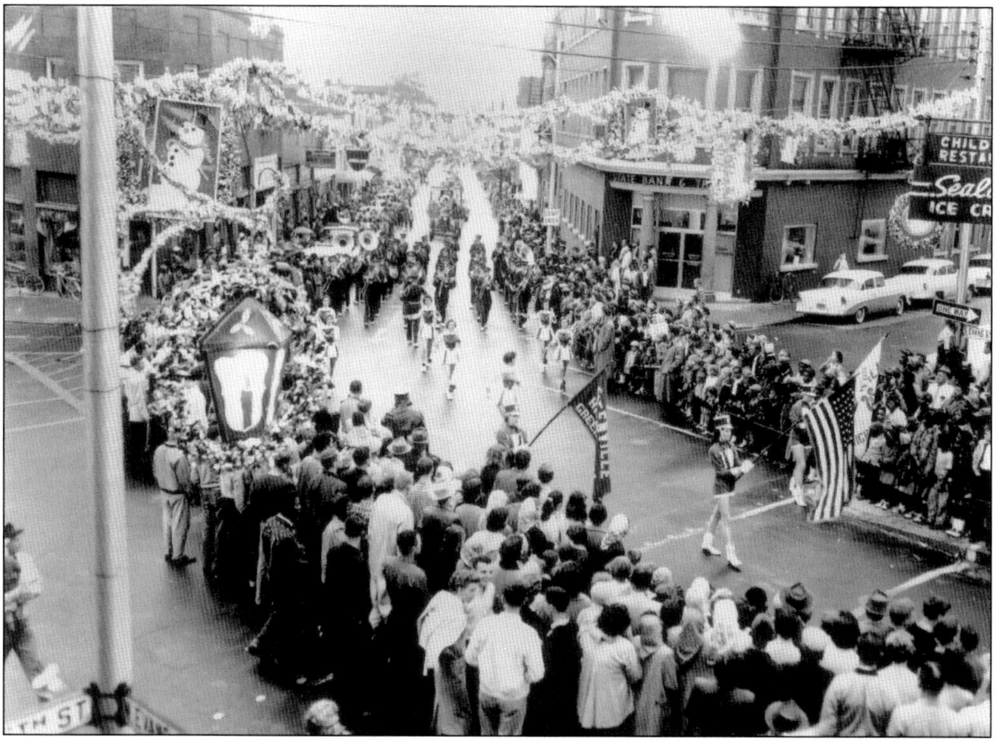

This was the Christmas parade in 1957 at Five Points. Christmas lights first appeared for the Christmas Parade downtown in 1927 through the efforts of the Merchants Association and the Woman's Club. They strung colored lights across Evans Street at Five Points and a few days later similar strings appeared on other blocks. In 1928, a 35-foot-tall Christmas tree was put up at Five Points in an effort to make Greenville the "best decorated town in eastern North Carolina." (Courtesy of ECMC.)

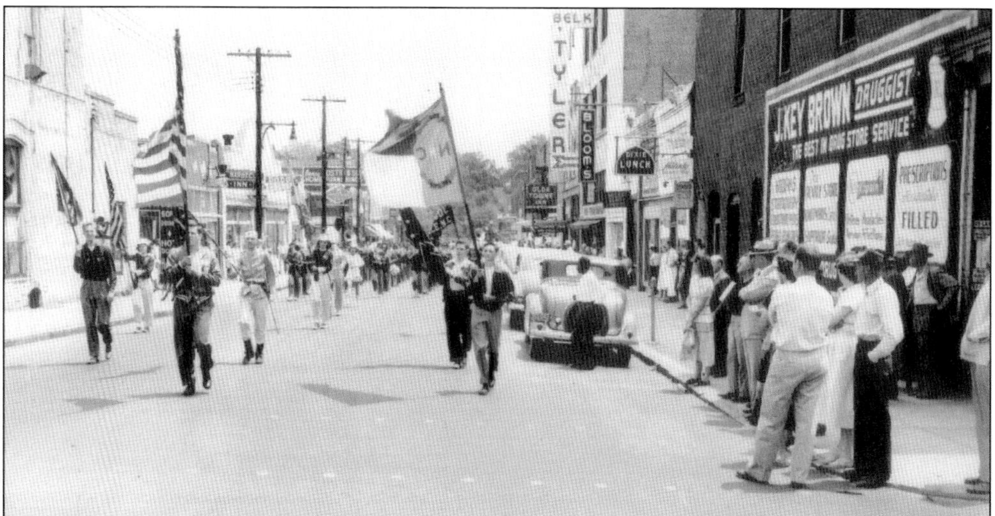

The Confederate Day parade marches down Fifth Street on May 10, 1950. A local school and bank holiday, Confederate Day was celebrated with a parade and the laying of wreaths at Greenville's two Confederate monuments. (Courtesy of ECMC.)

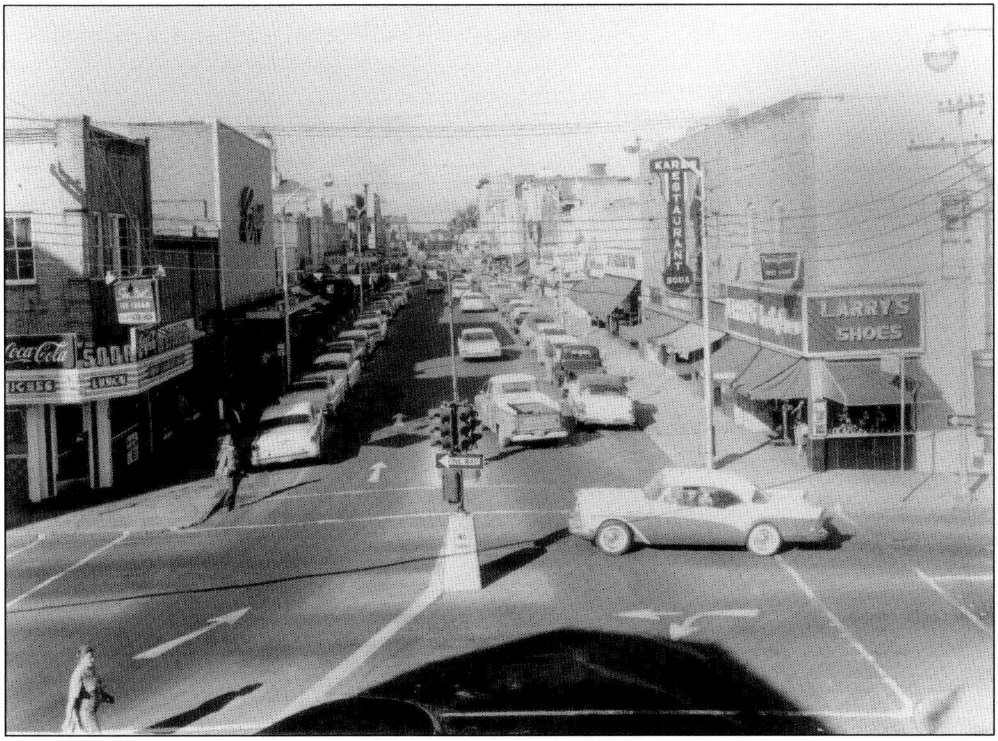

An Evans Street view looks north from Five Points about 1960. The first electric traffic light in Greenville was put on a pillar in the middle of Five Points in 1922, only the second one in the state at the time. (Courtesy of ECMC.)

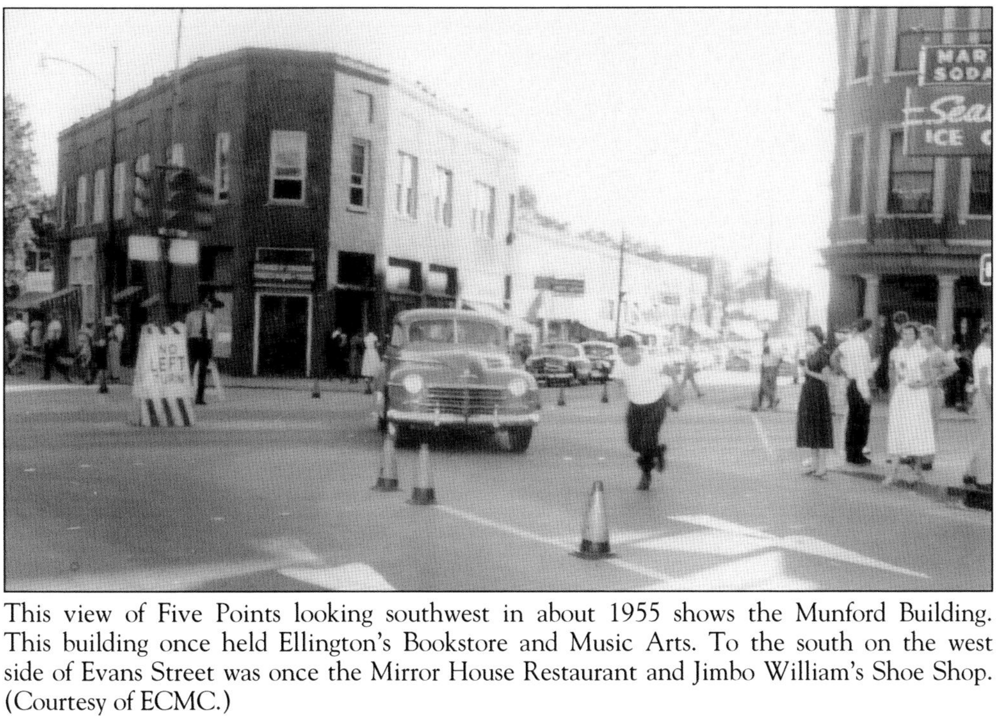

This view of Five Points looking southwest in about 1955 shows the Munford Building. This building once held Ellington's Bookstore and Music Arts. To the south on the west side of Evans Street was once the Mirror House Restaurant and Jimbo William's Shoe Shop. (Courtesy of ECMC.)

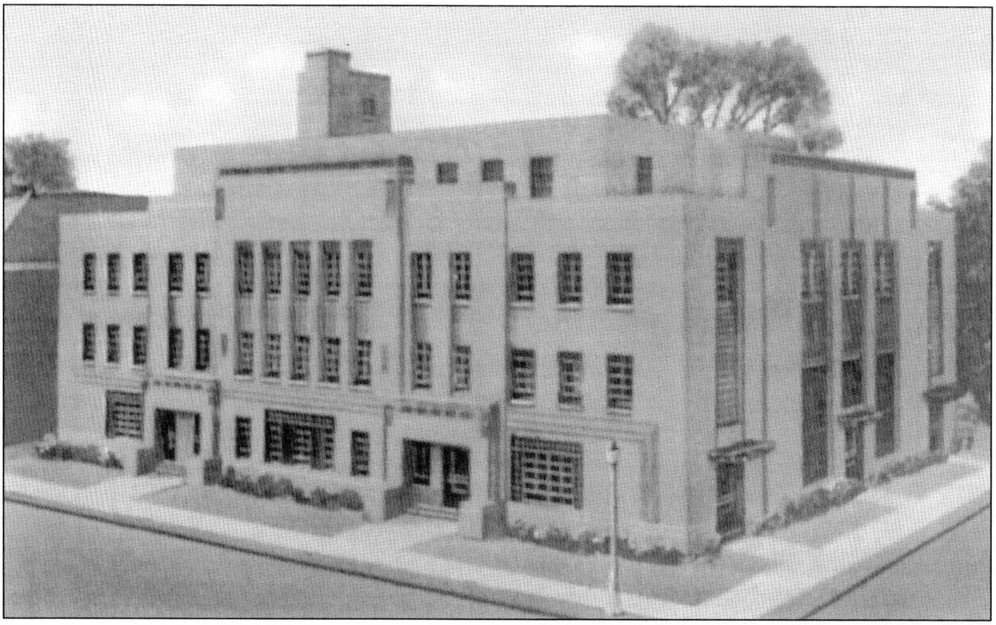

The Greenville City Hall, built in 1939–1940 on Fifth and Washington Streets, was designed by Frank Benton in the Art Deco style. The building had 10 offices and a jail on the top floor. During the Cold War, air sensing and radiation equipment was installed on the roof. (Courtesy of Roger Kammerer.)

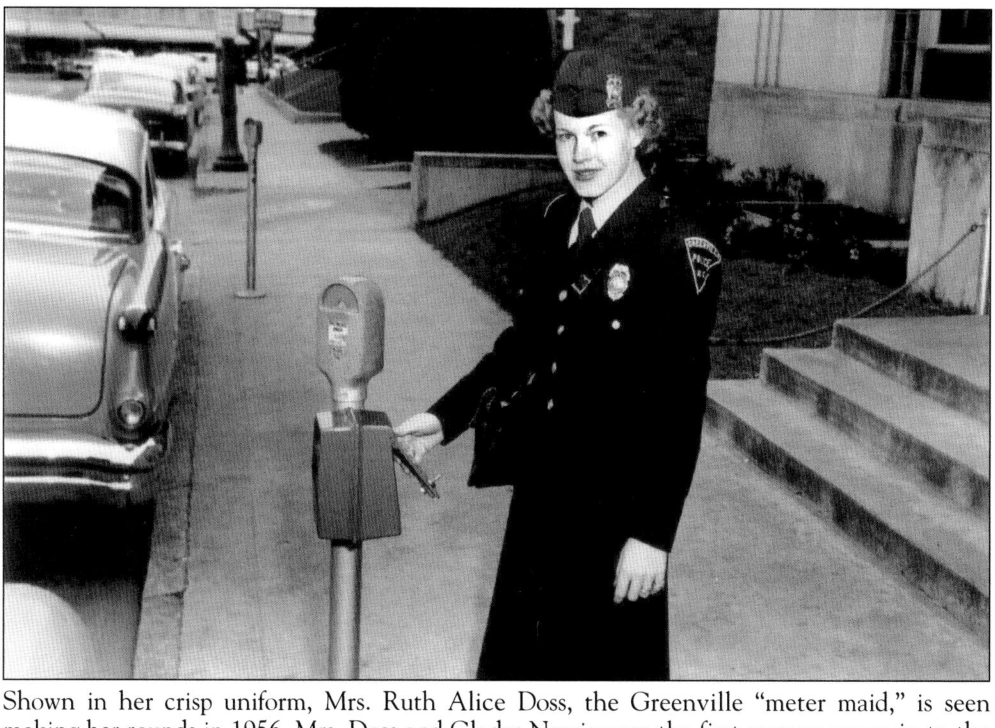

Shown in her crisp uniform, Mrs. Ruth Alice Doss, the Greenville "meter maid," is seen making her rounds in 1956. Mrs. Doss and Gladys Norris were the first women sworn in to the Greenville Police Department in 1954. Parking meters were first installed in town in 1948 and cost a penny for 13 minutes or a nickel for an hour. (Courtesy of ECMC.)

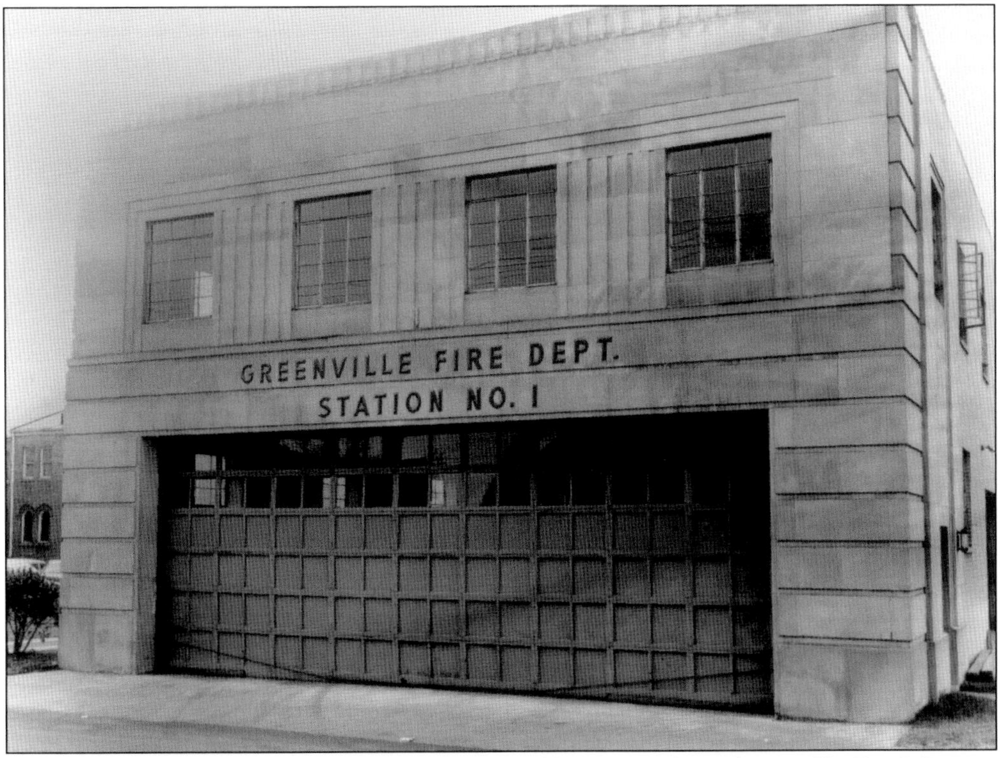

The Greenville Fire Station was built in 1939 on Fifth Street and was designed by Frank Benton in the Art Deco Style. It was torn down in 1996. (Courtesy of ECMC.)

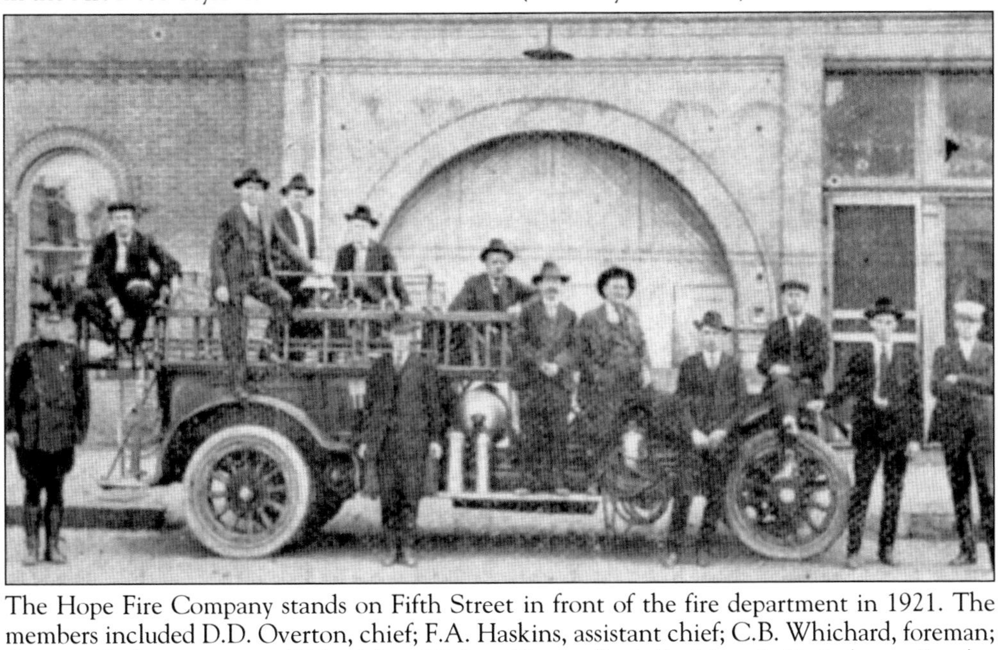

The Hope Fire Company stands on Fifth Street in front of the fire department in 1921. The members included D.D. Overton, chief; F.A. Haskins, assistant chief; C.B. Whichard, foreman; George Hodges, captain; E.H. Foley; Walter Harris; Fred Speight; A.C. Jackson; Stanley Moore; Elbert Smith; H.D. Mabe; D.M. Clark; George Cherry; and S.W. Snell. (Courtesy of Roger Kammerer.)

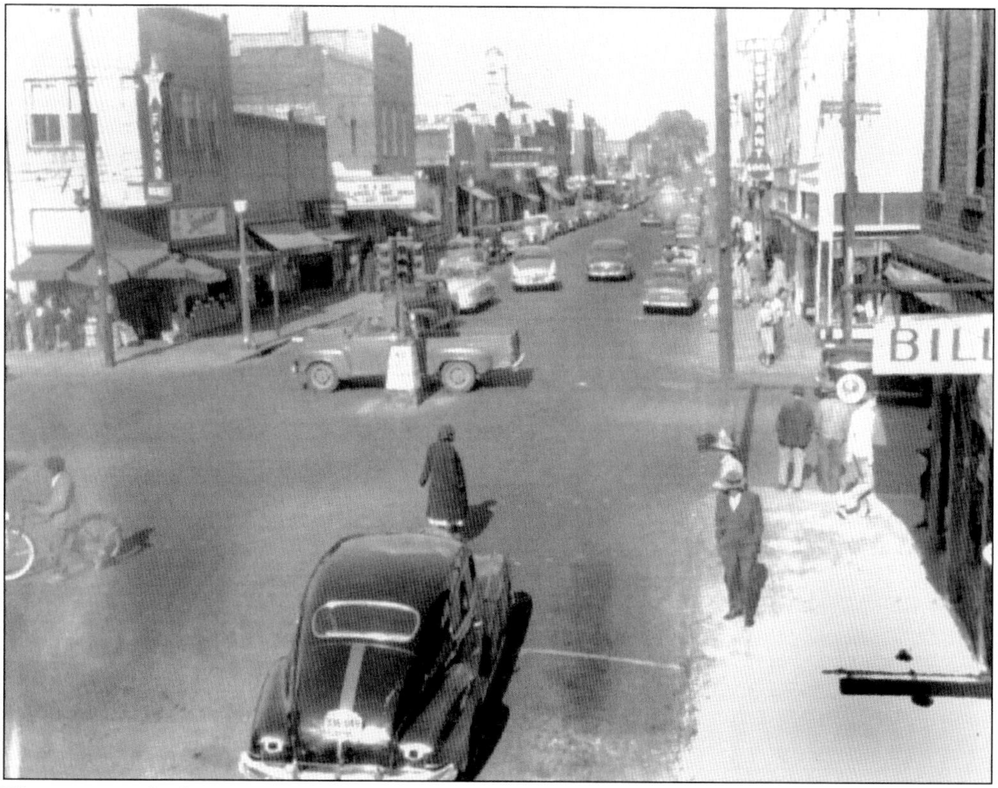

This is a view looking up Evans Street from Five Points in 1950. Notice the Colony Theater on the left, which opened in 1941 and closed in 1955. (Courtesy of Julian Vainright.)

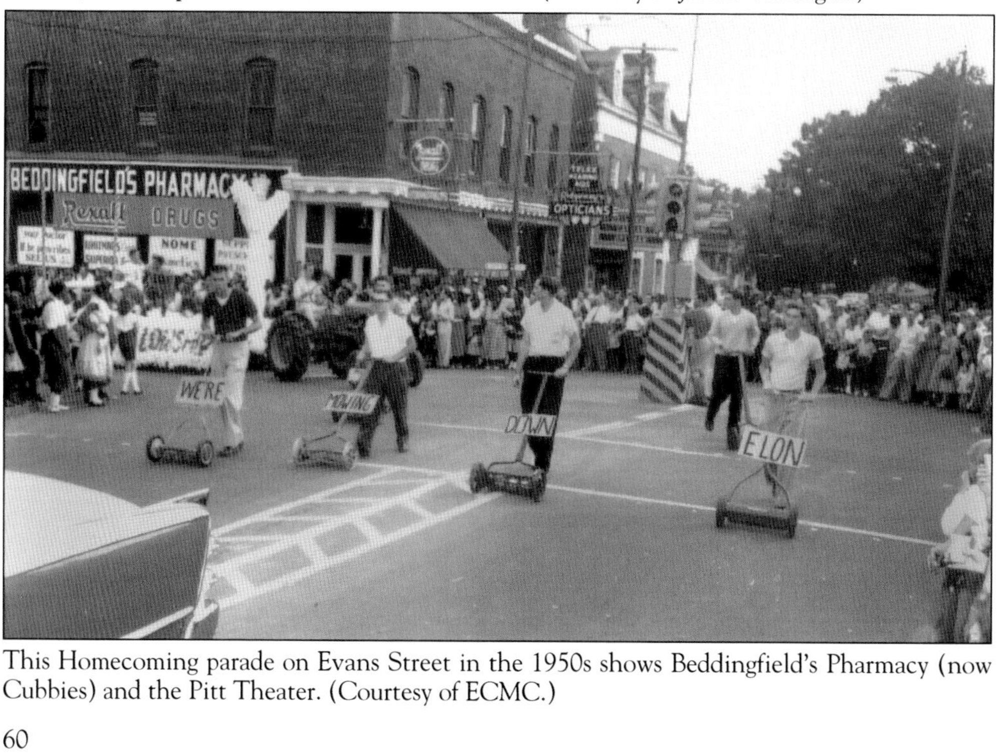

This Homecoming parade on Evans Street in the 1950s shows Beddingfield's Pharmacy (now Cubbies) and the Pitt Theater. (Courtesy of ECMC.)

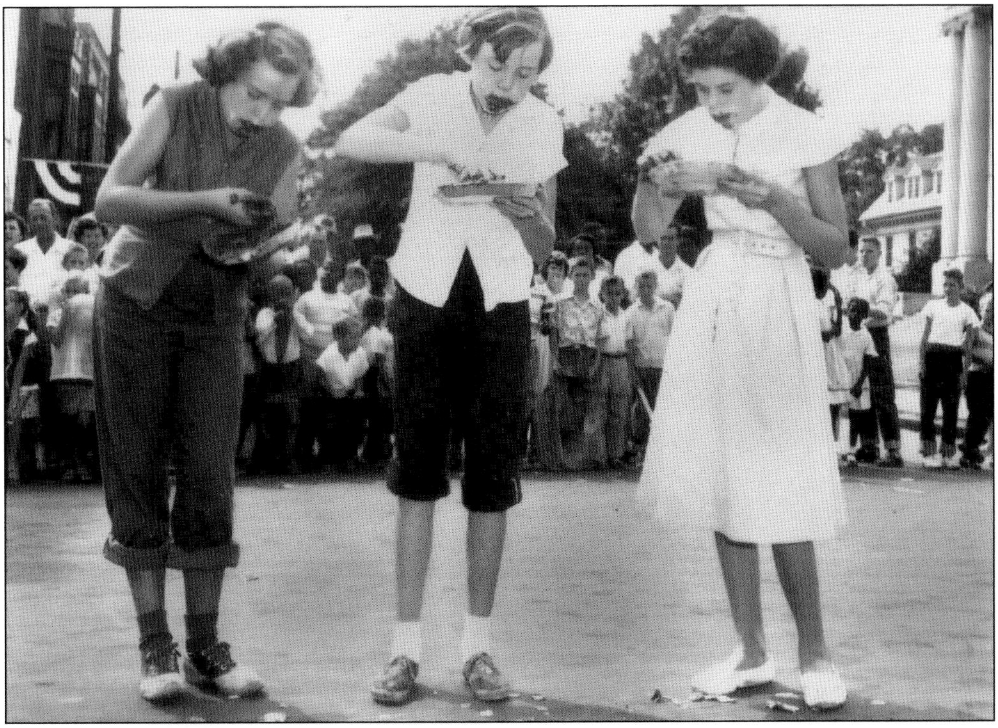

These girls participate in a pie-eating contest at Third and Evans Streets as part of a Merchants Association event in the 1950s. The Merchants Association sponsored Dollar Day, Cow Day, Turkey Day, Straw Hat Day, Farmers Day, and Hi Neighbor Day to enliven downtown business. (Courtesy of ECMC.)

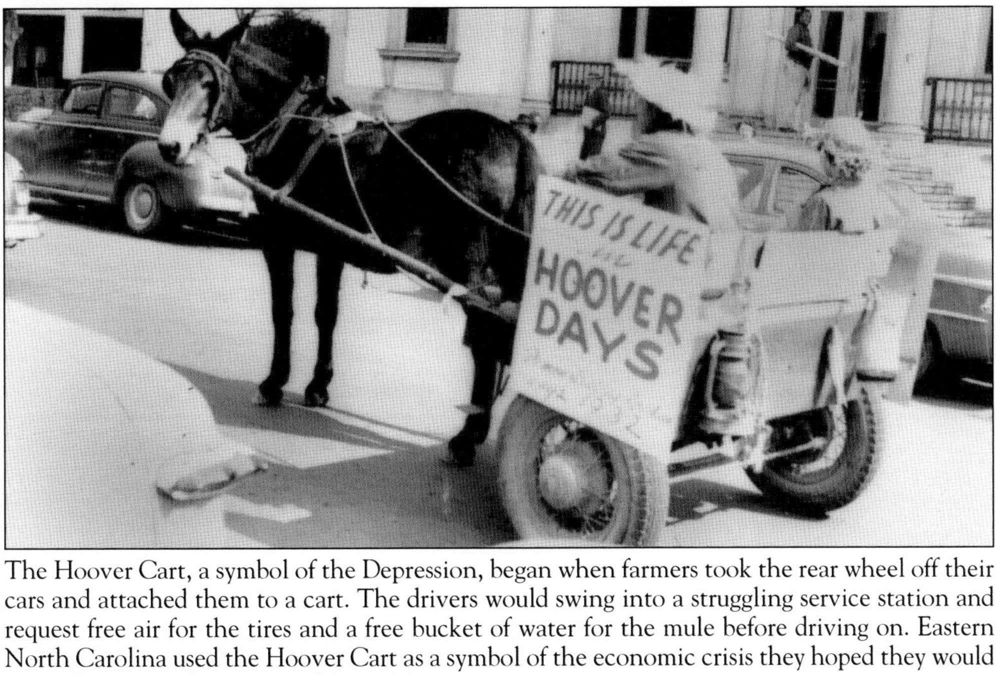

The Hoover Cart, a symbol of the Depression, began when farmers took the rear wheel off their cars and attached them to a cart. The drivers would swing into a struggling service station and request free air for the tires and a free bucket of water for the mule before driving on. Eastern North Carolina used the Hoover Cart as a symbol of the economic crisis they hoped they would never face again. (Courtesy of ECMC.)

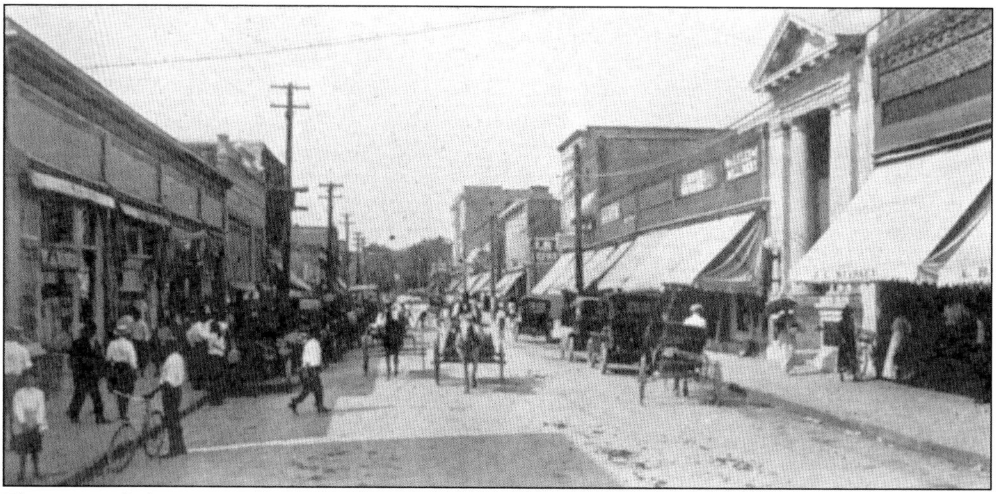

This typical day on Evans Street in 1914 shows both cars and wagons. Cars first appeared in Greenville in 1903, which made the newspaper lament "horseless vehicles should be run with horse sense." The greatest complaint by merchants at that time was that the sidewalks were covered in "bicycles, goat carts, and too much spit." (Courtesy of the *Illustrated City of Greenville, Pitt County, 1914.*)

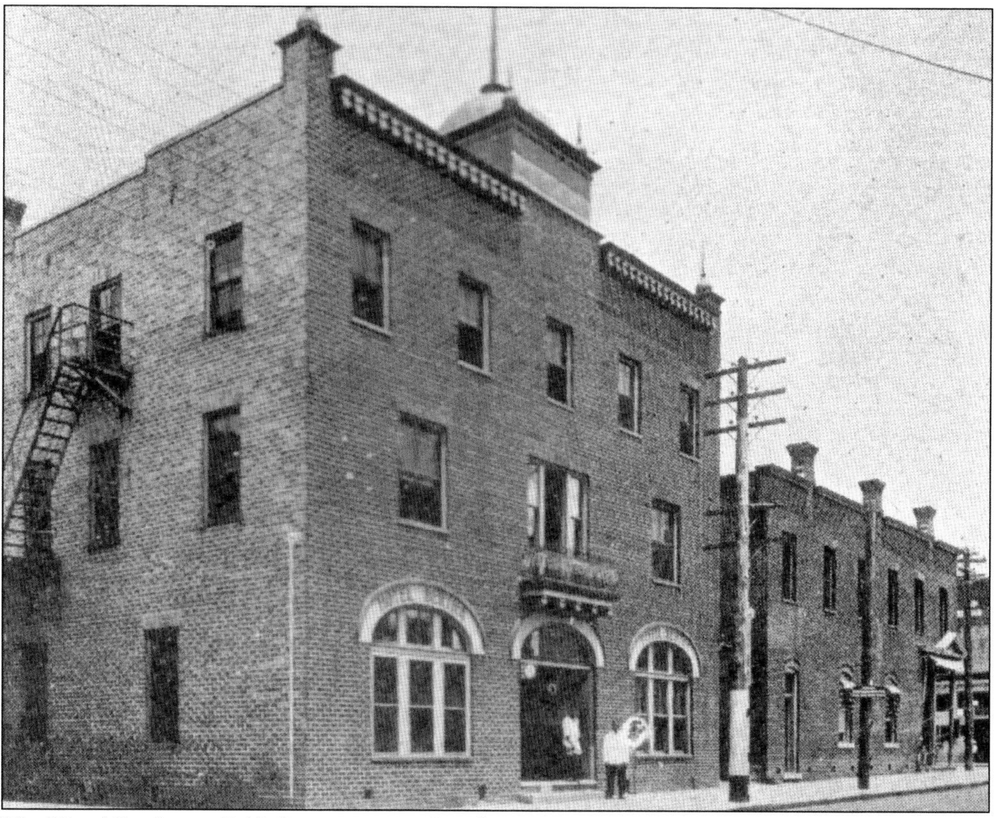

The Hotel Bertha on Fifth Street appeared in this manner in 1914. Built in 1900 by Benjamin F. Patrick, it was the first large commercial hotel in Greenville. It became known as the Princeton Hotel by 1919. (Courtesy of the *Illustrated City of Greenville, Pitt County, 1914.*)

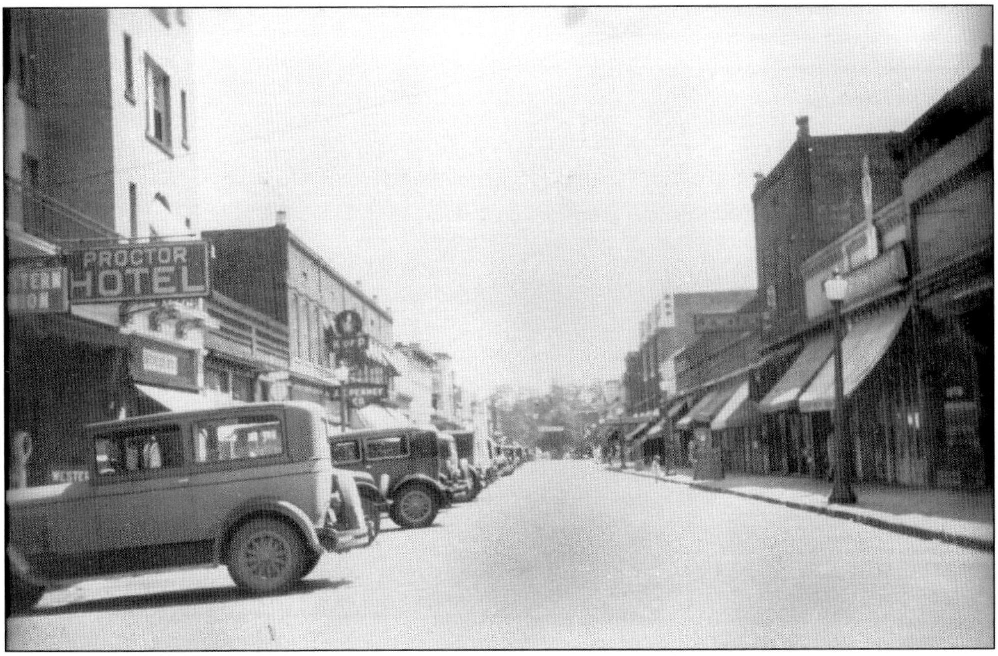

Evans Street is viewed looking south from Third Street in 1932. (Courtesy of Charles Horne Collection.)

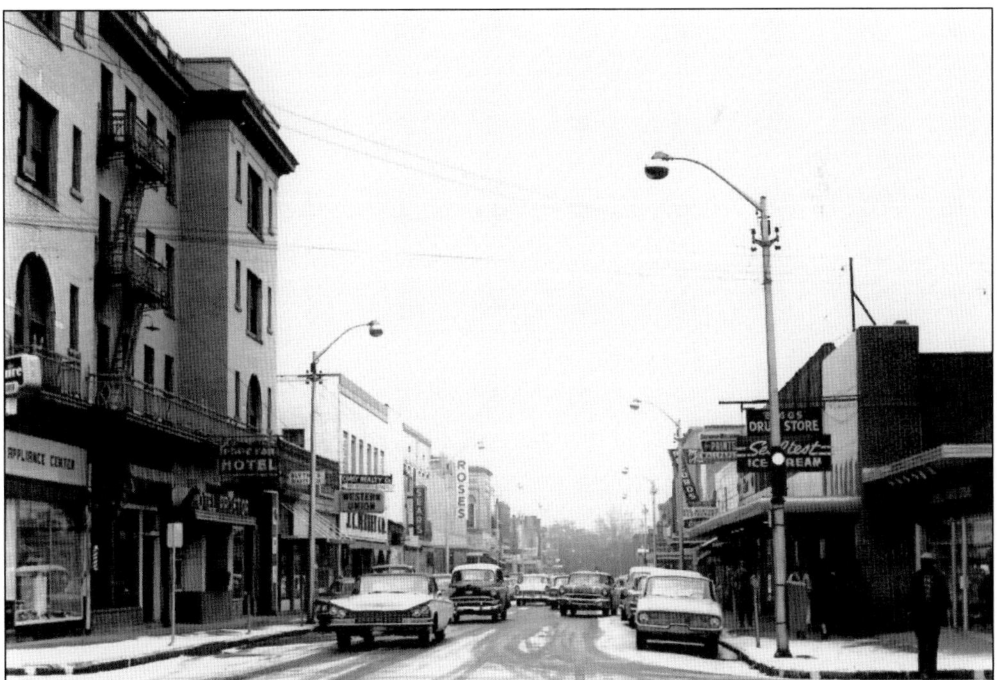

This is a comparison photo of Evans Street looking south from Third Street in about 1963. (Courtesy of ECMC.)

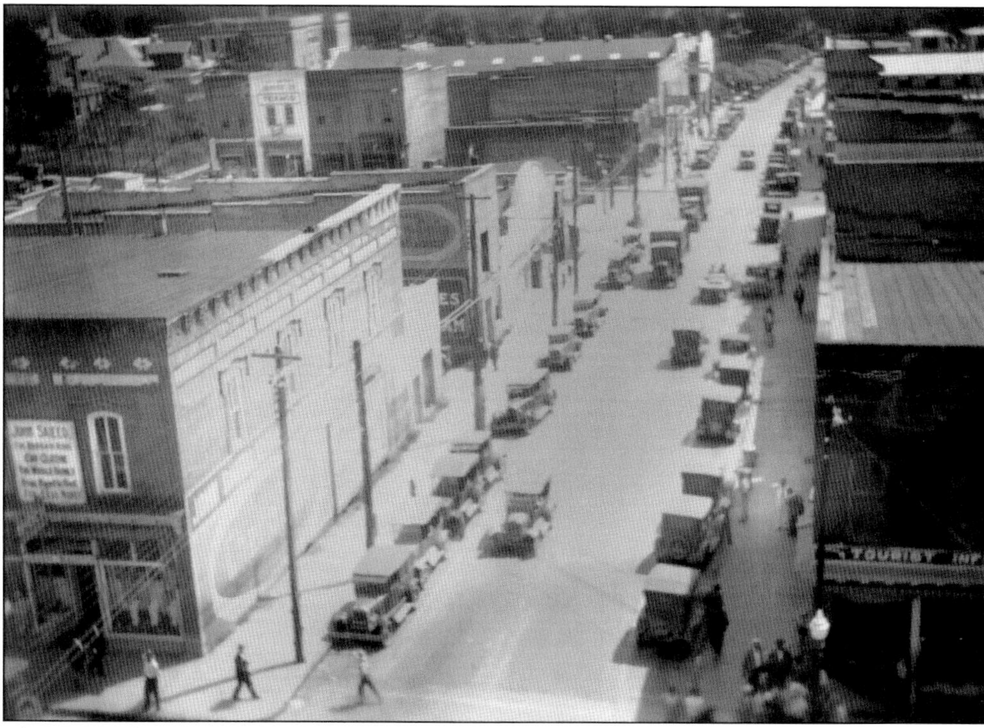

This unusual view looking down from the State Bank shows Fifth Street in the 1920s. Notice the unusual buildings on the left side of the street, where an ice cream factory, car dealership, and taxi cab company all were located. (Courtesy of Charles Horne Collection.)

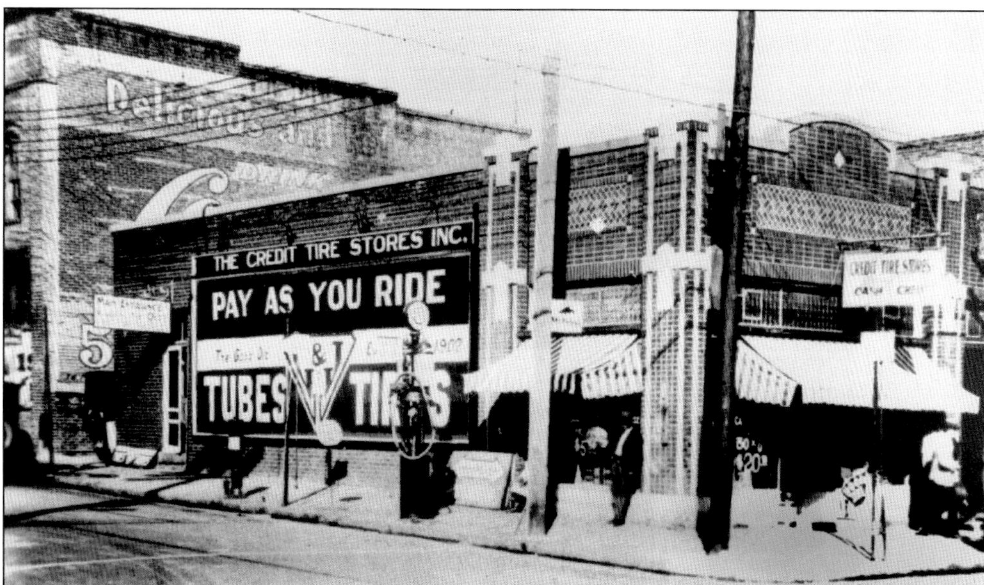

This Depression-era image of the Credit Store and gas station at the northeast corner of Fifth and Cotanche Streets was taken in 1935. The Credit Stores featured tires, batteries, and gas on credit. It did not last long in Greenville. (Courtesy of ECMC.)

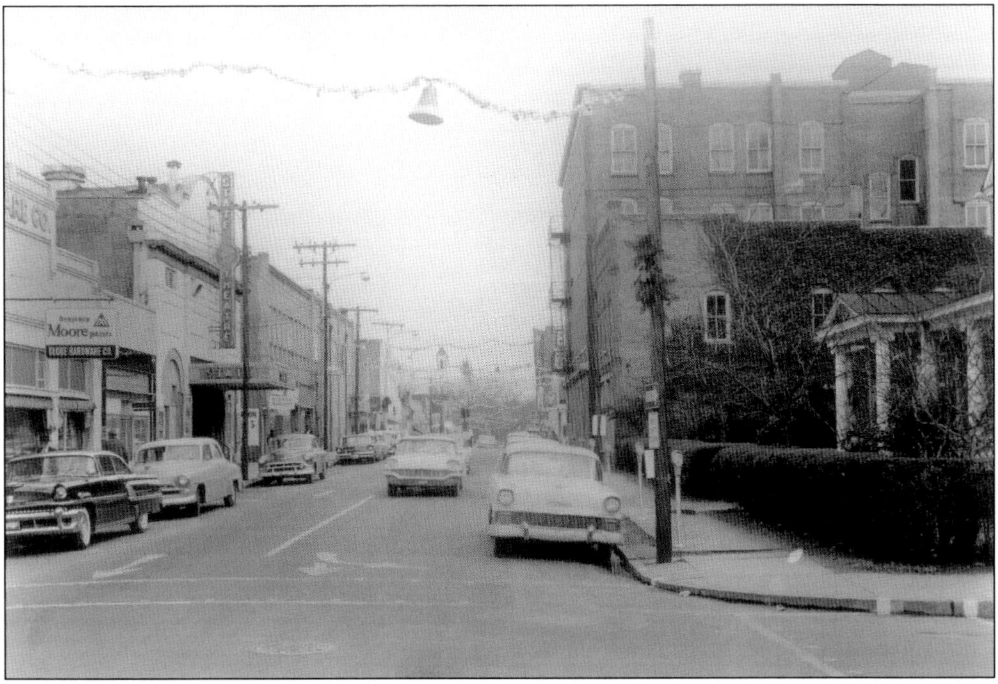

This scene shows Fifth Street at Christmas in 1959. Notice to the right the porch of the Humber House, the Humber Machine Shop, and the back of the State Bank. (Courtesy of ECMC.)

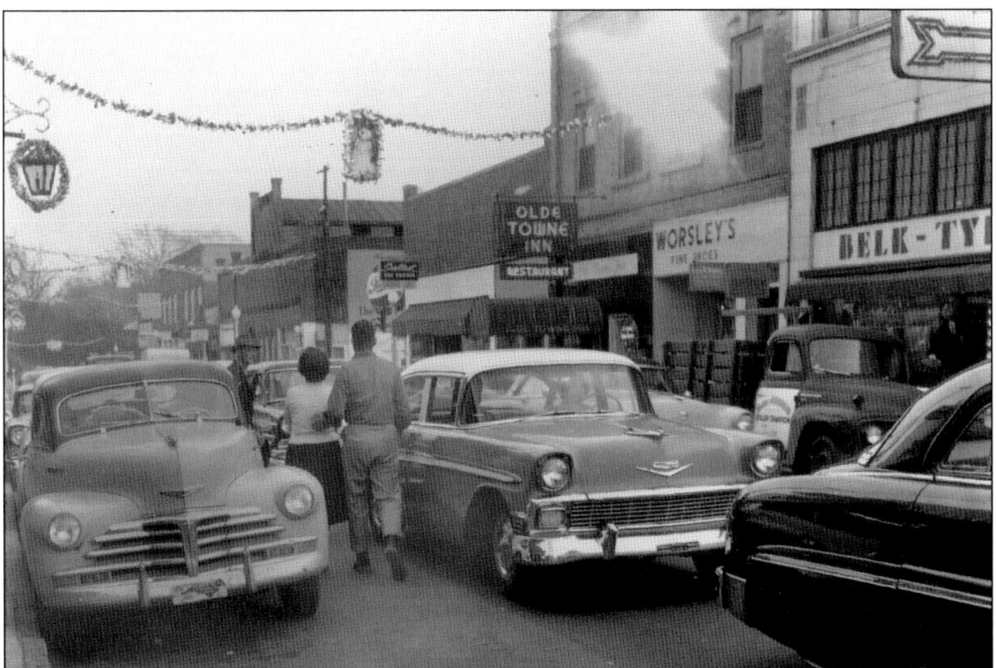

Another scene showing Fifth Street at Christmas in 1957 shows the Olde Town Inn, a Greenville landmark. It was the first air-conditioned restaurant in Greenville. (Courtesy of ECMC.)

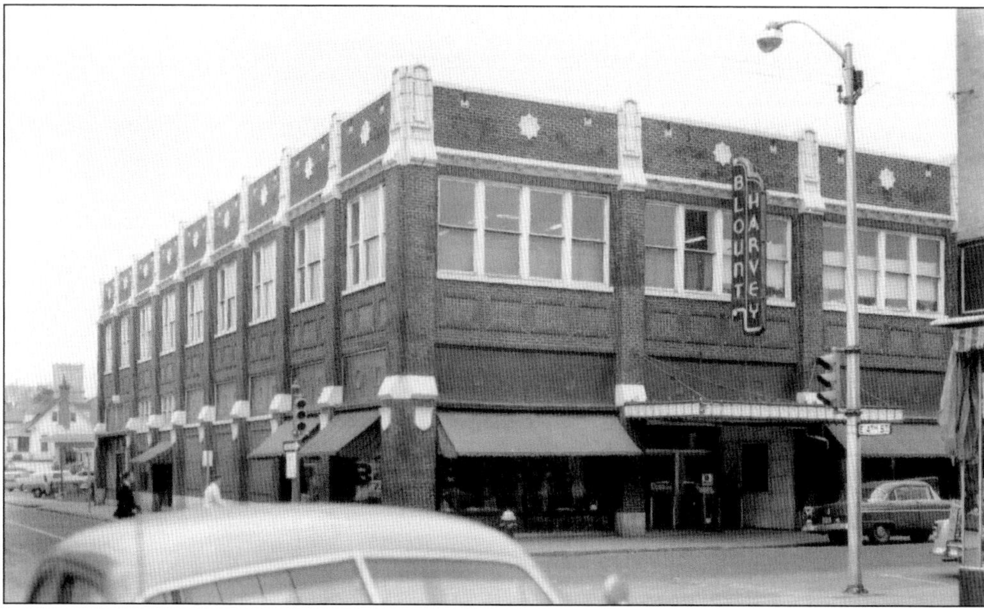

Located at the northwest corner of Evans and Fourth Streets, the Blount-Harvey Building is pictured in 1956. Blount-Harvey was organized in 1920 as a successor to the J.R. & J.G. Moye Company, which was situated across the street. Blount-Harvey's made Greenville the shopping mecca of Eastern North Carolina. (Courtesy of ECMC.)

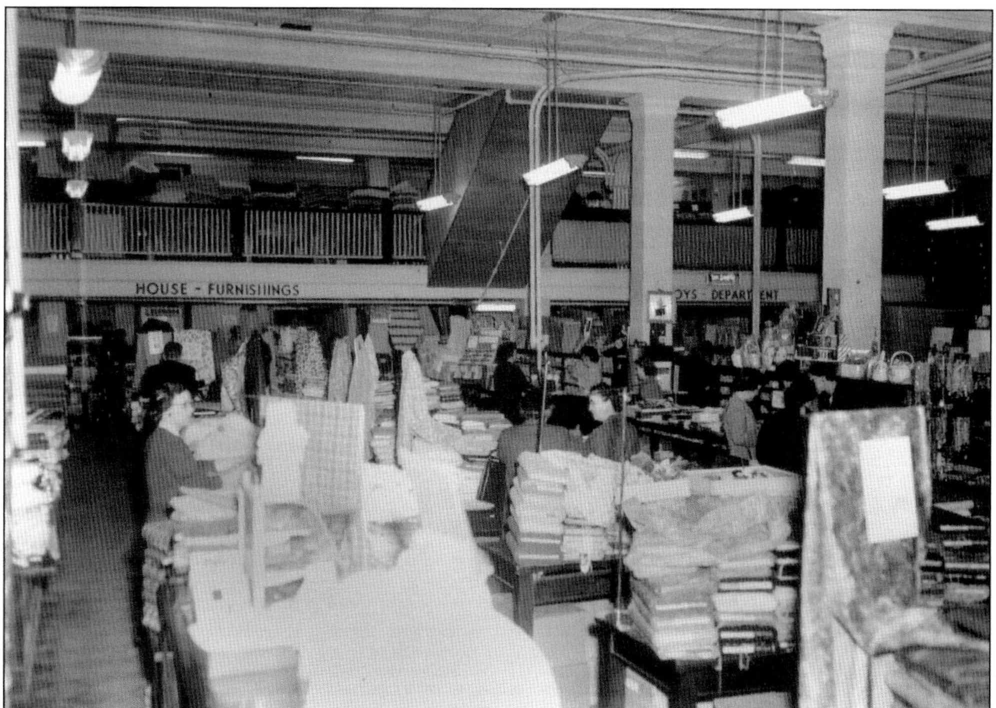

This photograph reveals the interior of the Blount-Harvey department store in 1956. Blount-Harvey's carried everything from farm implements to silk scarves. In 1938, a tea room was opened on the balcony. (Courtesy of ECMC.)

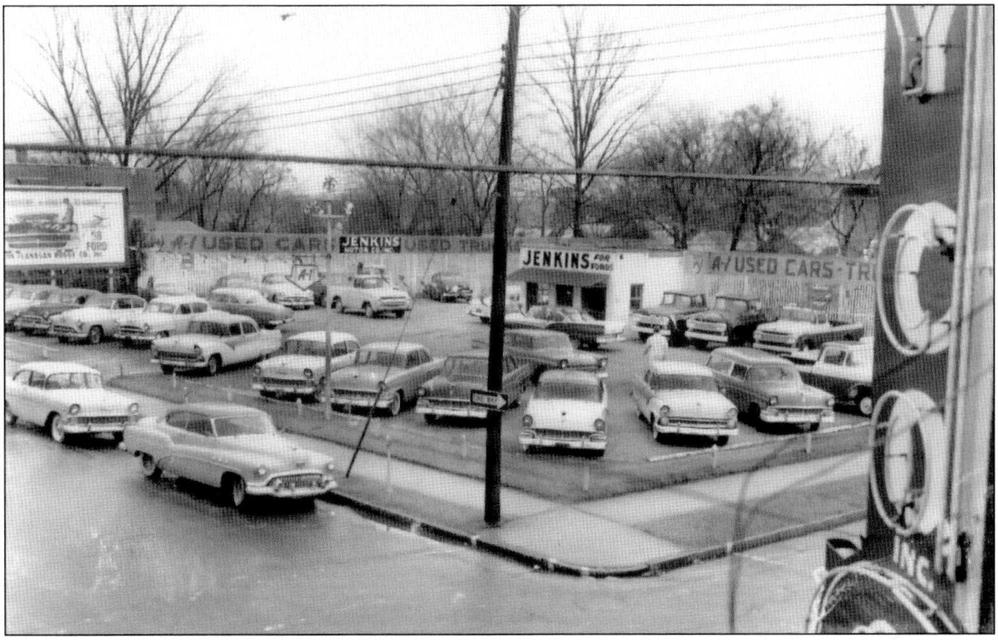

The Jenkins Motor Company at Fourth & Cotanche Streets is the subject of this 1958 view. Jenkins sold used cars in connection with Flanagan's Ford Dealership. Local boys would "borrow" cars with keys left inside for a date and would return them at the end of the evening. Mr. Jenkins knew, but he didn't worry about it. (Courtesy of ECMC.)

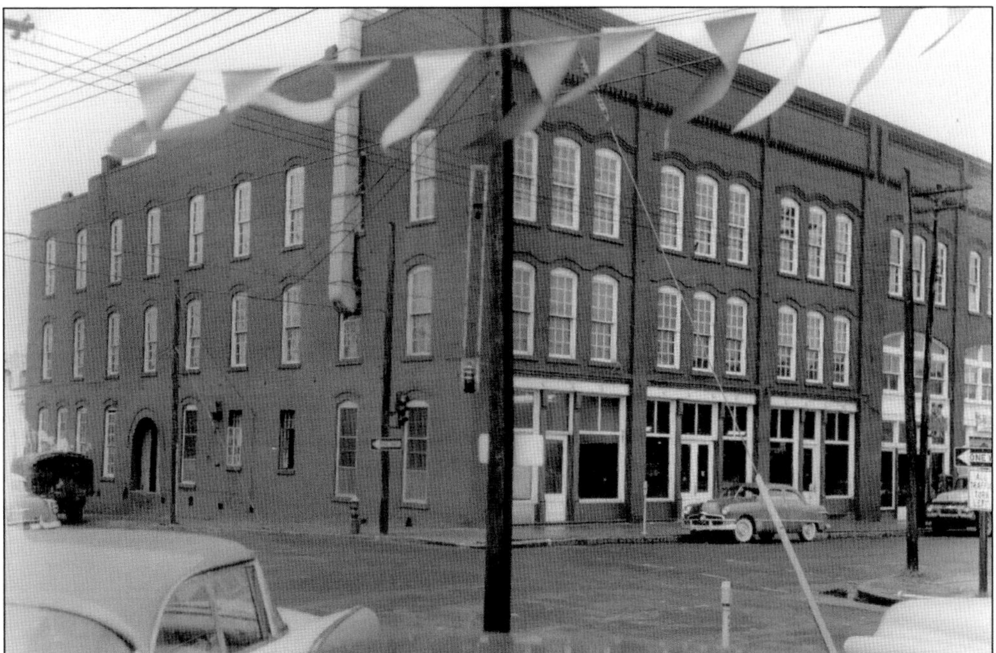

The John Flanagan Buggy Company and undertaking business was built in 1907 on the southwest corner of Fourth and Cotanche Streets. In 1914, it became a franchised dealer of Ford and Lincoln automobiles, while still making buggies until 1920. They sold the franchise in 1958 and closed. The building was razed in 1966–1967. (Courtesy of ECMC.)

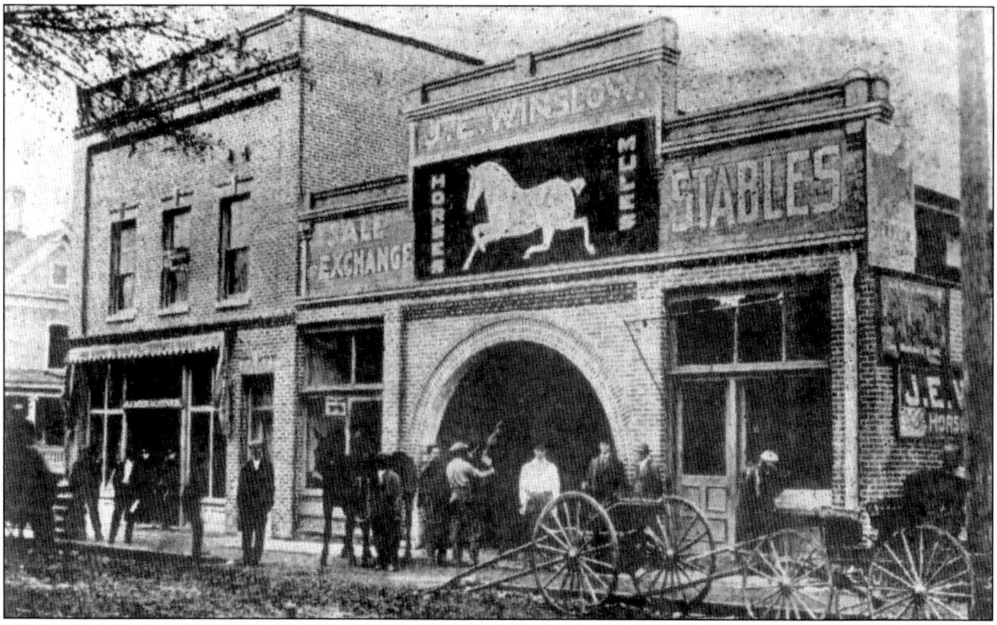

These stables were built in 1903 on Fifth Street by J.E. Winslow, a noted horse and mule dealer. In 1947, it became the Globe Hardware Company. It was restored in 1999 by owner Herb Wilkerson as part of the Greenville's Facade Grant Program. The two-story building to the left, built in 1910, included the Hines-Murphrey Coca-Cola Bottling Works at ground level and a Masonic lodge and the Greenville Public Library on the second floor. (Courtesy of *The Bicentennial Book, A Greenville Album.*)

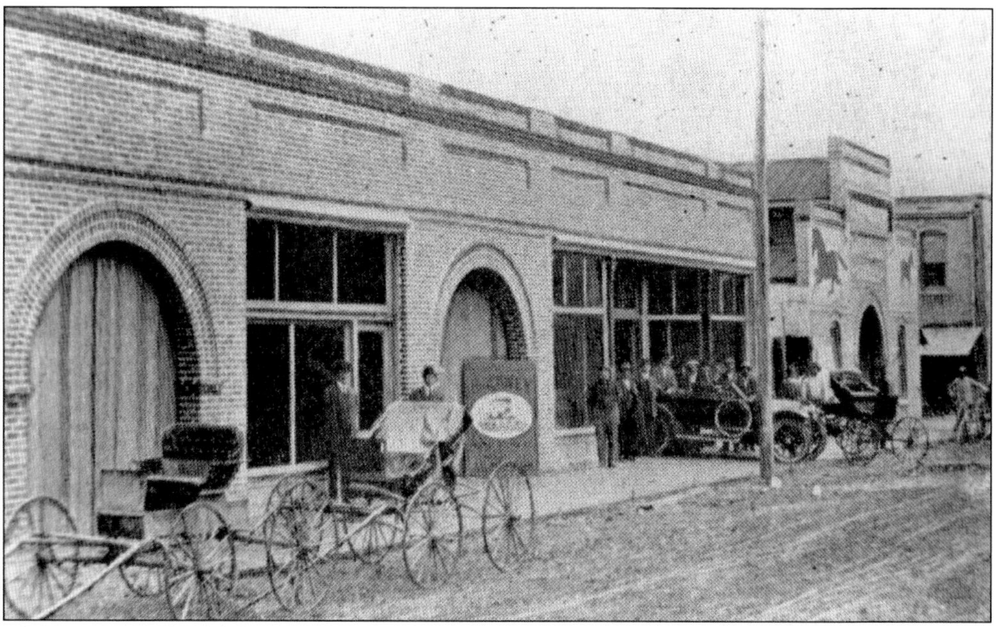

This rare view highlights the Washington Street side of the J.E. Winslow Stables *c.* 1914. Winslow also operated a farm implement company in the store to the left. He sold these buildings in 1918 to the Utility Garage and Machine Shop and the Sam White Motor Company and opened new stables on Clark Street. (Courtesy of ECMC.)

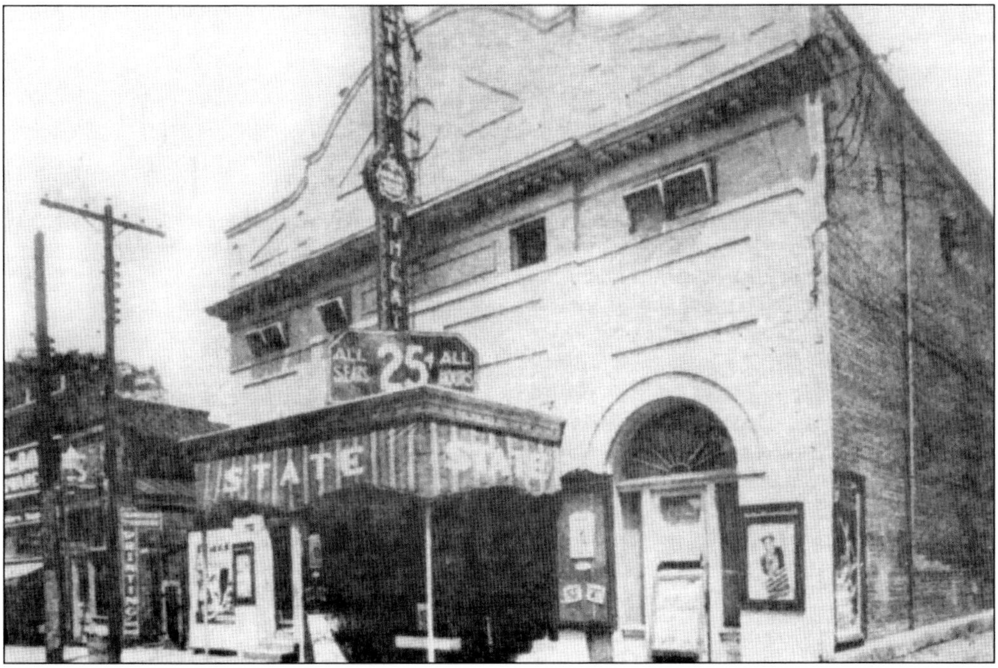

The State Theater, shown here about 1930, was built in 1914 by Samuel T. White. It seated 700 people and hosted nationally known traveling shows. In 1918, William Jennings Bryan spoke here. In 1930, it became known as the State Theater, but was renamed the Park Theater in 1973. It eventually became the property of Carmike Cinemas; they ran it as a $1.50 movie house until closing in 1999. (Courtesy *The Bicentennial Book, A Greenville Album*.)

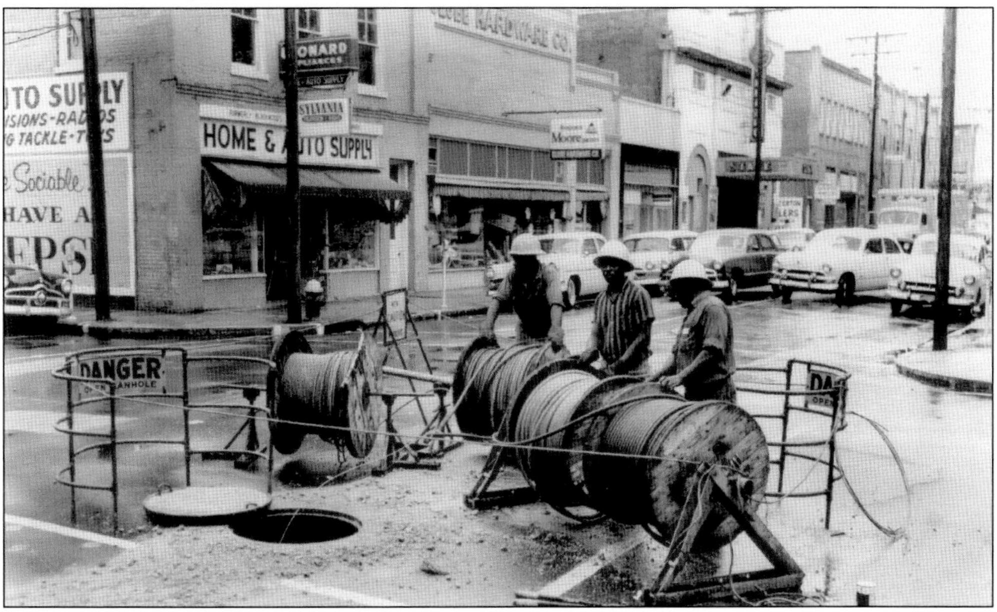

Fifth Street looking east in 1958 included the Home and Auto Supply, Globe Hardware Company (Winslow Stables), and the State Theater. The Home and Auto Supply burned in 1962 and was replaced by Wachovia Bank with the first drive-through teller in the city. (Courtesy of ECMC.)

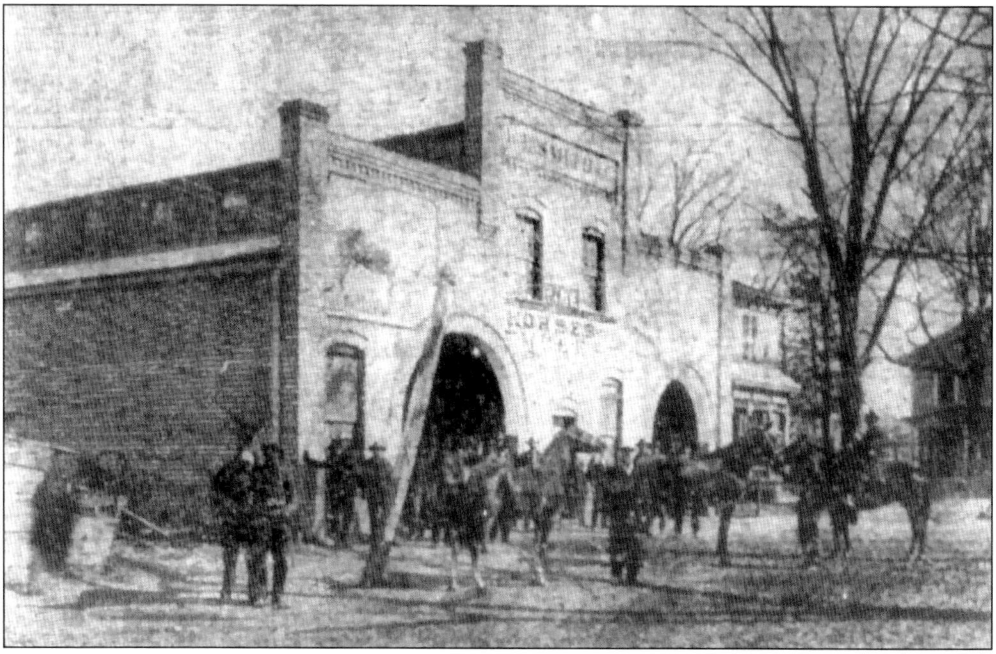

Robert Lee Smith built these stables on Fourth Street in 1903 and ran feed, sale, and exchange stables for horses and mules for many years. The stables, shown here in 1907, were 60 feet by 275 feet and fronted on Third and Fourth Streets. In later years this building was the Colonial grocery store and the Buccaneer night club. (Courtesy of Ross-Kammerer Photo Archive.)

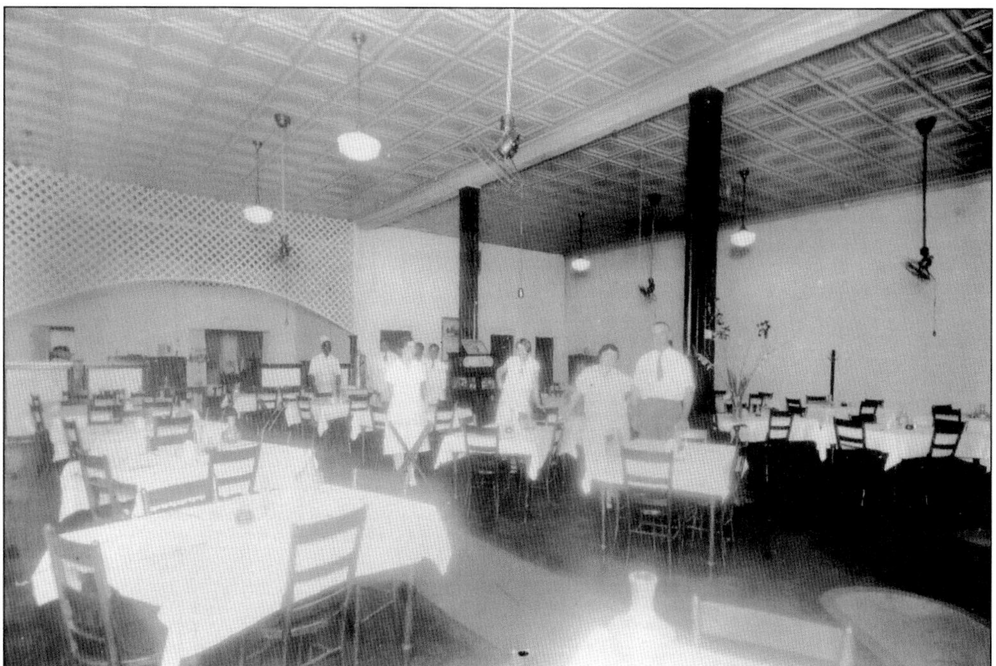

The Kitlow Cafeteria was opened in 1921 on Evans Street by Alex Blow and J.B. Kittrell. In 1926, it became known as the Service Cafe under the management of Gay Heath and Emily Johnston. (Courtesy of Charles Horne Collection.)

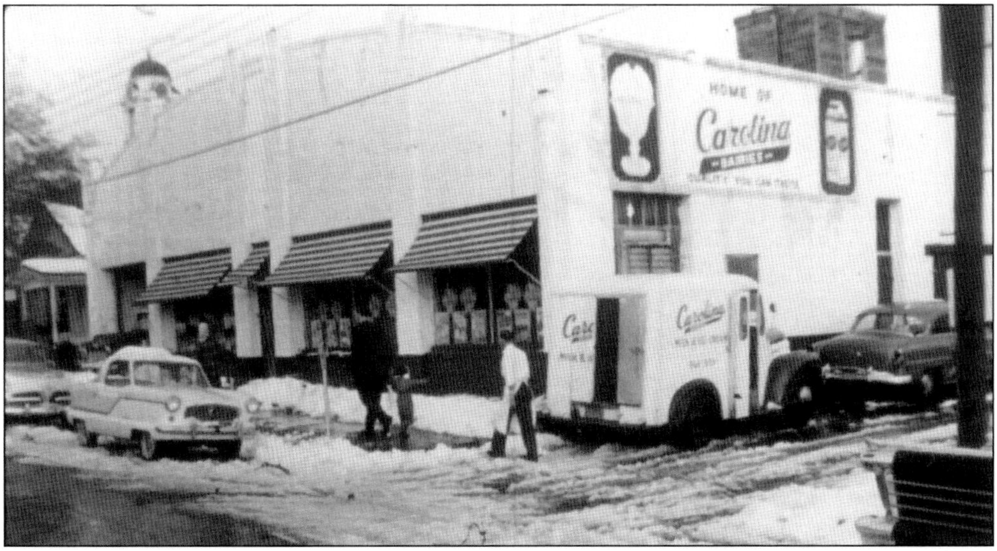

The Carolina Dairies Dairy Bar was located on the east side of Washington Street between Third and Fourth Streets. A hailstorm once broke out all the plate-glass windows. It was operated in conjunction with Harvey's Dairy at West End Circle until 1962 when they sold this building and dairy and moved to Memorial Drive. It was demolished by 1975. (Courtesy of Alex Albright.)

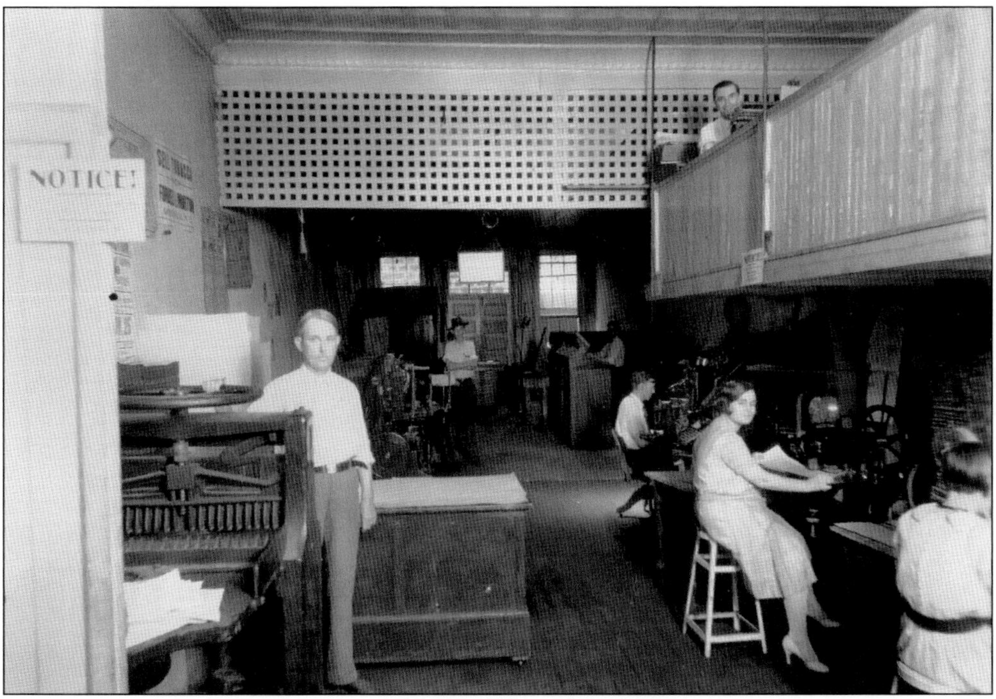

Henry W. Renfrow, who lived from 1879 to 1937 and was a native of Wilson County, moved to Greenville in 1912 and established Renfrow Printing Company on Evans Street. Renfrow had one of the largest and best-equipped printing plants in Eastern North Carolina and did all the printing for the tobacco warehouses. The business was later owned by J. Con Lanier, S.W. Parker, and W.H. Whichard. It ended in the 1980s. (Courtesy Charles Horne Collection.)

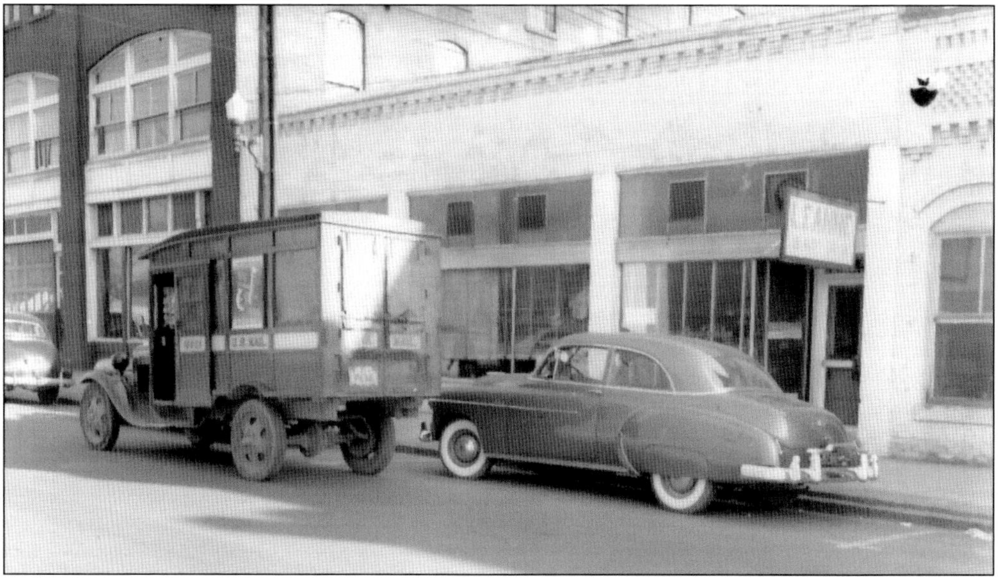

The old mail truck on Fourth Street sits in front of the businesses beside the John Flanagan Buggy Company in 1950. (Courtesy of ECMC.)

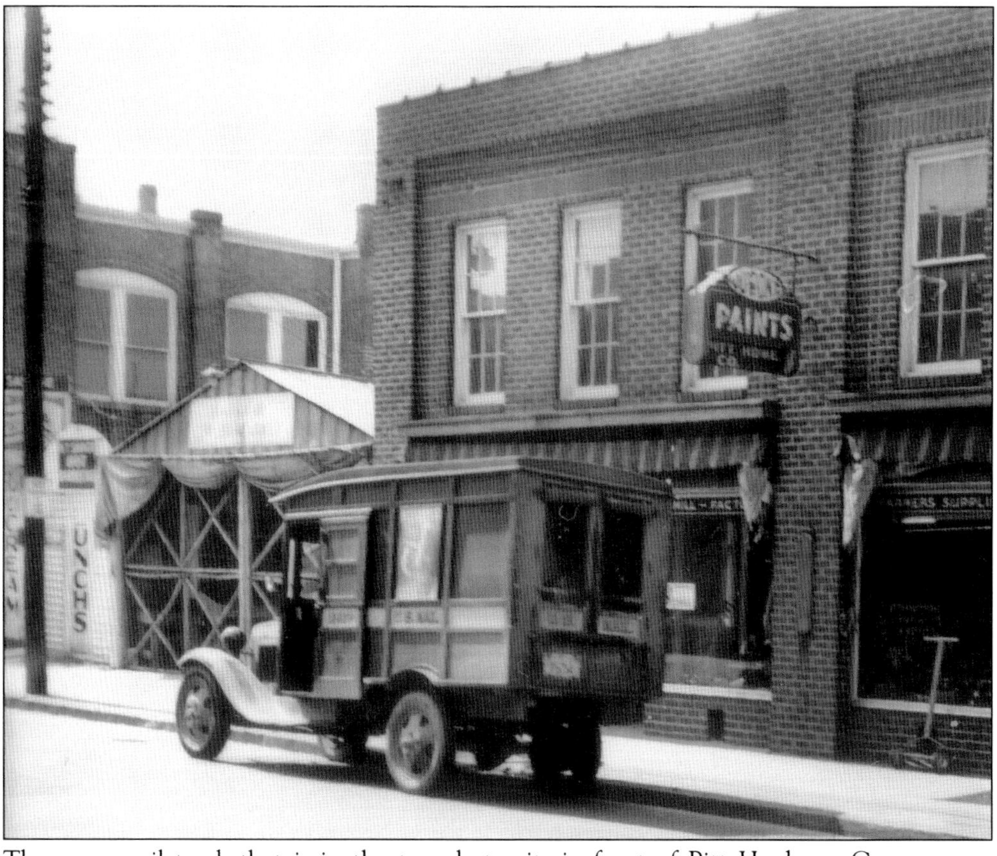

The same mail truck that is in the top photo sits in front of Pitt Hardware Company on Dickinson Avenue. Notice Savage's Barbecue tent to the left. (Courtesy of ECMC.)

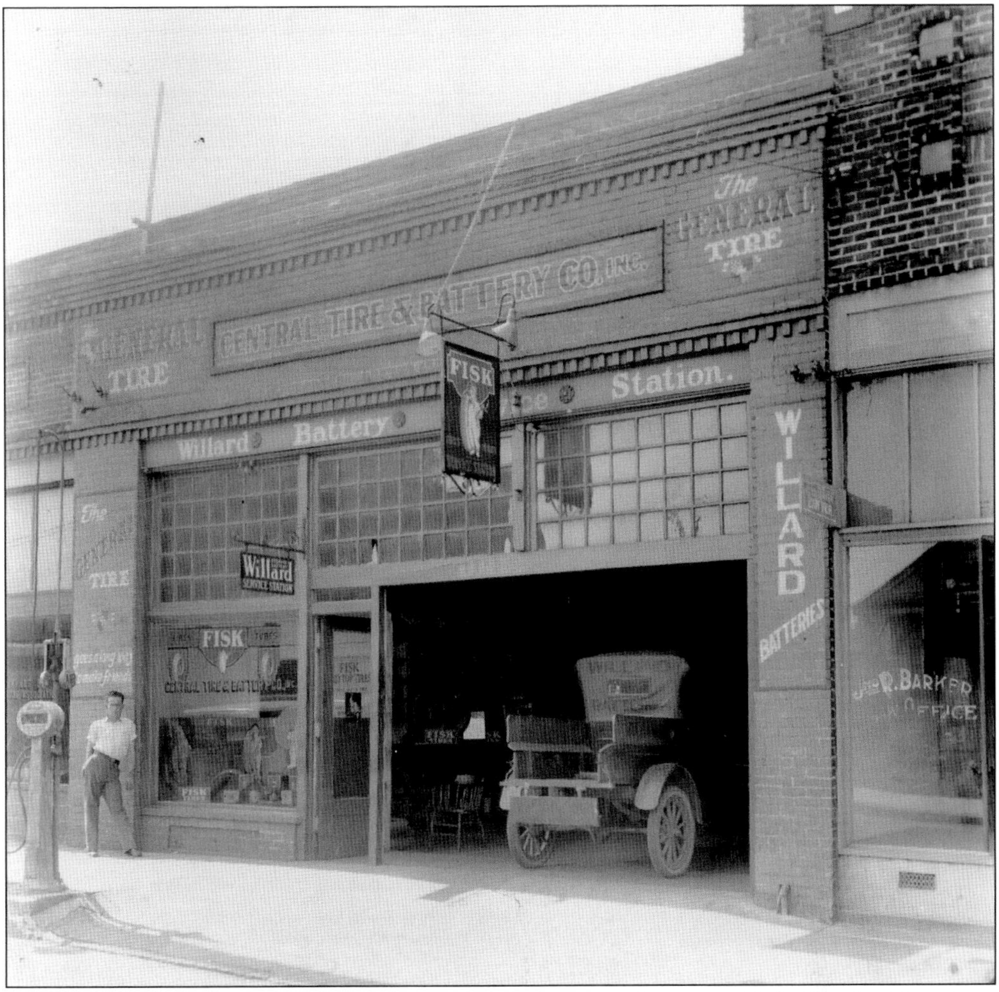

The General Tire and Battery garage on Fourth Street is shown c. 1925. The building later became the home of Cox Florist. Cox Floral service began in 1937 in the home of Marie Cox and was moved to East Fifth Street in 1940. In 1955 the business became a full-time florist operation. (Courtesy of Charles Horne Collection.)

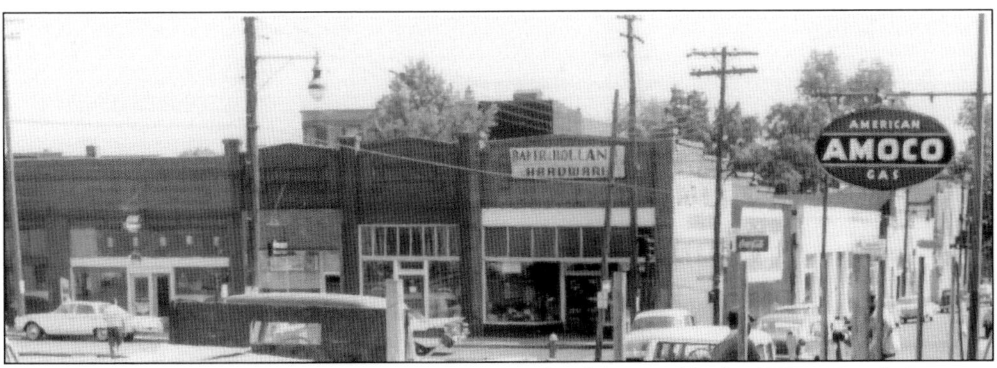

This photo illustrates the businesses on the south side of the 100 block of West Fourth Street in 1960. Cox Florist is still in the same location. (Courtesy of ECMC.)

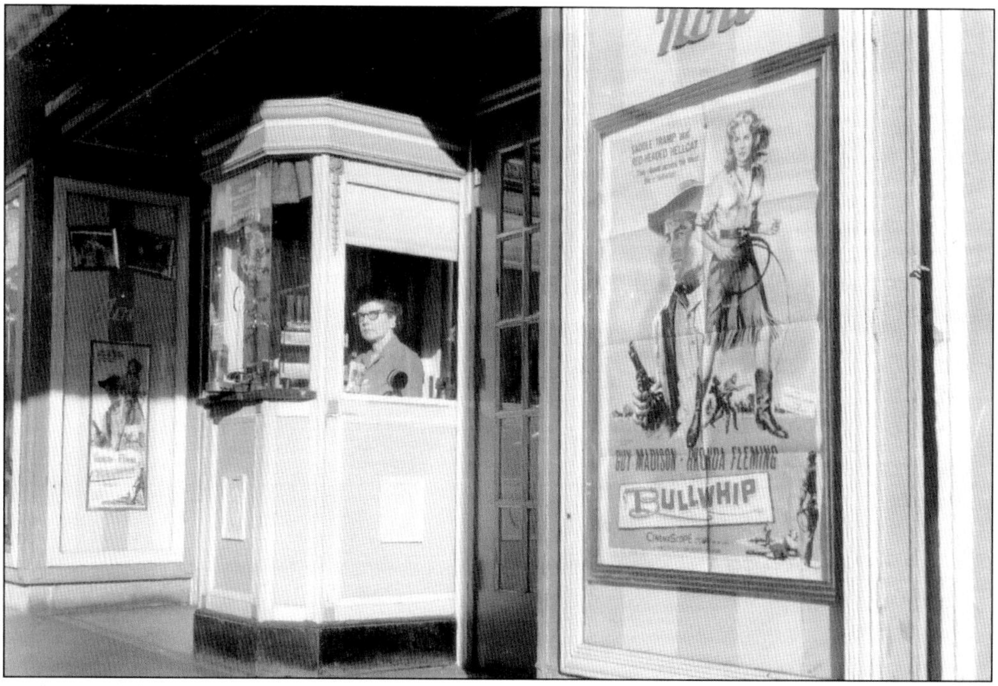

In front of the Pitt Theatre in the ticket booth in 1957 is Mrs. Sallie B. Reagan, wife of Bratha M. Reagan. Bratha ran the Deluxe Beauty & Barber Shop on Evans Street. (Courtesy of ECMC.)

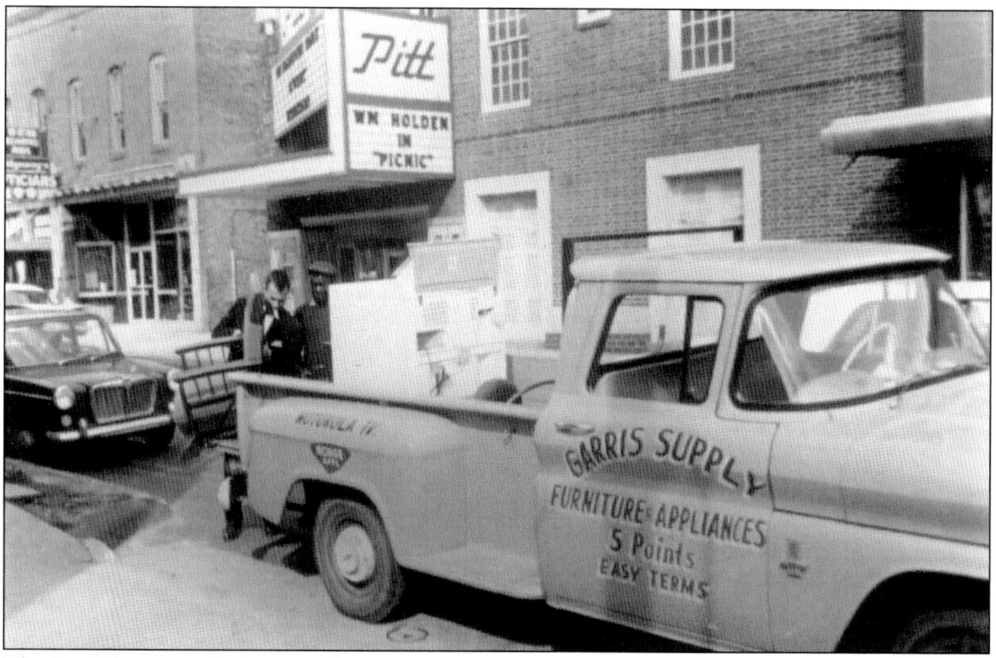

The Pitt Theatre, which opened in January 1934, was built and owned by C.H. Edwards. With its 999 seats, the Pitt Theatre was where Will Rogers and Constance Bennett appeared and where *Gone With the Wind* was first shown in Greenville. It burned in August 1979 and was torn down in 1980. (Courtesy of Alex Albright.)

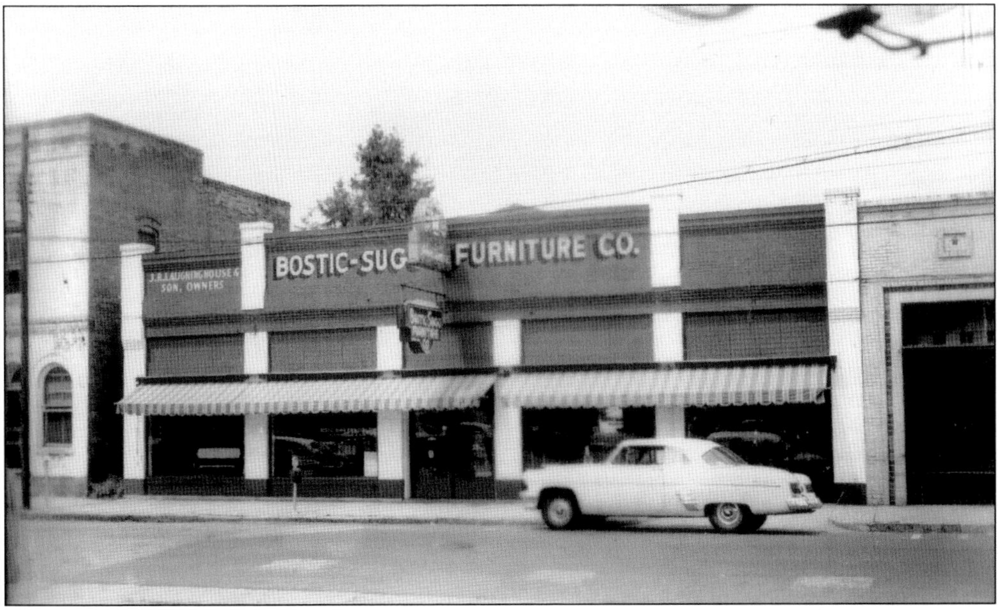

The Bostic-Sugg Furniture Company on Third Street looked like this in 1953. Begun in 1938 by Berry Bostic and M.D. Sugg, the store was originally located on East Fifth Street. It was later owned by J.R. and Billy Laughinghouse. Bostic-Sugg moved to their present store on Tenth Street in 1965. (Courtesy of ECMC.)

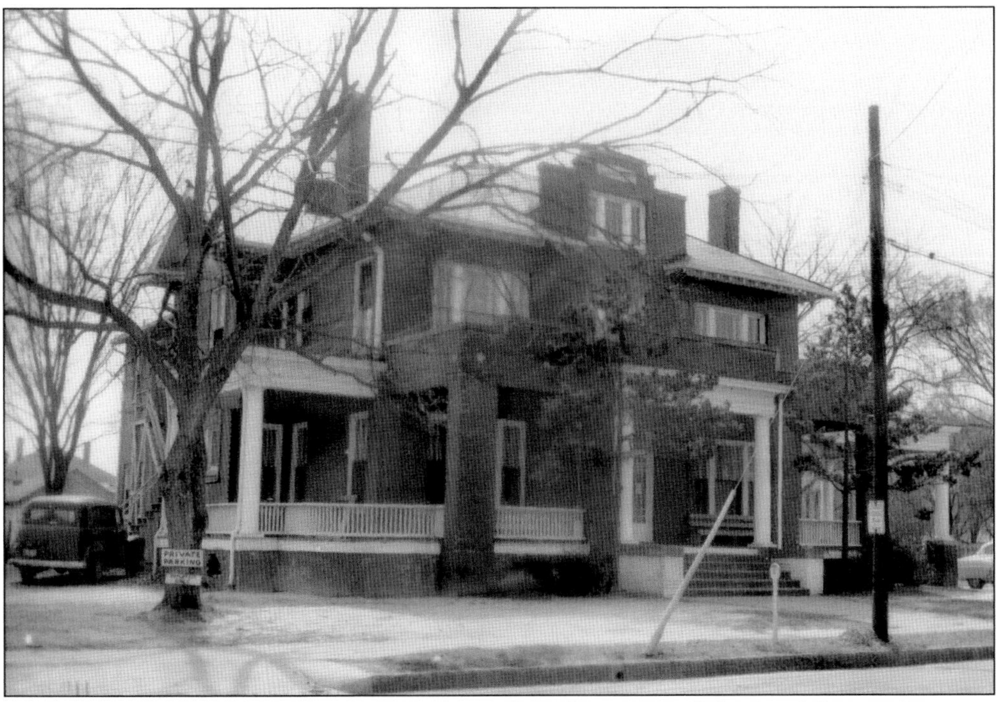

The Pitt County Health Department was located on the corner of Third and Greene Streets in 1956. It was built in 1917 by L.W. Tucker, former Pitt County Sheriff; in 1935, it was purchased by the county and used as the Health Department until 1951. It was torn down in 1985 by Planters Bank for a parking lot. (Courtesy of ECMC.)

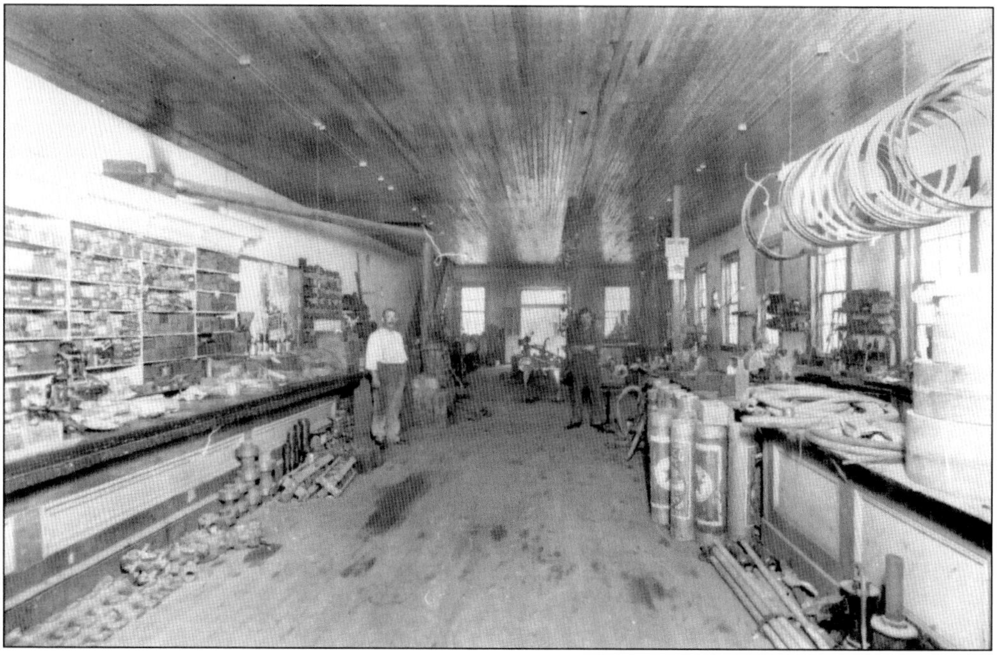

This photo shows the interior of R.L. Humber's Machine Shop on Fifth Street about 1910. It was oiginally built by O.P. Humber; his son R.L. Humber rebuilt the shop out of brick in 1904. (Courtesy of North Carolina Archives.)

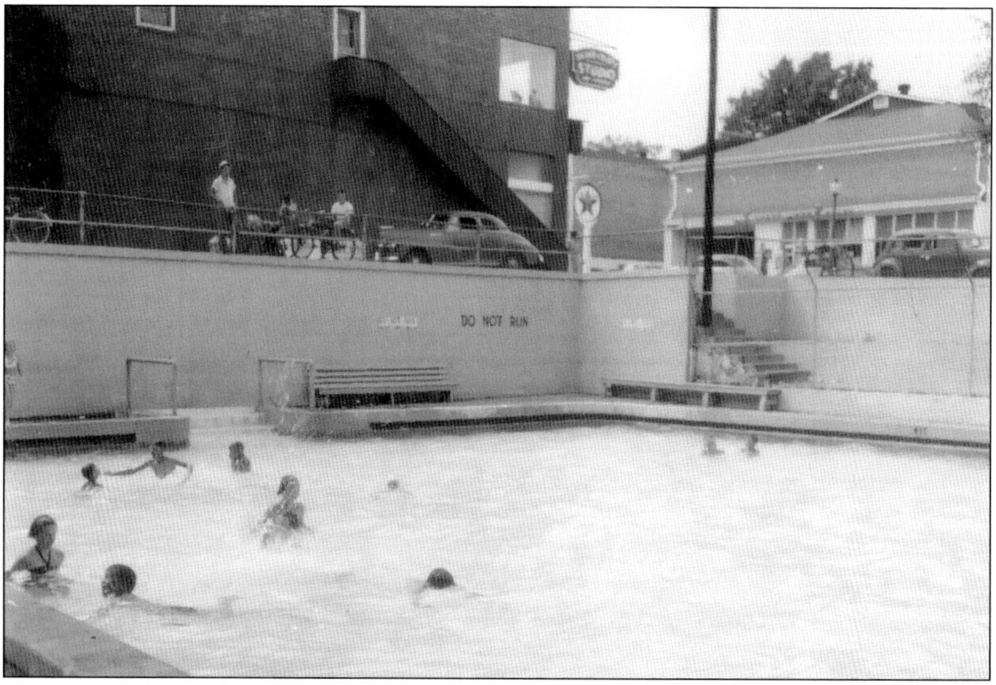

The City Pool, seen here in 1951, was built at the southeast corner of Fifth and Reade Streets in 1934 with government funds. It had a kiddie pool and a park beside it. It was closed during epidemics of infantile paralysis and polio, was condemned in 1951, and was filled in as Greenville's first city-owned, public, off-street parking lot. (Courtesy of ECMC.)

The lovely Connie Midyette stands beside "Lively Louie, the Talking Trash Can" at Five Points in 1958. It was a city trash can that said "thank you" as part of the city's Clean up-Paint up Campaign. A loud speaker in the can was connected to a tape recorder in what is now Cubbies. (Courtesy of ECMC.)

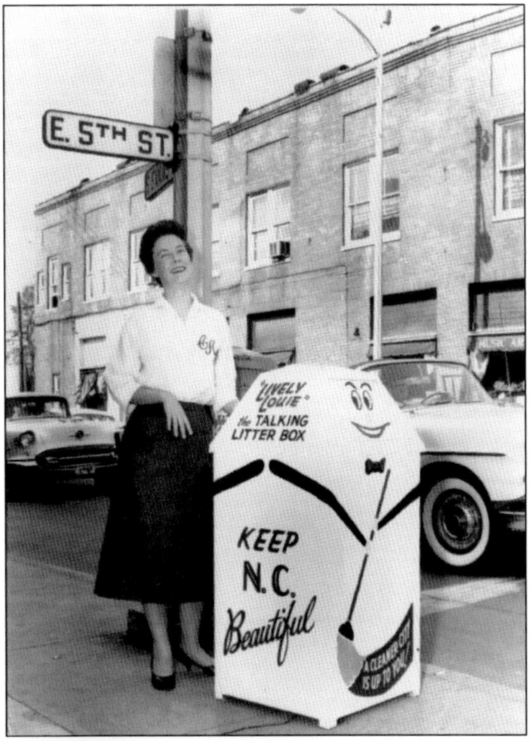

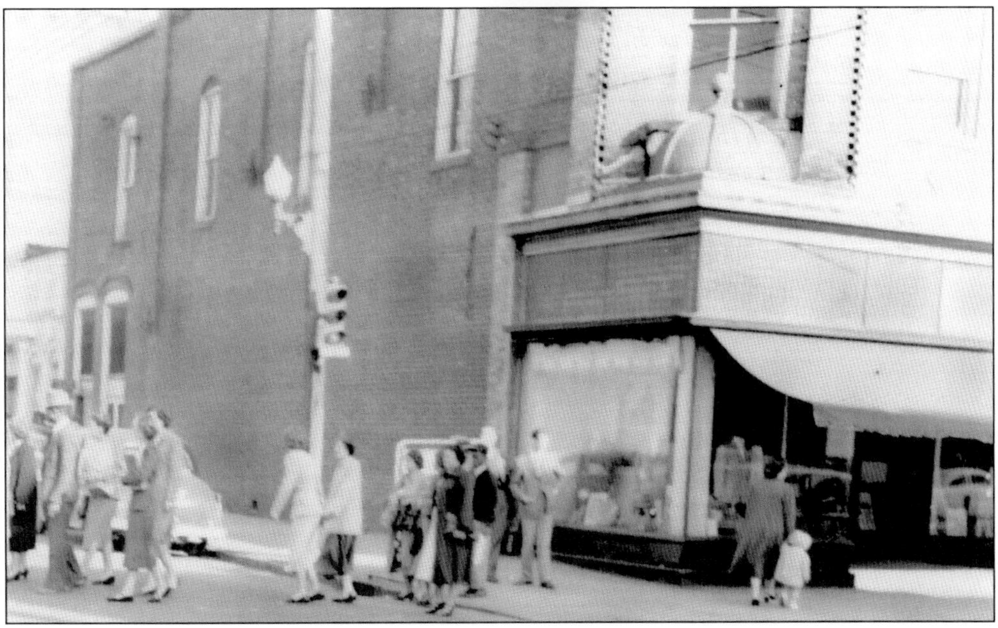

Frank Wilson (1866–1945) established a men's clothing business in 1893. Following a fire in 1899, he moved his store to Fourth and Evans where he became known as the "King Clothier." The store was renovated in 1917 to include a balcony in the rear with a shoe department beneath it. He added a boy's department on the second floor in 1920. In 1945, his son Thomas E. Wilson purchased the store from his father's estate and, along with C.A. "Clink" Bowen, operated it until it closed. Notice the crown on the corner. (Courtesy of ECMC.)

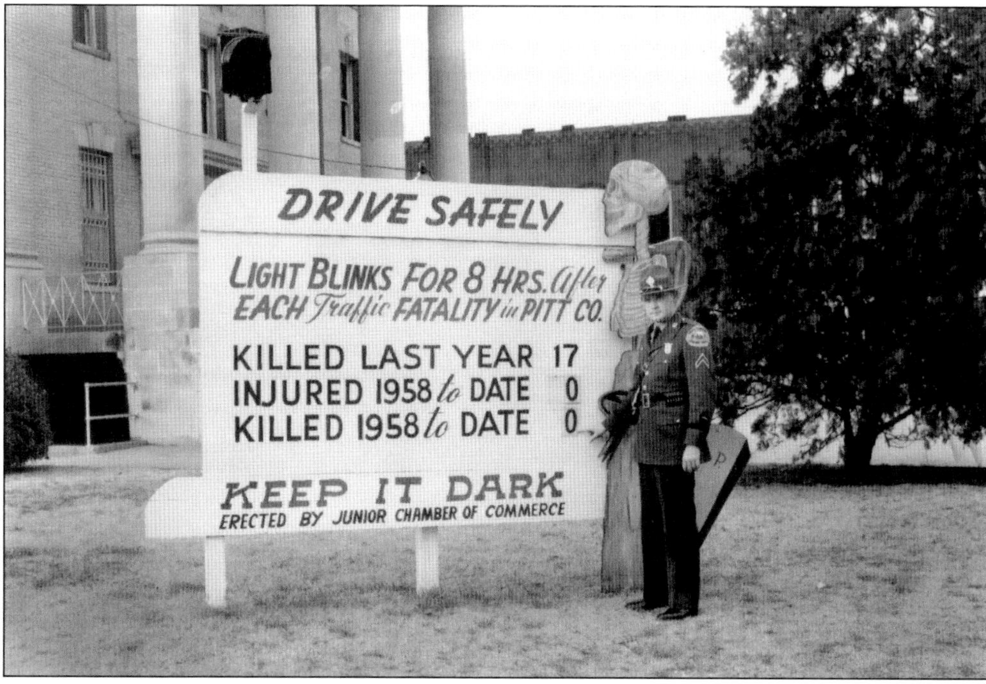

This highway patrol promotion in 1958 was among many things featured on the courthouse lawn over the years. In 1952, the Lion's Club Newsstand opened to aid their blind program. It was operated by Preston Cherry of Bethel, a blind veteran of World War II. (Courtesy of ECMC.)

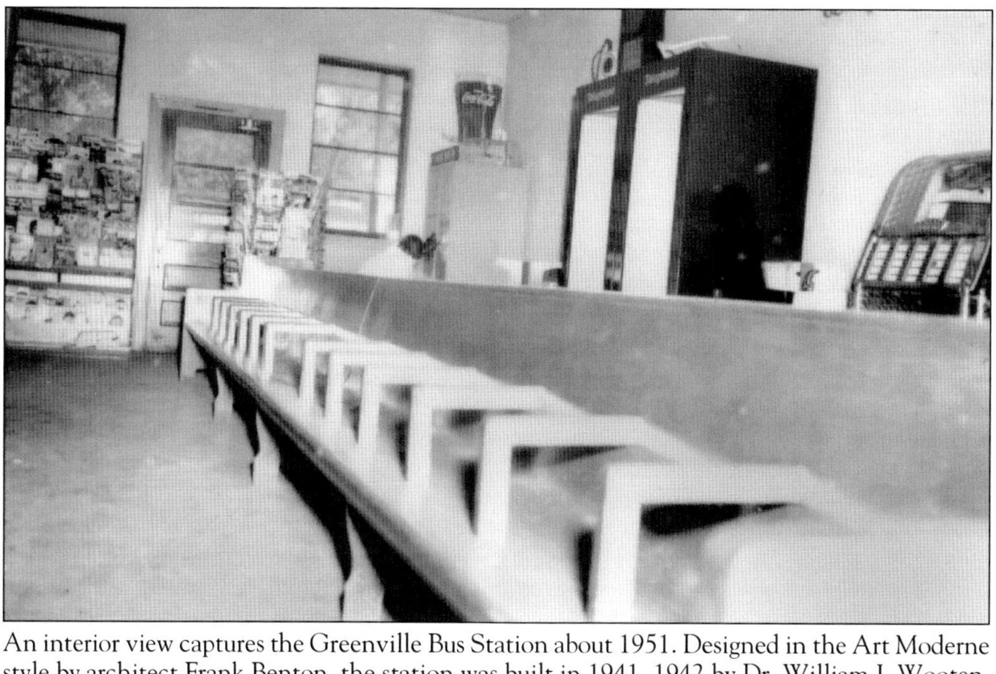

An interior view captures the Greenville Bus Station about 1951. Designed in the Art Moderne style by architect Frank Benton, the station was built in 1941–1942 by Dr. William I. Wooten. He leased it to the Carolina Coach Company and it became known as Union Station. It had a lunch counter then. (Courtesy of ECMC.)

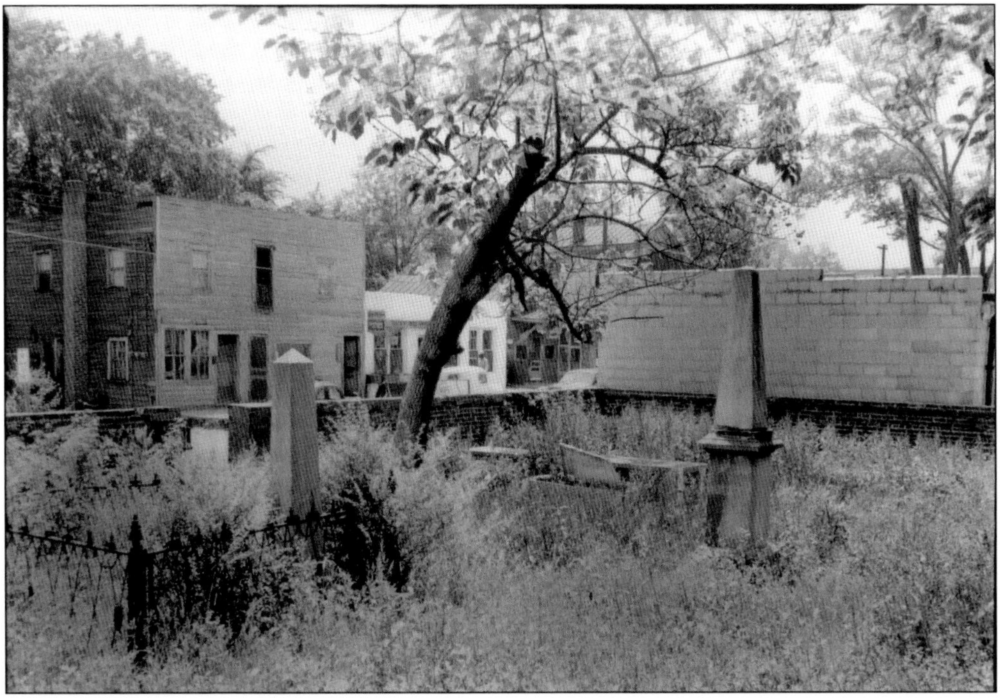

A rare view of the Evans Family Cemetery was taken on the west side of Evans Street in 1955. This cemetery holds the remains of the descendants of the founding family of Greenville. A number of graves were moved when the street was widened in 1968. (Courtesy of ECMC.)

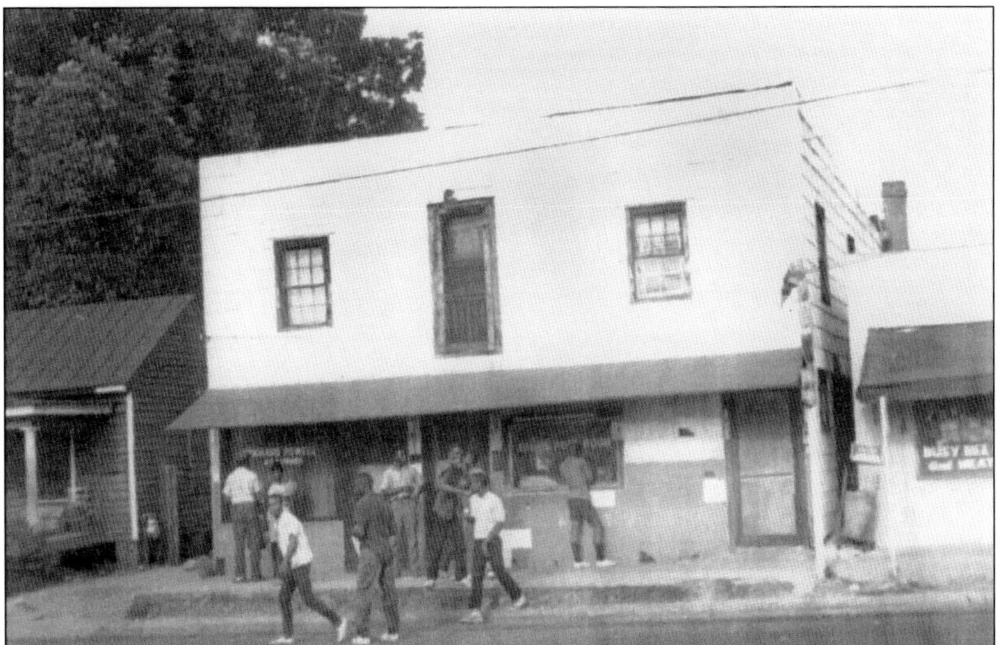

Located at 115 Evans Street in 1965, this building held the law office of Richard Powell and the billiard hall of Ernest C. Adams. To the right was the Busy Bee Grocery and the Service Barber Shop. (Courtesy of ECMC.)

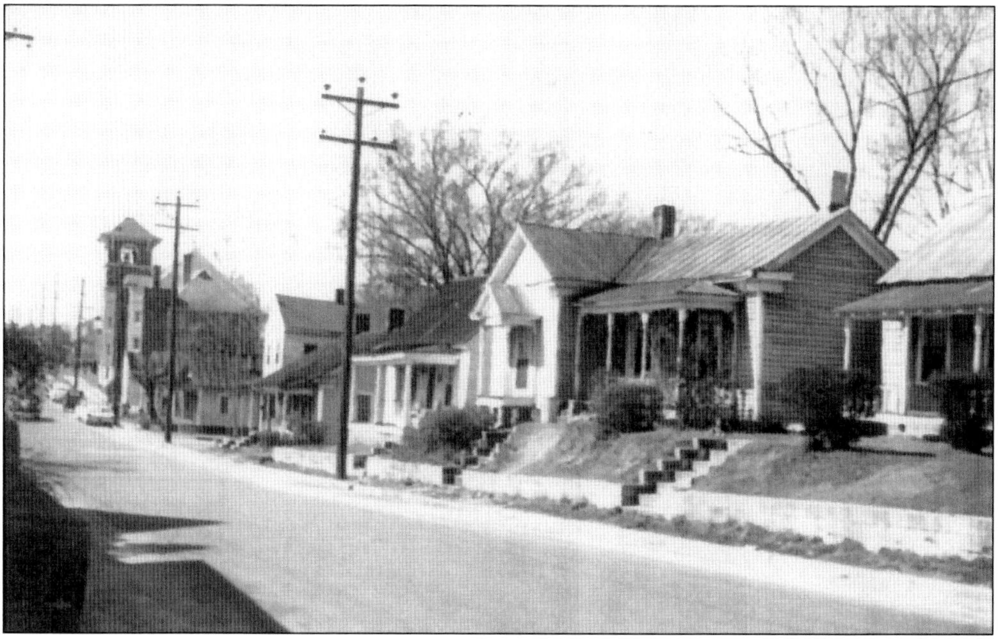

This view of First Street was taken about 1965 and shows the area down near the river, which was called the "Tenderloin" section and was considered the red-light district. It is now the site of the Town Commons. (Courtesy of ECMC.)

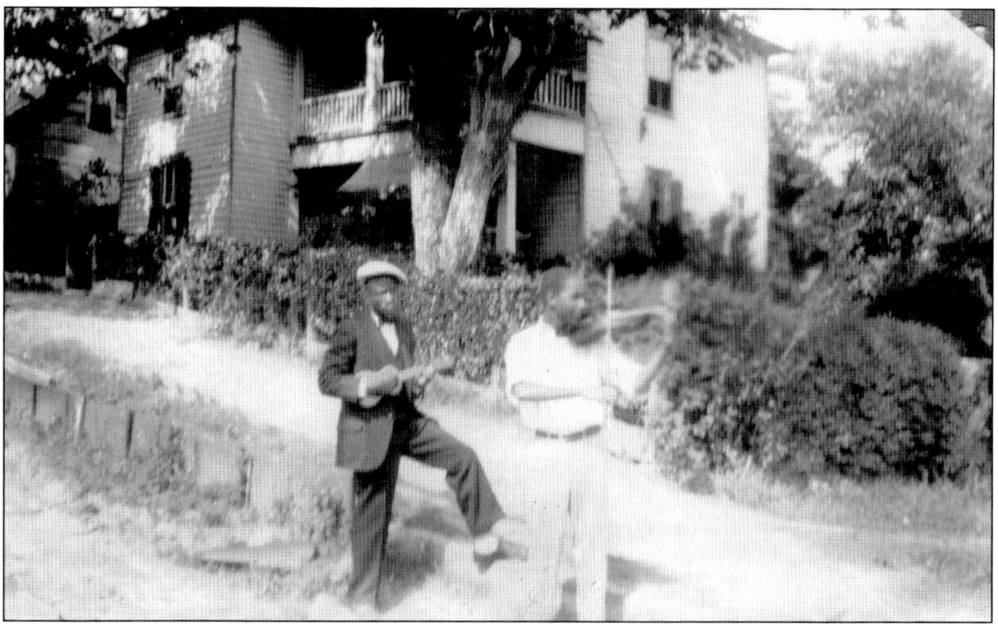

Two unknown musicians play in front of the Wiley P. Norcott home on the corner of Third and Reade Streets. (Courtesy of Lonnie Norcott.)

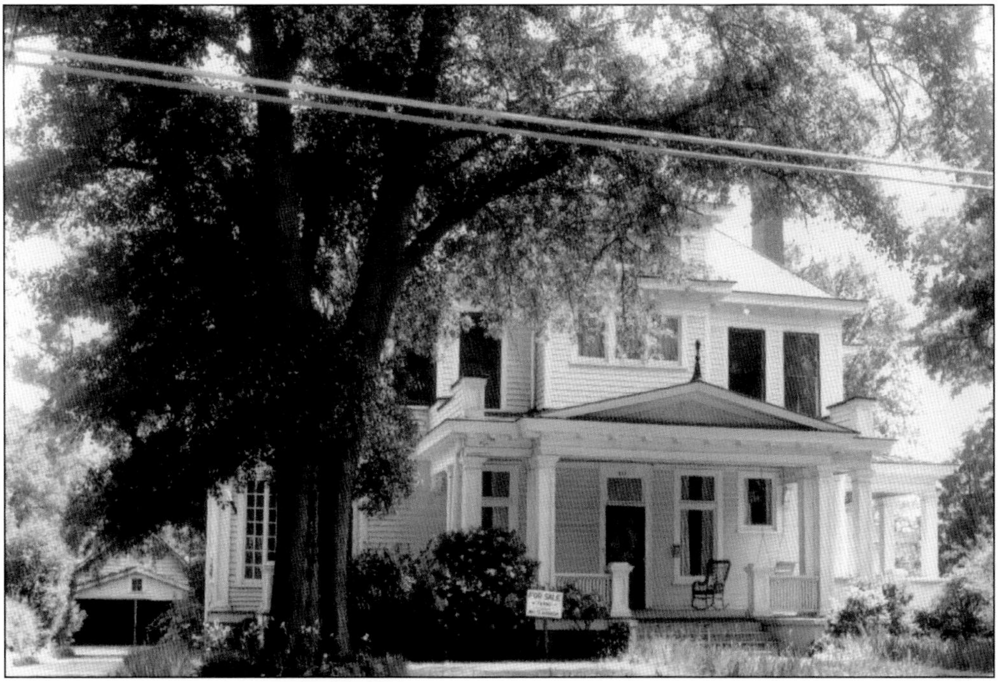

The Travis and Ione M. Hooker Home, shown here as it looked in 1956, was located on West Fifth Street. It was built in 1908 and burned down. Ione used to sing in concert with the noted Osceola Band. (Courtesy of ECMC.)

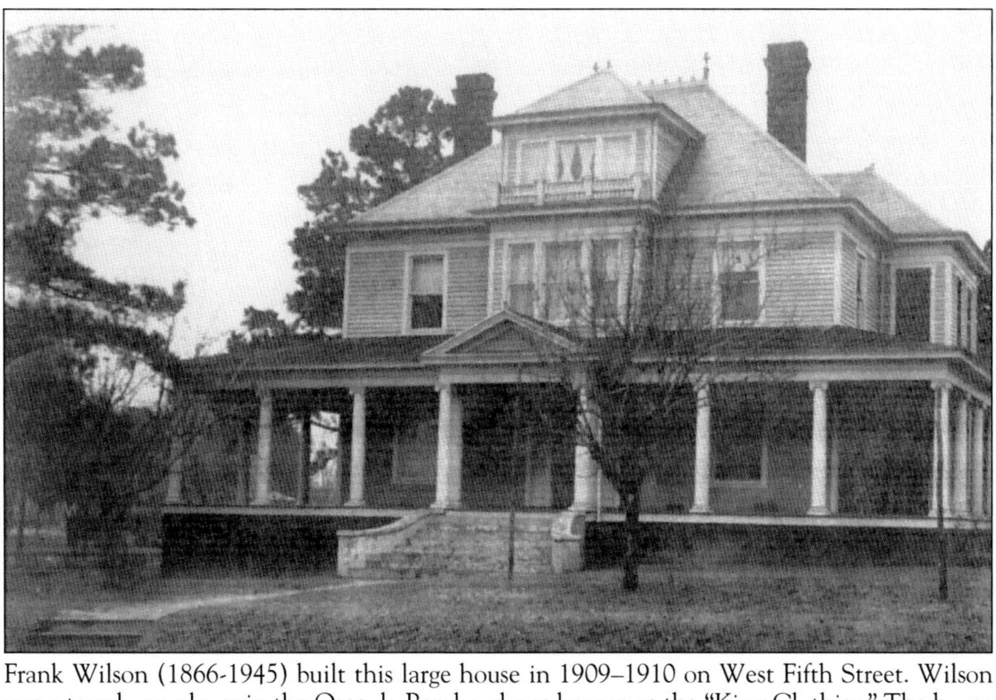

Frank Wilson (1866-1945) built this large house in 1909–1910 on West Fifth Street. Wilson was a trombone player in the Osceola Band and was known as the "King Clothier." The house was destroyed by fire. (Courtesy of ECMC.)

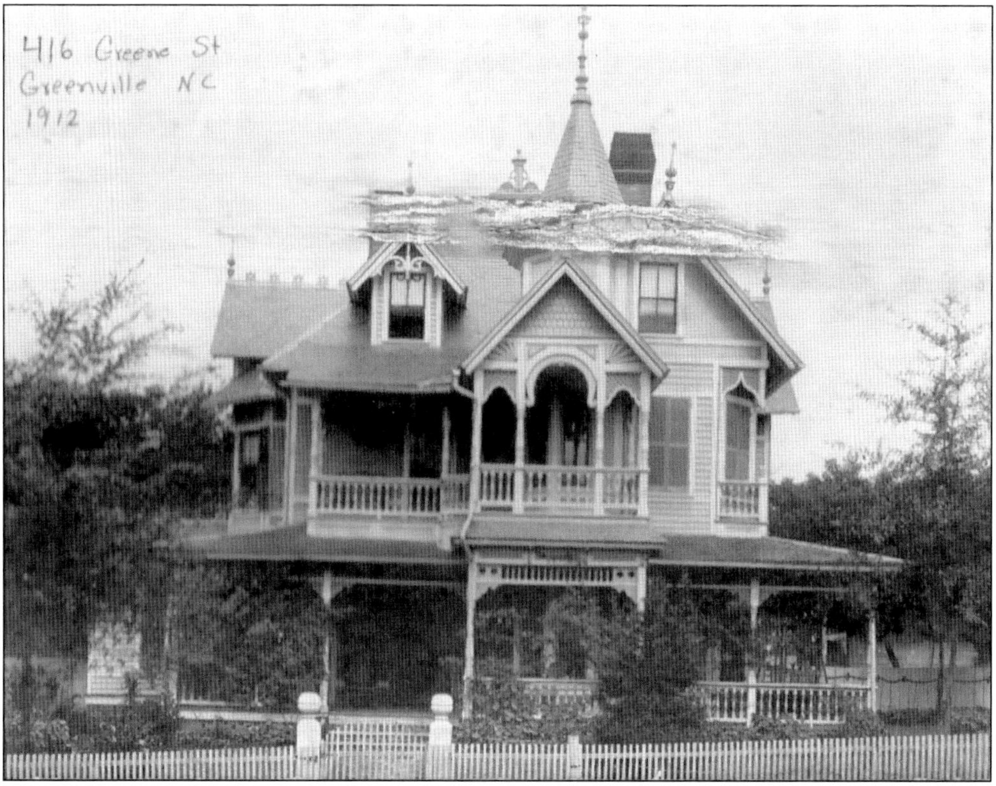

Pictured in 1912, this house at 416 Greene Street was built by John L. Wooten in 1895. Wooten had a pharmacy and soda fountain on Evans Street and later became Pitt County Auditor. The house was demolished in 1936. (Courtesy of Dr. John L. Wooten.)

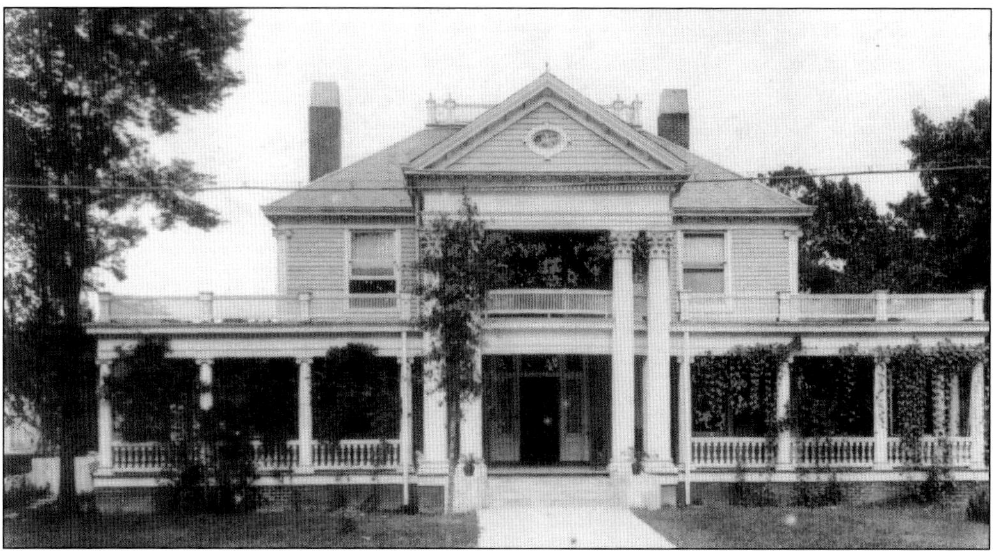

The Dr. E.A. Moye House was built on Evans Street in 1897. Dr. Elbert Alfred Moye Jr. (1869–1914) was a civic leader and owner of numerous businesses. His pharmacy and soda fountain opened in 1909 and later became J. Key Brown's Drug Store, then Beddingfield's Pharmacy, and now Cubbie's. The house was torn down in 1961. (Courtesy of Jimmy Moye.)

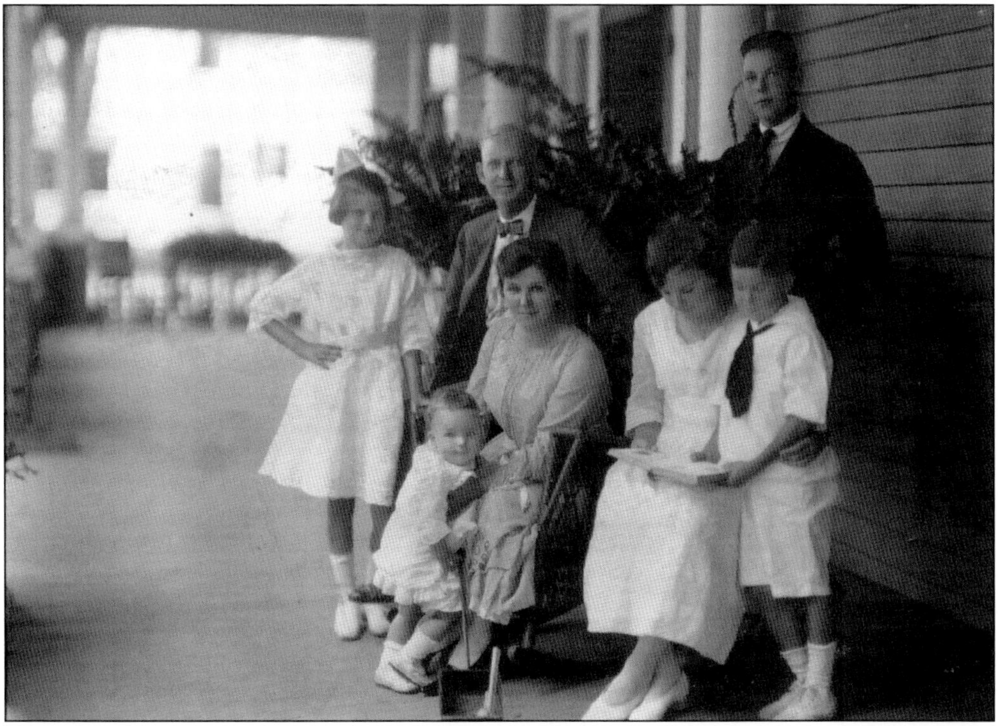

The G.B.W. Hadley family pose on their front porch about 1920. They are, from left to right, (front) Herbert Hadley, Clara Bruce Forbes Hadley, Rose Hadley Fambrough, and Jacob Milton Hadley; (back) Jane Forbes Hadley, G.B.W. Hadley, and George Hadley. (Courtesy of Mrs. Laura Bruce Nichols.)

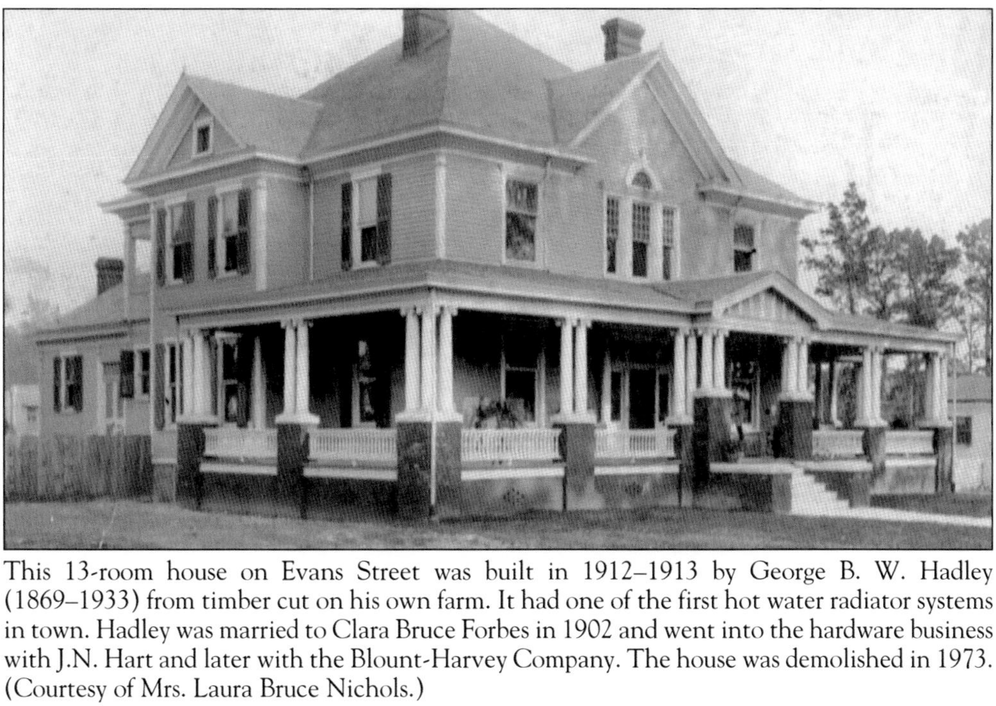

This 13-room house on Evans Street was built in 1912–1913 by George B. W. Hadley (1869–1933) from timber cut on his own farm. It had one of the first hot water radiator systems in town. Hadley was married to Clara Bruce Forbes in 1902 and went into the hardware business with J.N. Hart and later with the Blount-Harvey Company. The house was demolished in 1973. (Courtesy of Mrs. Laura Bruce Nichols.)

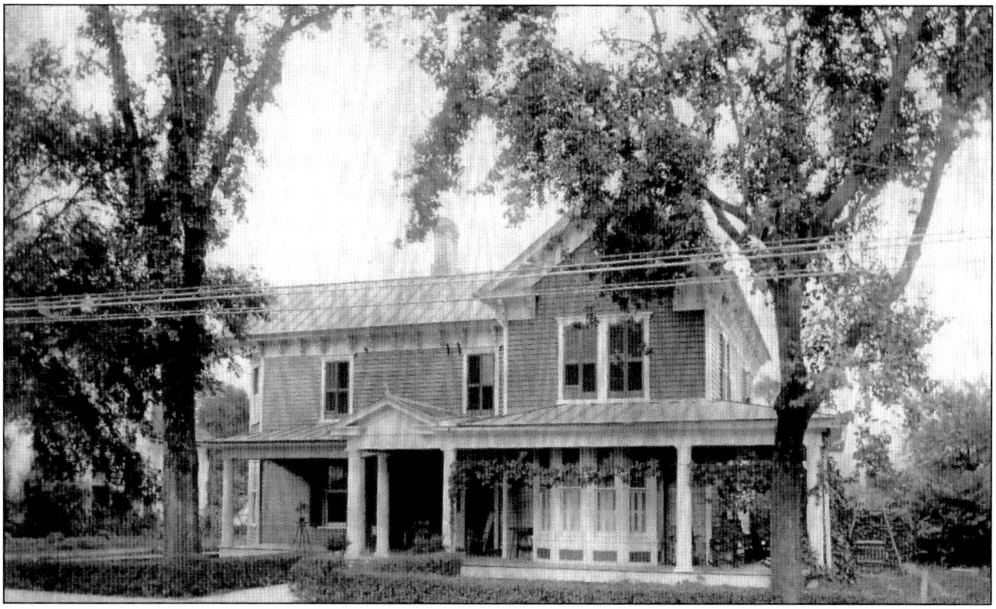

Built about 1910, the James Brown House was located at what is now the intersection of Reade Street and Dickinson Avenue. It was demolished in 1972. (Courtesy of Courtside Cafe.)

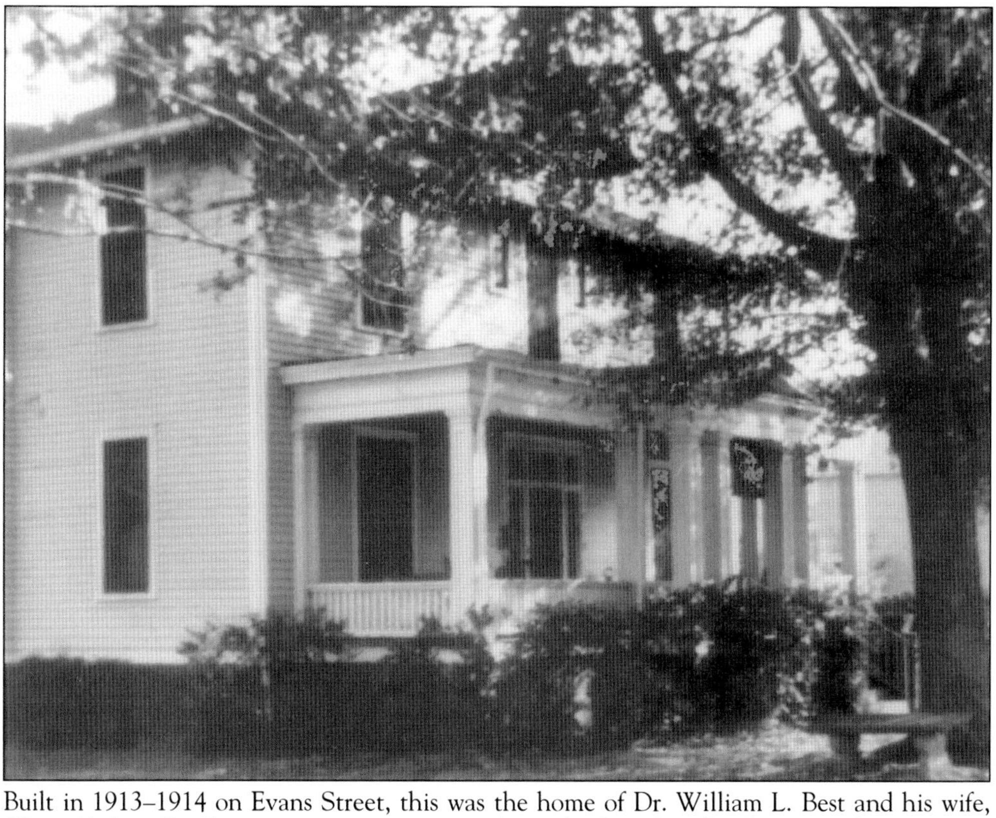

Built in 1913–1914 on Evans Street, this was the home of Dr. William L. Best and his wife, Glenn Forbes. Dr. Best was an optometrist and ran the Best Jewelry Company from 1901 to 1973. (Courtesy of Jimmy Moye.)

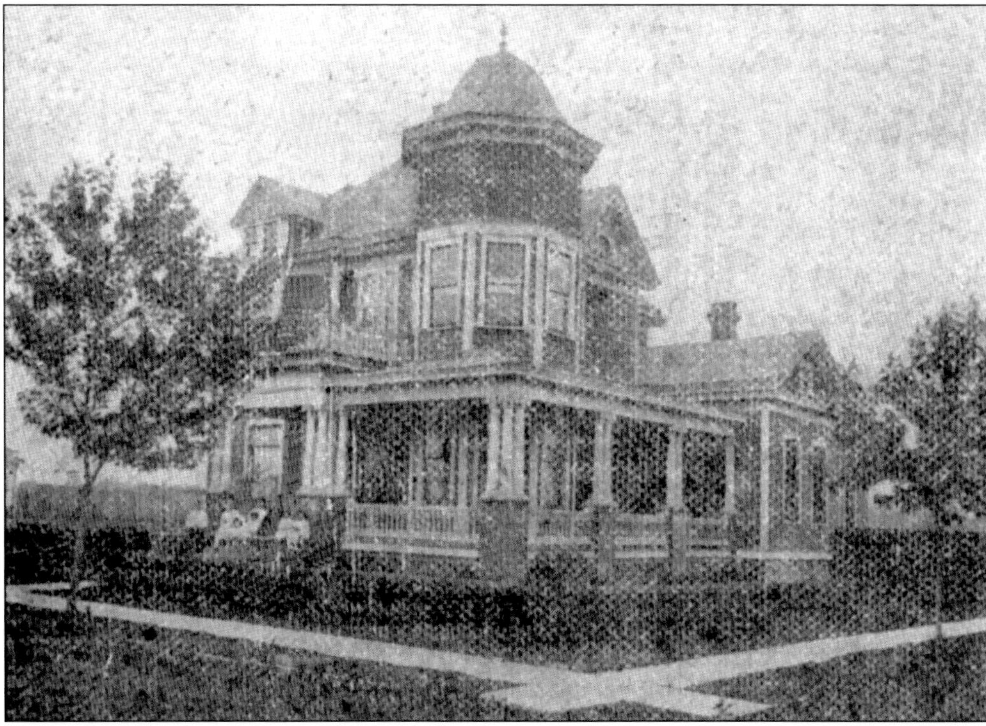

The York/Overton House, 1002 West Fourth Street, as it appeared in 1921, was built in Greenville Heights by C. V. York in 1908. C.V. York was a noted architect and a developer of Greenville Heights. He was also the Greenville weather observer and part-owner of a number of businesses. In 1910, the house was sold to D.D. Overton, who was fire chief, building inspector, and owner of a large hogshead factory. (Courtesy of Roger Kammerer.)

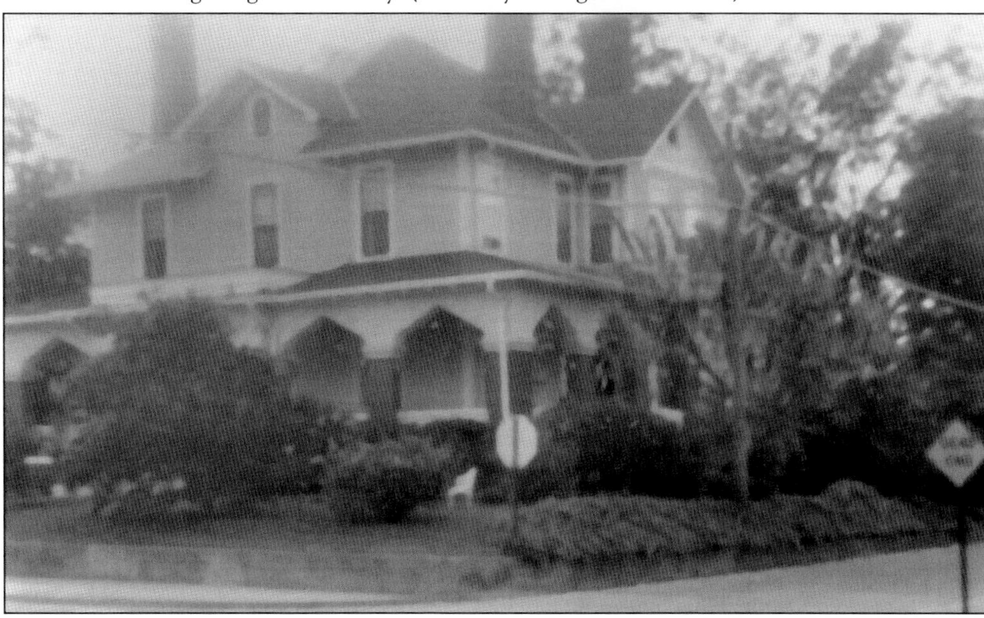

The Smith/Forbes House, located at the corner of Evans and Eighth Streets, was built about 1907. (Courtesy of Jimmy Moye.)

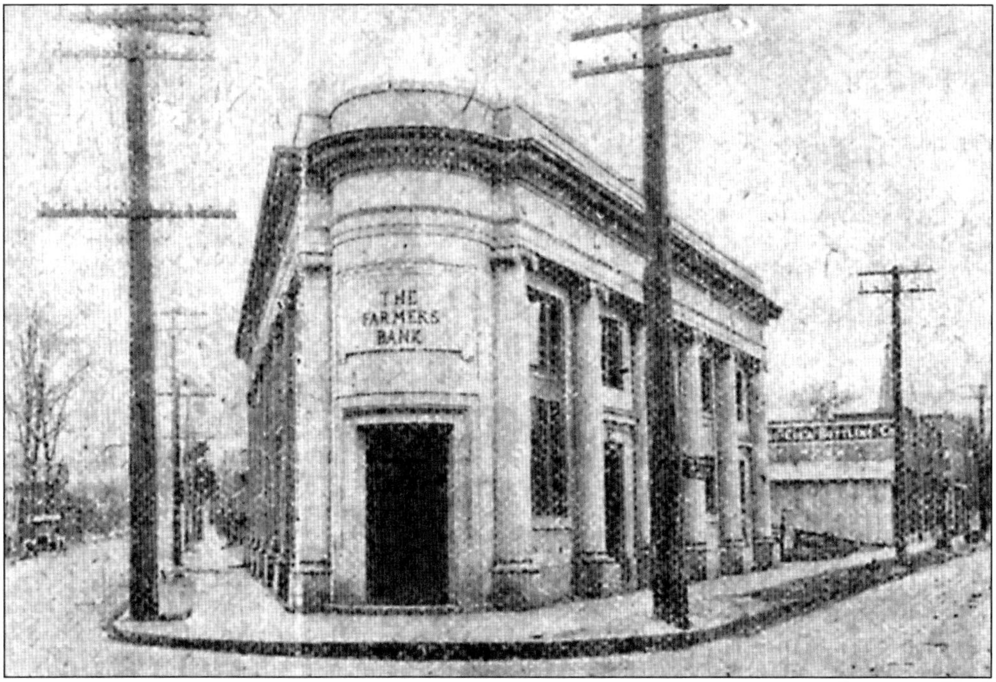

One of four triangular buildings in town, The Farmers Bank was built on the corner of Pitt Street and Dickinson Avenue in 1920. It later served as a branch of the Guaranty Bank & Trust Co. and the Wachovia Bank. It was torn down in 1962 and the drive-in window was kept there. (Courtesy of Roger Kammerer)

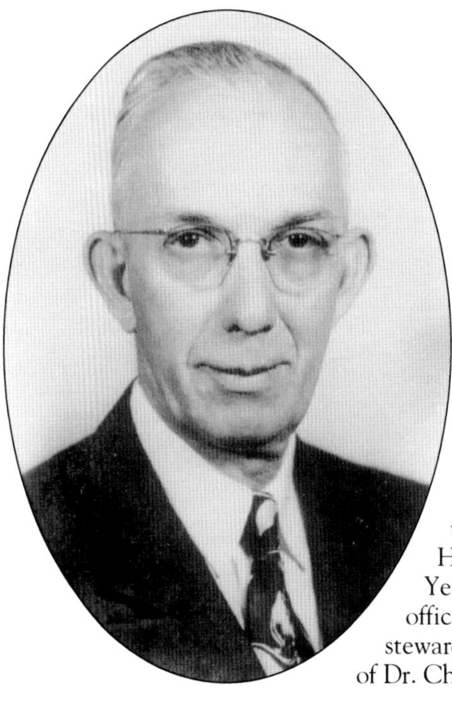

Dr. Karl B. Pace (1888–1968), a native of Chatham County, graduated from UNC at Chapel Hill and Jefferson Medical College. He was a captain in the Medical Corps of the U.S. Army in World War I. He returned to Greenville in 1919 and was a general practitioner for more than 50 years. A founder of the Pitt Community Hospital, Pace was named American Doctor of the Year for 1955 by the AMA. He was a Mason, an officer and member of numerous medical societies, and a steward of Jarvis Memorial Methodist Church. (Courtesy of Dr. Charles Pace.)

Five

Tobacco Town

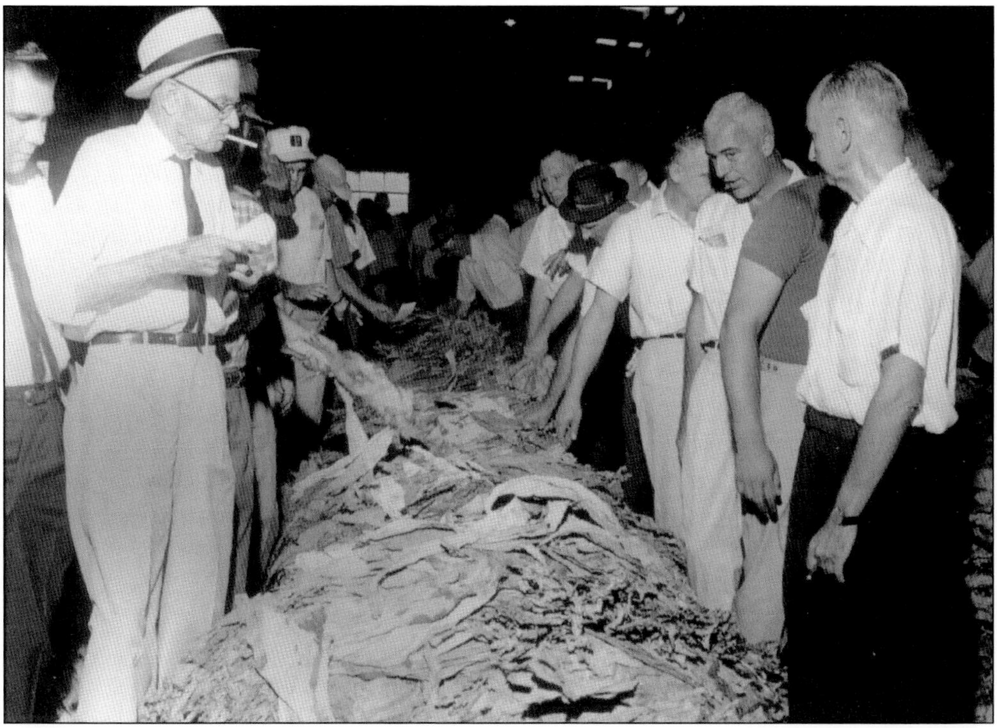

This image depicts the once familiar spectacle of a tobacco auction as it looked in 1962. In the years after World War II, the tobacco market in Greenville grew to be one of the largest in the state. The days and weeks of the tobacco market were clearly different than the rest of the year. Electric currents flowed through the entire town out of the sights, sounds, and activity in the tobacco district—around which the rest of the town revolved. Even the air smelled differently. The warehouses that hosted the tobacco market were large features of Greenville's landscape and were equally impossible to miss, no matter what the season. These warehouses and the activity they generated placed Greenville among the greatest tobacco marketing centers in the world. (Courtesy of ECMC.)

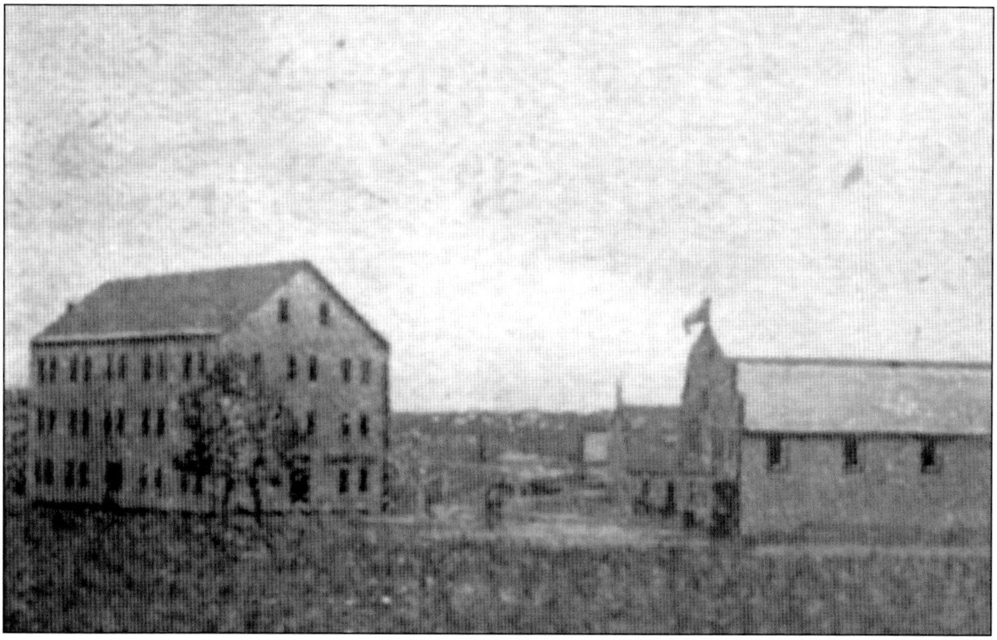

This old "Tobacco Town" photograph along Ninth Street from 1895 shows O.L. Joyner's four-story prize house on the left and the Eastern and Greenville Tobacco Warehouses on the right. (Courtesy of Roger Kammerer.)

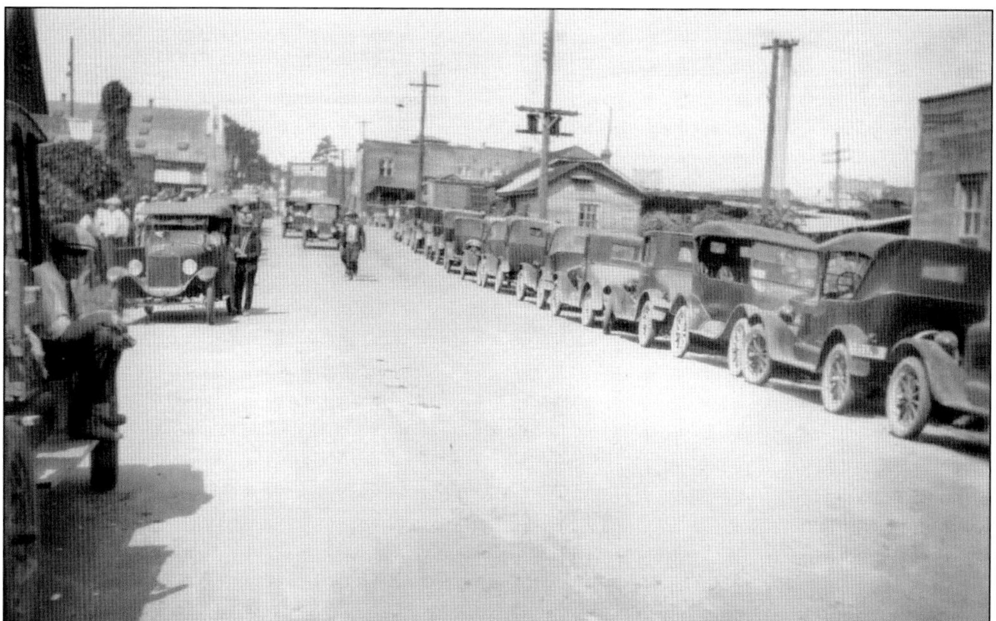

This is Ninth Street looking west from Washington Street in the 1920s. In the early days, John Clark and Alfred Forbes gave a bugle or trumpet blast to announce the start of a tobacco auction, which would send people running. (Courtesy of Charles Horne Collection.)

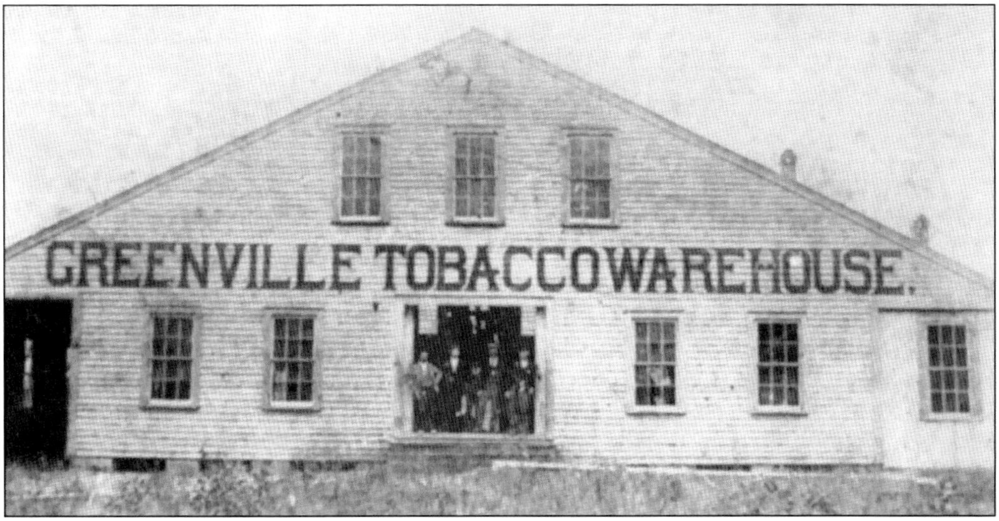

The Greenville Tobacco Warehouse, the first tobacco warehouse in town, was built in 1891 on Ninth Street by a stock company headed by R.J. Cobb, a merchant and cotton broker. It was managed by Evans & Company for many years, which was owned by Leon F. Evans, the father of Tobacco culture in Pitt County. It fell in a snowstorm in 1897 and was rebuilt. (Courtesy of ECMC.)

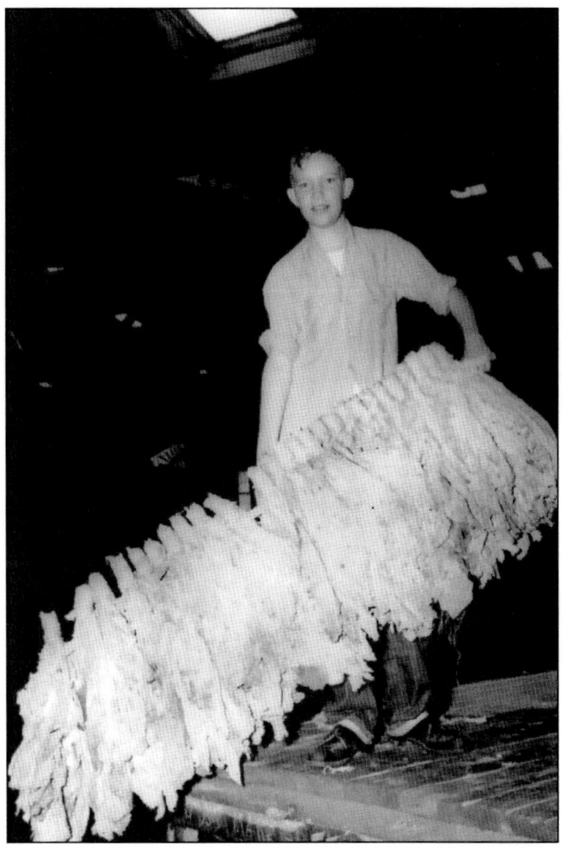

Richard McLawhorn of Winterville is shown unloading his tobacco at the Fifth Annual Junior Tobacco Show and sale in 1956. The sale, at the New Carolina Warehouse, was sponsored by the Tobacco Board of Trade. Eleven 4-H and FFA farm youths entered the show in hopes of receiving prizes starting at $50. (Courtesy of ECMC.)

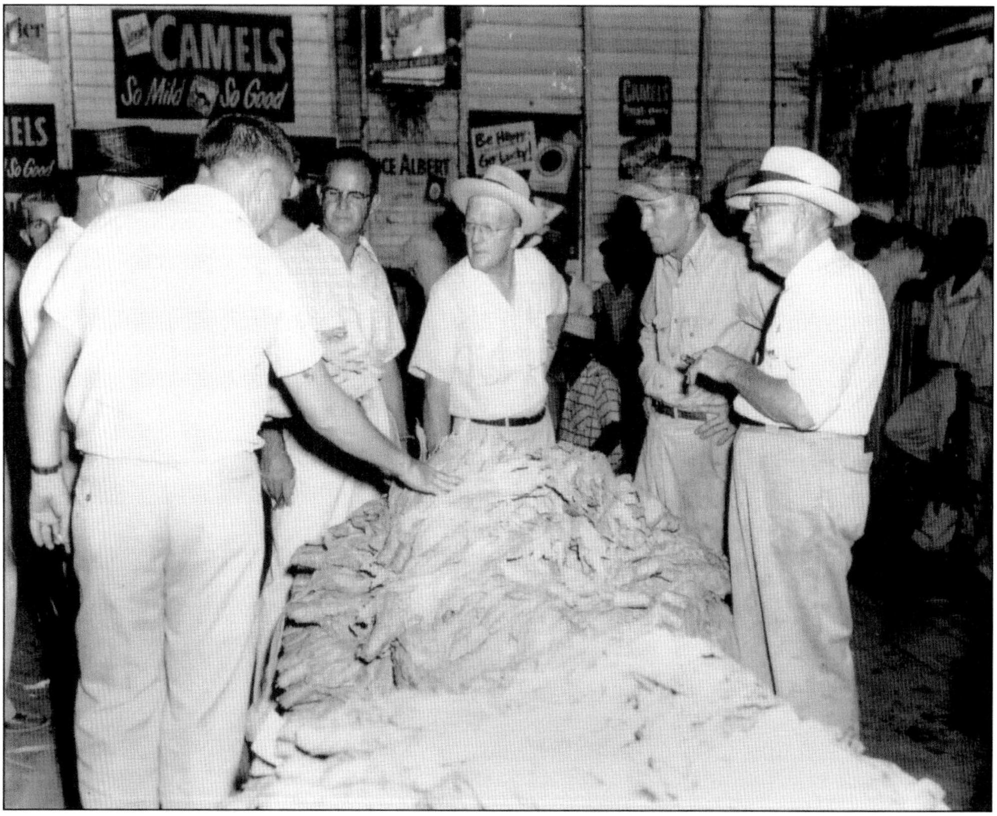

A tobacco farmer, buyers and auctioneer are shown discussing the grade of a pile of leaf in 1957. (Courtesy of ECMC.)

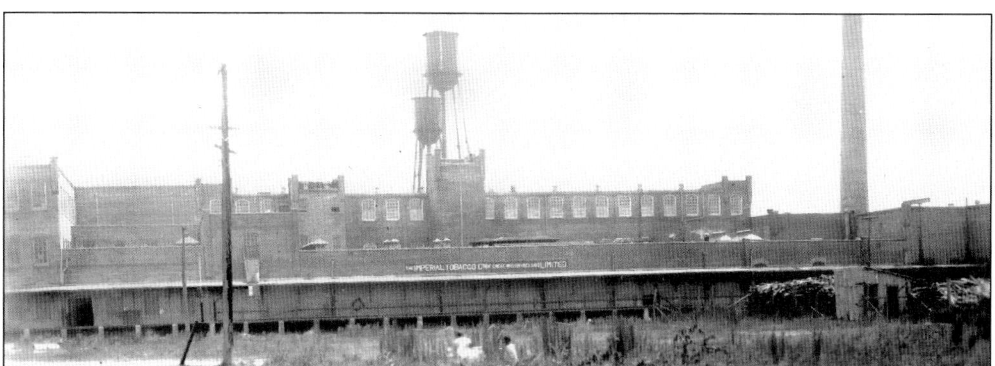

The Imperial Tobacco Company was located on Atlantic Avenue in 1932. It was built in 1902 on Clarks Field, then owned by C.T. Munford, who laid out the streets in the tobacco district. In the 1930s, Imperial bought 10 to 15 million pounds each season on the Greenville market. The large plant was managed by C.W. Shuff. (Courtesy of Charles Horne Collection.)

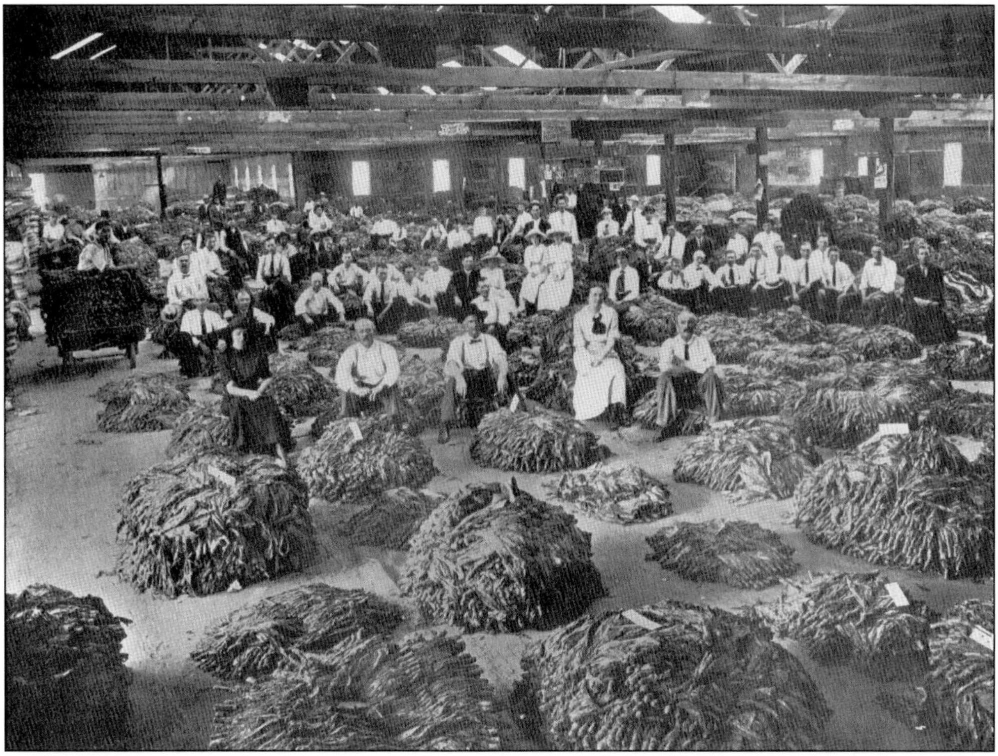

This 1914 image shows the interior of the Centre Brick Warehouse—owned by J.F. Brinkley, W.L. Rice, and D.S. Spain—and a tobacco sale of 93,762 pounds, which averaged over $24 per hundred pounds at auction. (Courtesy of "Illustrated City of Greenville" [pamphlet] Pitt County, 1914.)

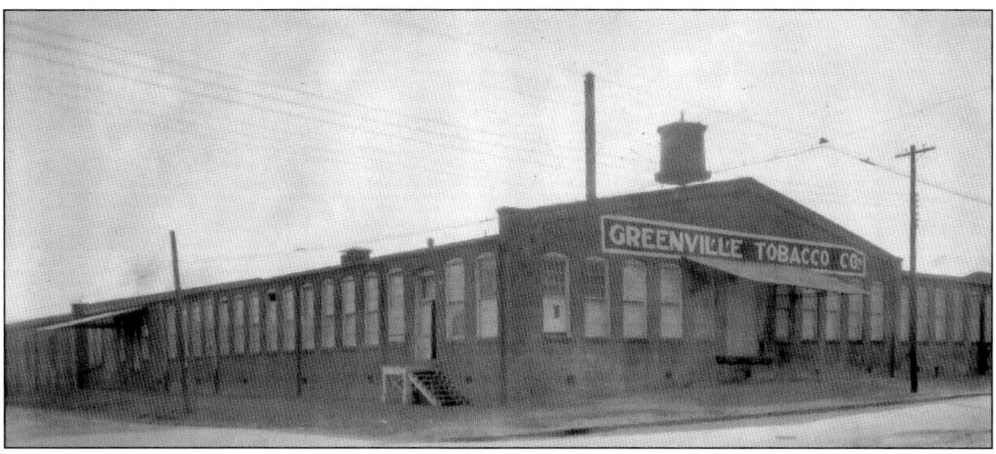

The Redrying and Stemming Factory of the Greenville Tobacco Company is shown in 1932. It bought 5 to 10 million pounds of tobacco on the Greenville market every year. (Courtesy of Charles Horne Collection.)

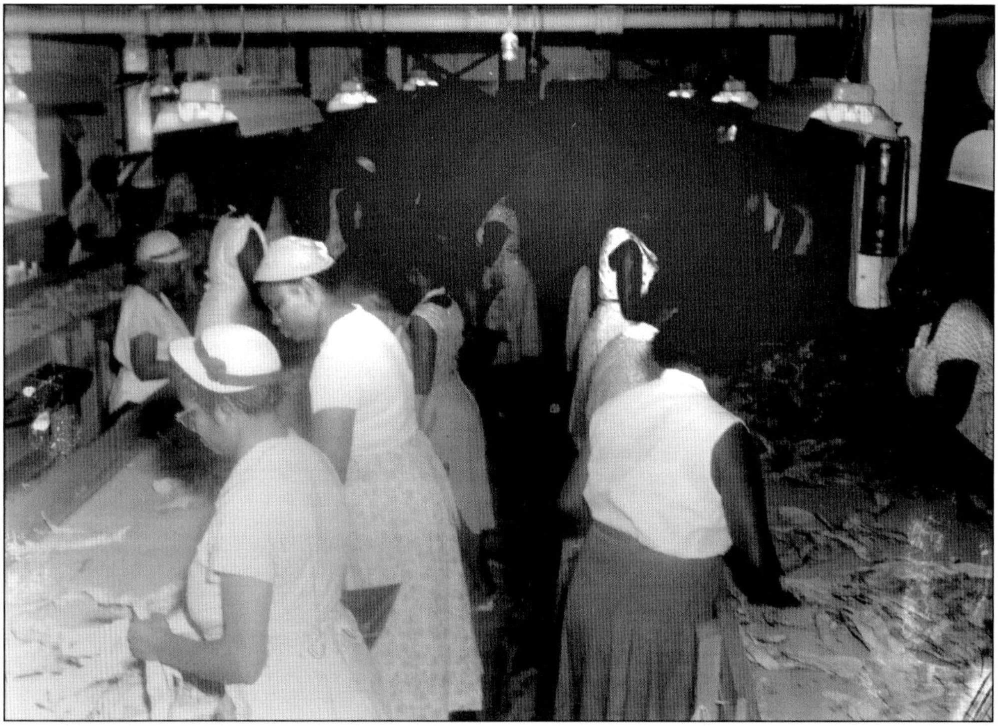

Women sort Georgia tobacco leaves at the Imperial Tobacco factory in 1957. Experienced workers sort to prevent the mixture of graded tobacco. "Green" tobacco (all tobacco as marketed) is redried and packed here before being sent to other plants in the United States and other countries where it is made into various products. (Courtesy of ECMC.)

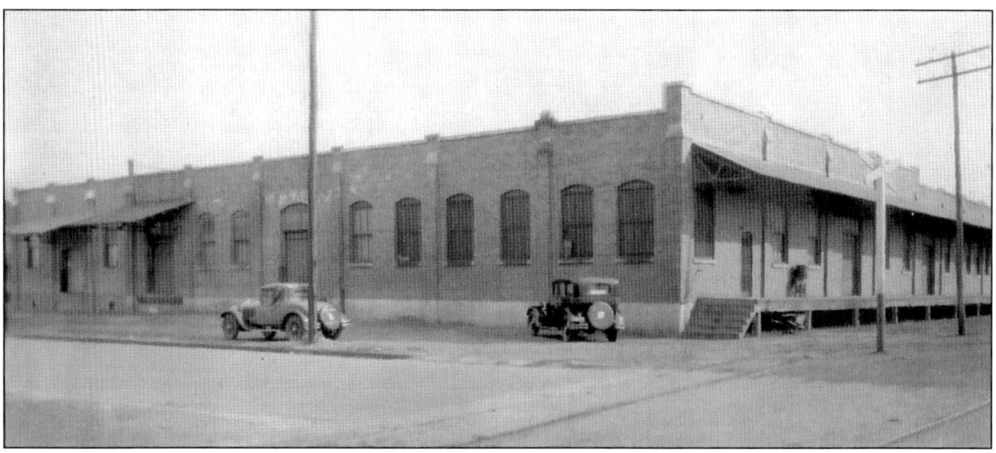

This is an unknown tobacco factory on the Greenville market in the 1930s. (Courtesy of Charles Horne Collection.)

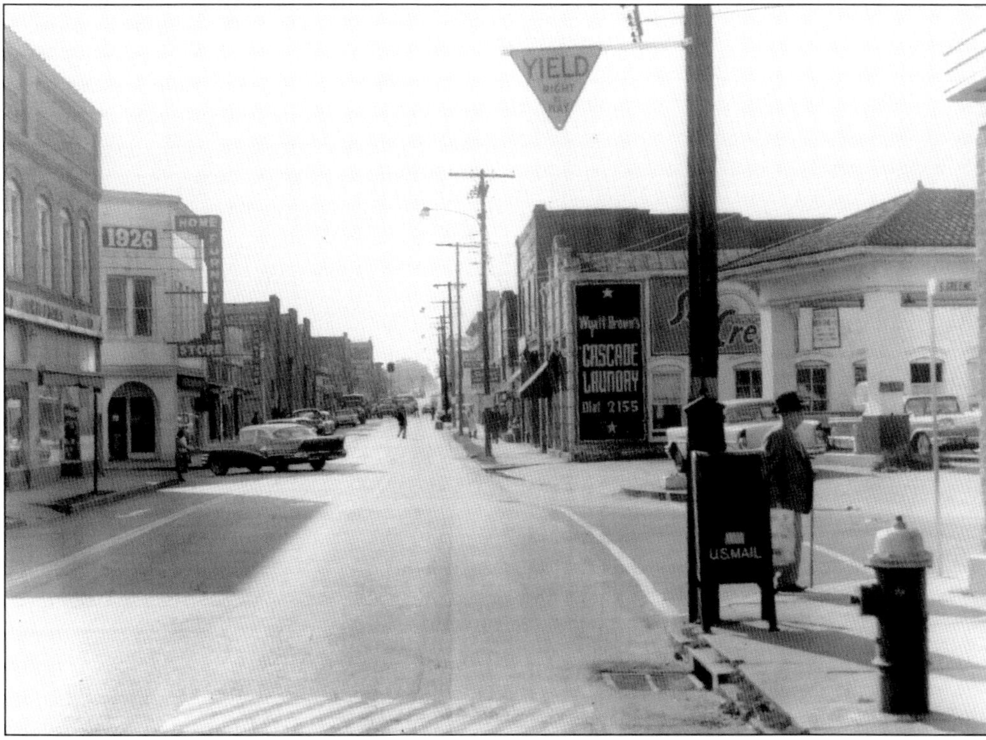

Dickinson Avenue is viewed looking west from about Greene Street in 1959. (Courtesy of ECMC.)

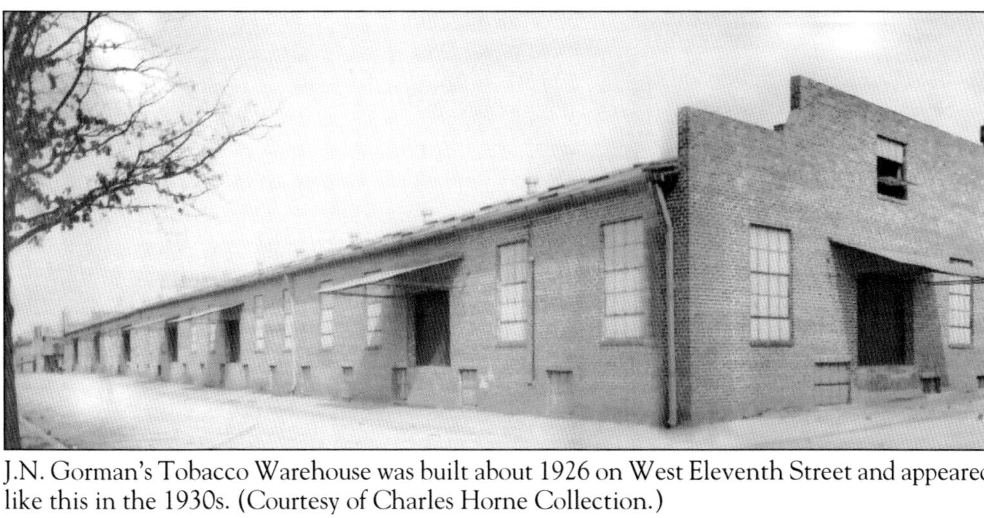
J.N. Gorman's Tobacco Warehouse was built about 1926 on West Eleventh Street and appeared like this in the 1930s. (Courtesy of Charles Horne Collection.)

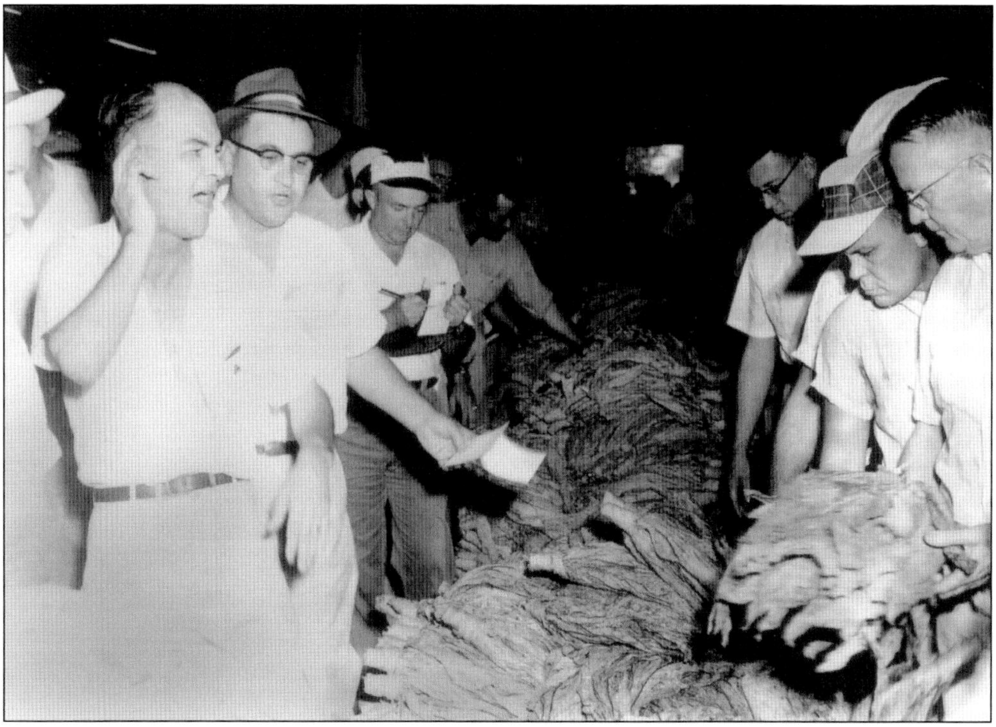

An auction takes place at the Farmers Warehouse on the north side of the river in 1957. The Farmers Warehouse, owned by the Tripp brothers, covered 25 acres and was said to be the largest tobacco auction warehouse in the world. The auctioneer at left was Ray Oglesby of Winterville. (Courtesy of ECMC.)

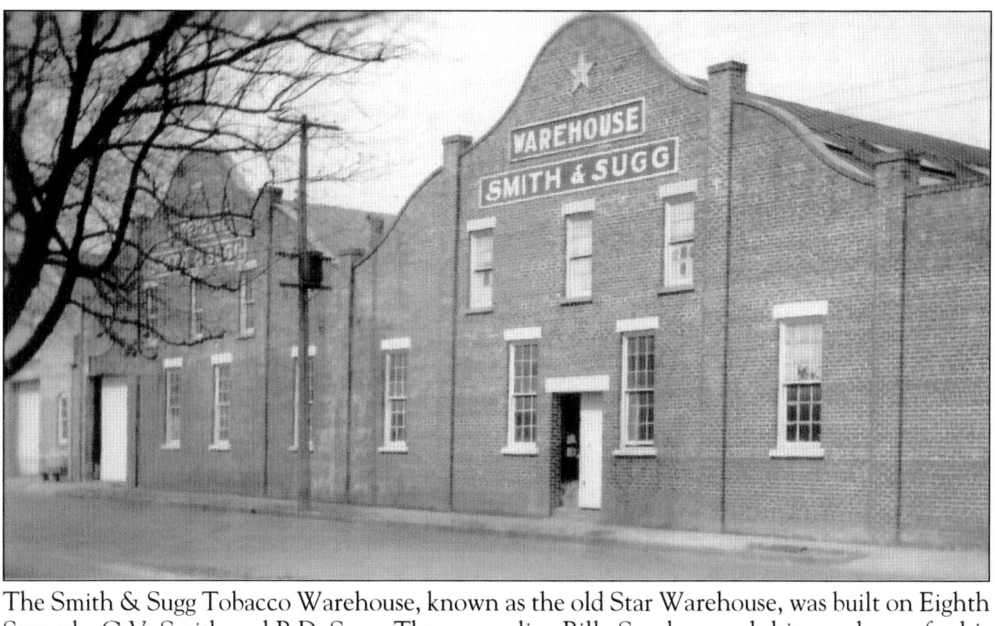

The Smith & Sugg Tobacco Warehouse, known as the old Star Warehouse, was built on Eighth Street by G.V. Smith and B.D. Sugg. The evangelist, Billy Sunday, used this warehouse for his services in the 1930s. (Courtesy of Charles Horne Collection.)

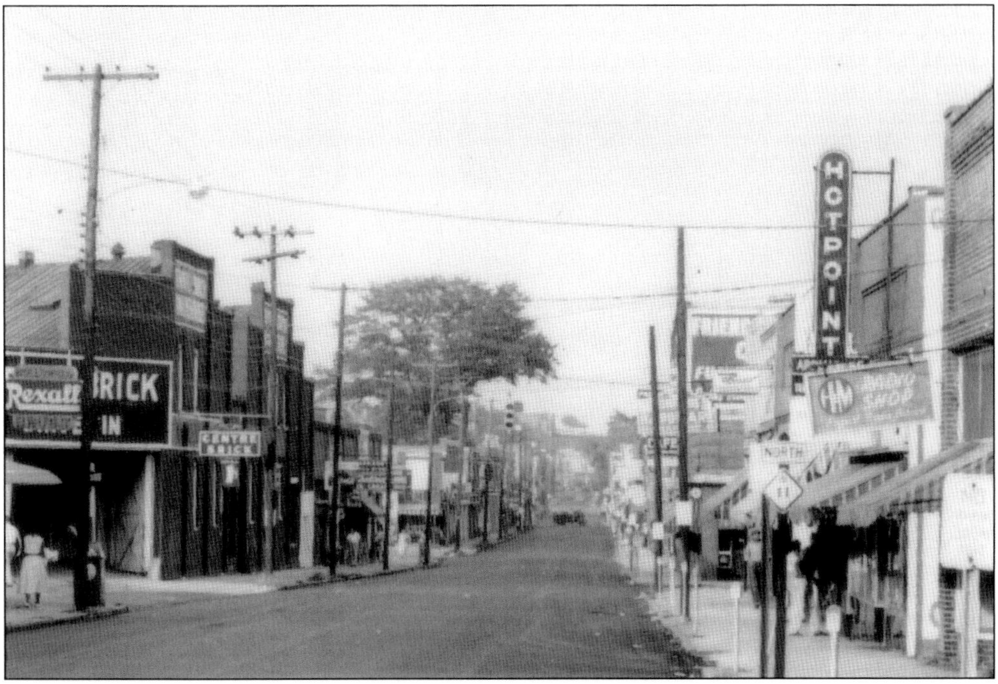

The businesses pictured on Dickinson Avenue looking east from Grand Avenue back toward Atlantic Avenue are Centre Brick Warehouse and Karl's Food Market (owned by Karl G. Cahoon), both on the left, and Ken's Furniture (owned by Kenneth W. Brown) on the right. (Courtesy of ECMC.)

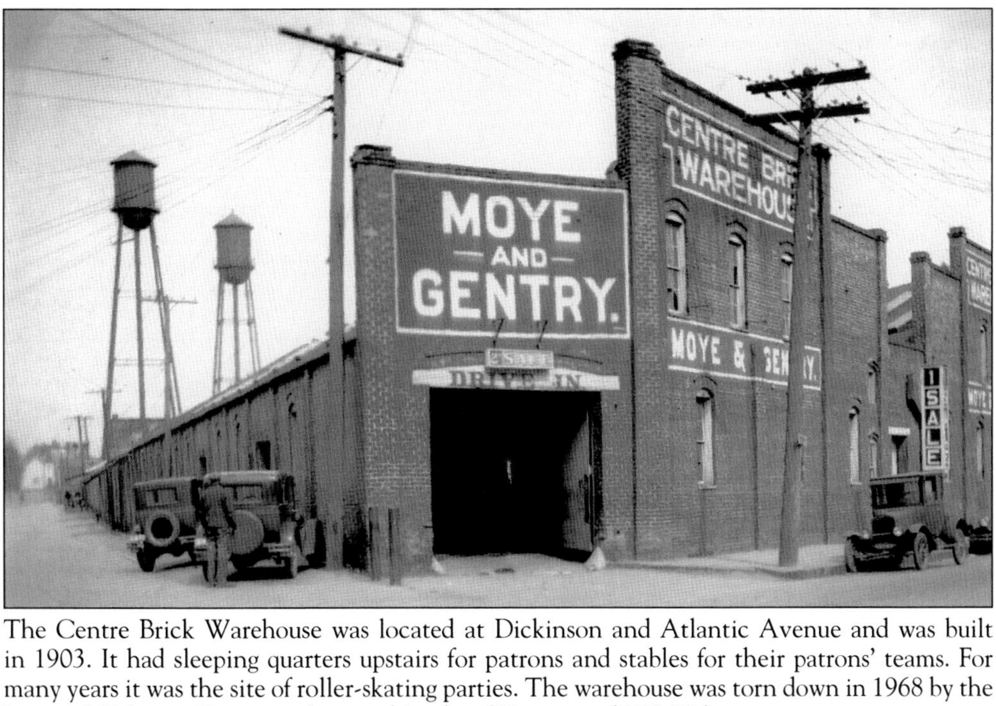

The Centre Brick Warehouse was located at Dickinson and Atlantic Avenue and was built in 1903. It had sleeping quarters upstairs for patrons and stables for their patrons' teams. For many years it was the site of roller-skating parties. The warehouse was torn down in 1968 by the Imperial Tobacco Company for a parking lot. (Courtesy of ECMC.)

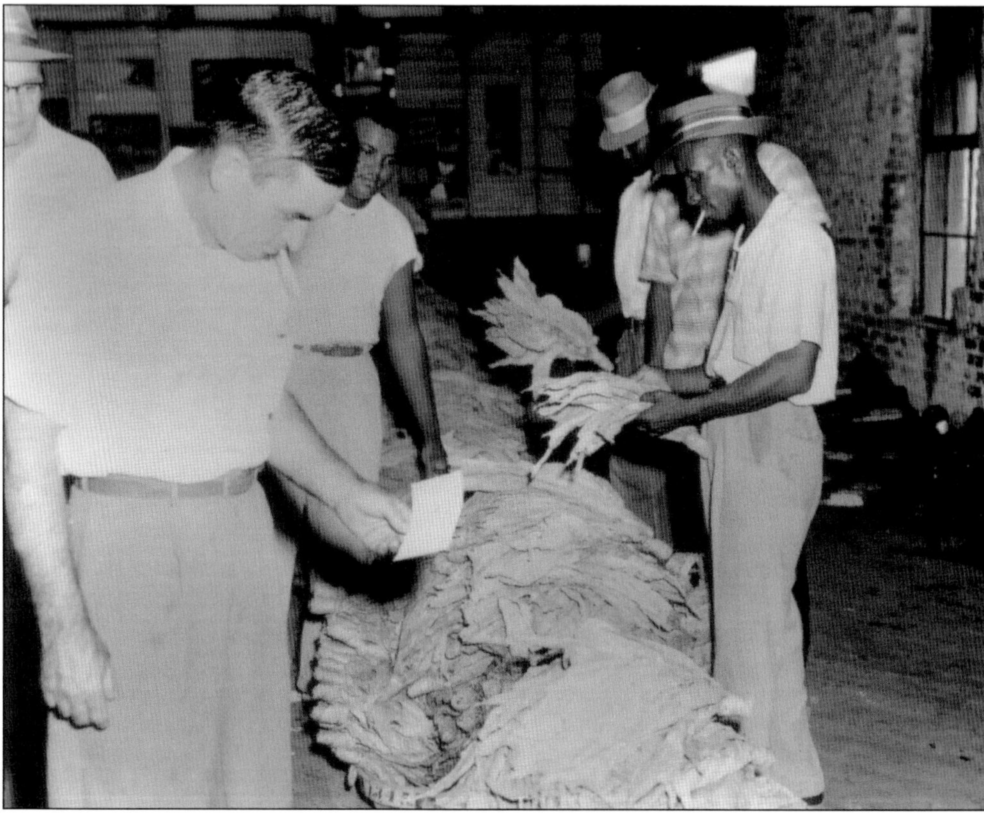

This scene depicts a tobacco auction on the Greenville market in 1957. (Courtesy of ECMC.)

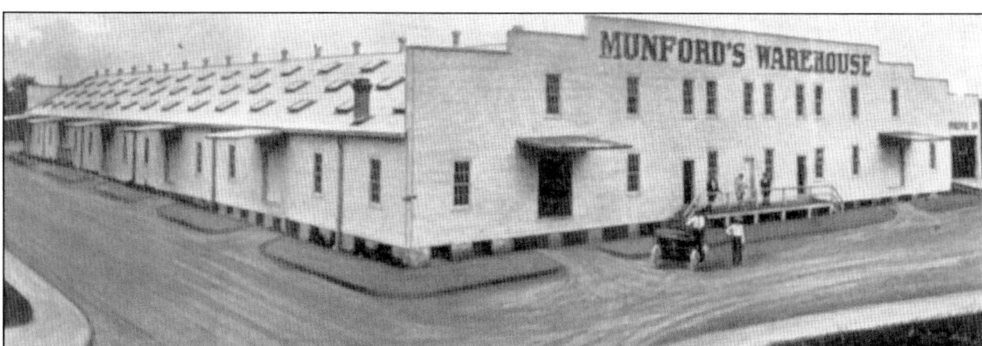

Munford's Tobacco Warehouse was built in 1913 and owned by C.T. Munford and R.H. Knott. When it was built, it was the largest tobacco warehouse in Eastern North Carolina. (Courtesy of "Illustrated City of Greenville" [pamphlet] Pitt County, 1914.)

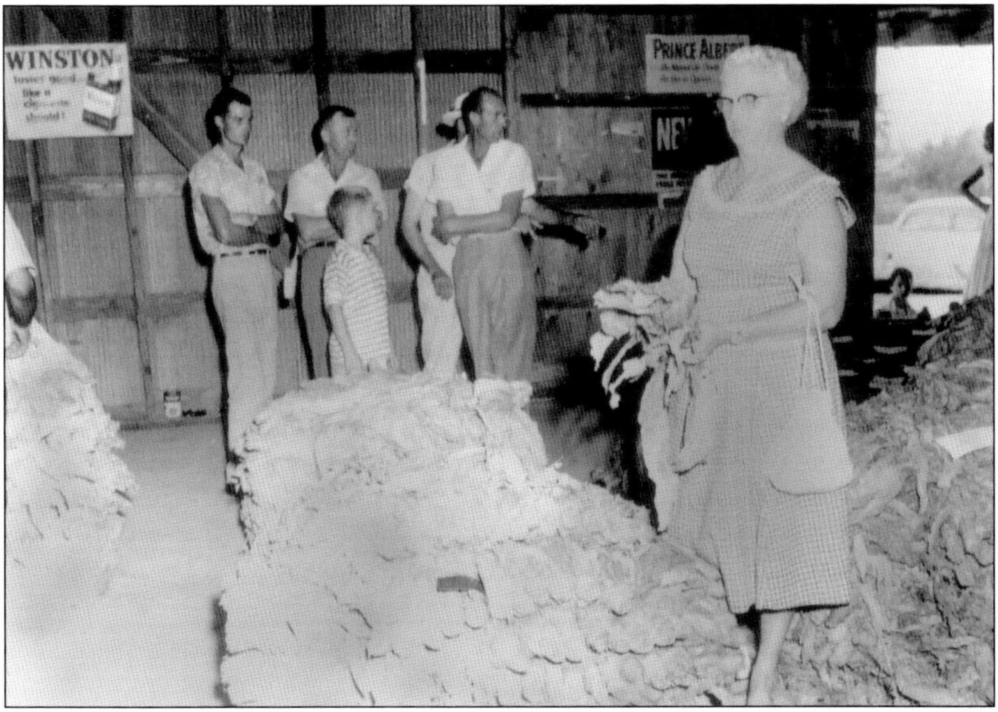

Having 1,516 pounds of tobacco on the warehouse floor, Mrs. Fannie Bell House was selling her tobacco on the Greenville market in 1957. Her case was unusual—she handled the farm by herself while her two sons were off at college. Mrs. House, who actively engaged in farming since 1942, complained that her crops in 1957 were struck down by weather, mixed seeds, and government regulations reflecting discounted varieties. (Courtesy of ECMC.)

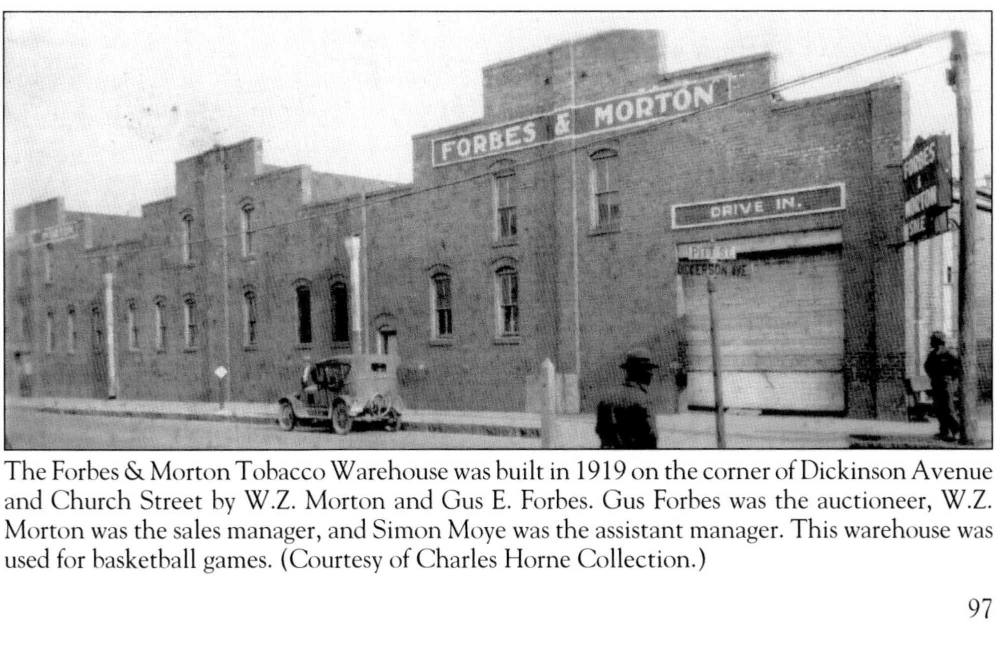

The Forbes & Morton Tobacco Warehouse was built in 1919 on the corner of Dickinson Avenue and Church Street by W.Z. Morton and Gus E. Forbes. Gus Forbes was the auctioneer, W.Z. Morton was the sales manager, and Simon Moye was the assistant manager. This warehouse was used for basketball games. (Courtesy of Charles Horne Collection.)

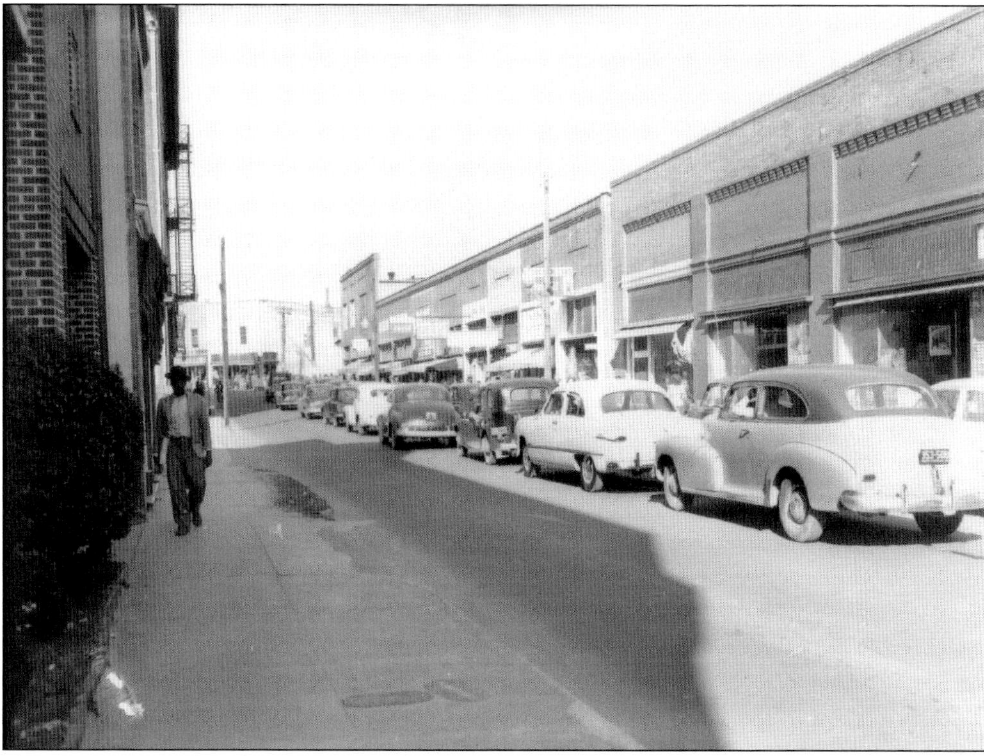

Shown is a view of Dickinson Avenue looking east from the sidewalk in front of the telephone building about 1956. The Dixie Gray Cafe is the only recognizable business in this photo. These businesses were torn down, along with the State Bank in 1975, thus changing this part of Dickinson Avenue. (Courtesy of ECMC.)

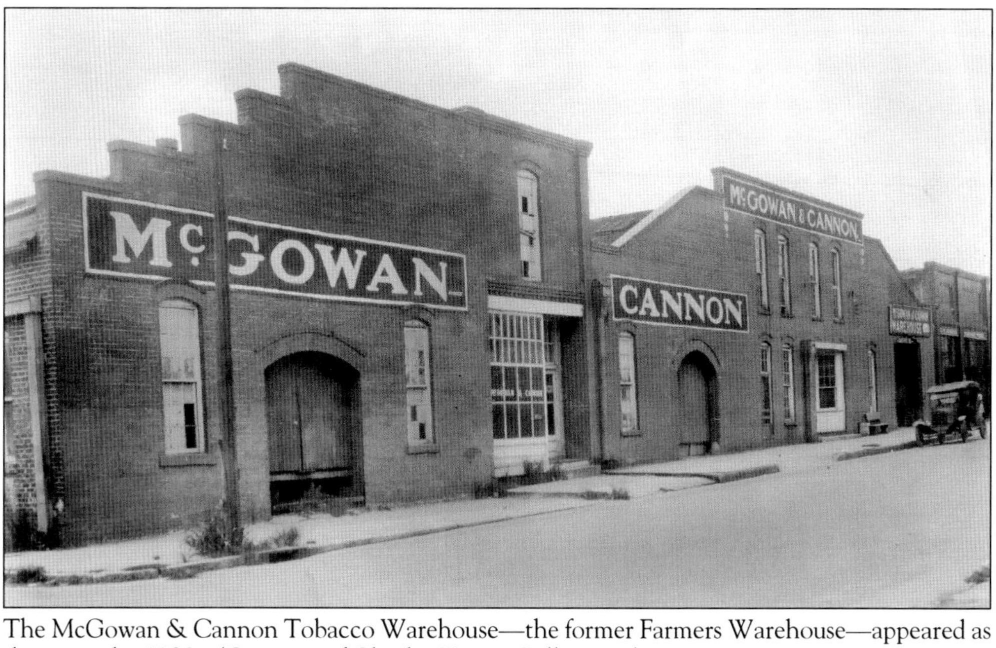

The McGowan & Cannon Tobacco Warehouse—the former Farmers Warehouse—appeared as shown in the 1930s. (Courtesy of Charles Horne Collection.)

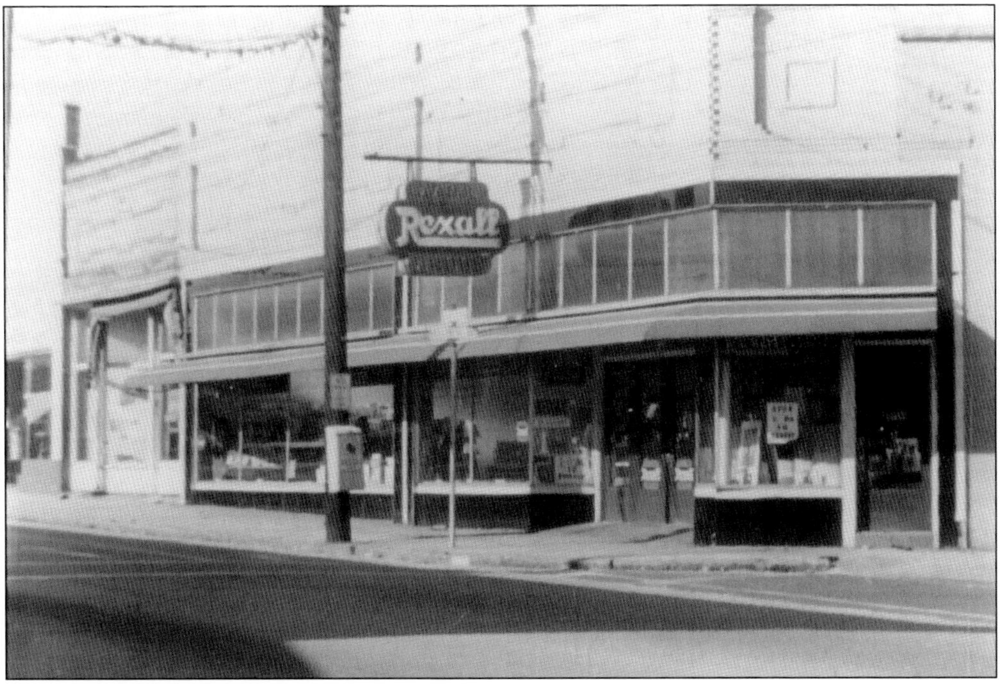

A local landmark, Clyde Hollowell's Drug Store was located at the northwest corner of Atlantic Avenue and Dickinson Avenue. Hollowell bought the business in 1940, and in 1962 Clarence Johnson became a partner. They built a new store across the street in 1963 on the former site of C.H. Edwards Hardware Co. The old store became Avenue Pharmacy (the name on the sign), also a part of Hollowell's. Orange-aid was the featured item at the soda fountain at Hollowell's Drug Store. (Courtesy of Alex Albright.)

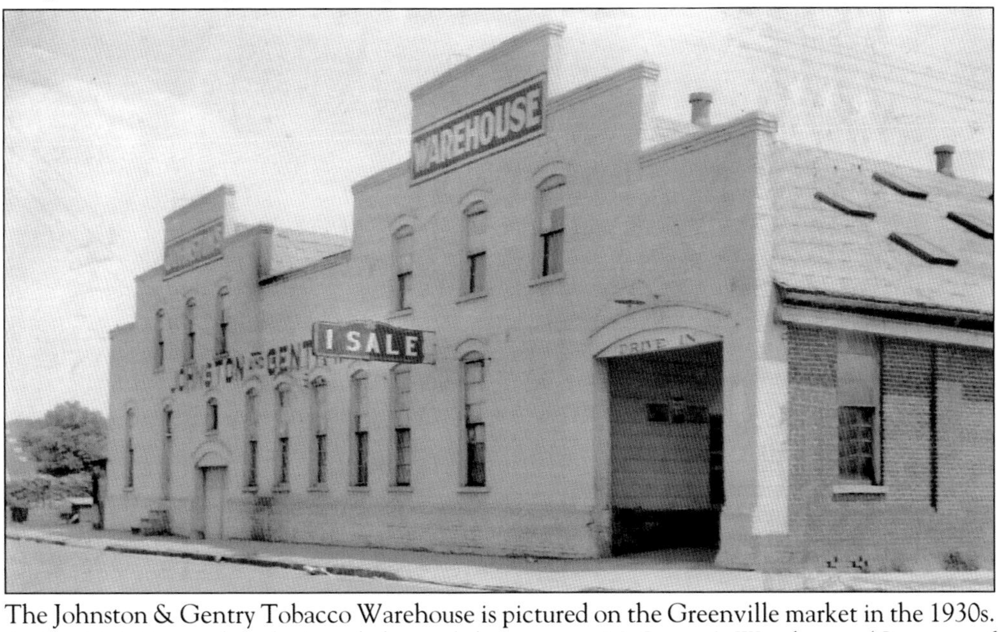

The Johnston & Gentry Tobacco Warehouse is pictured on the Greenville market in the 1930s. C. Hugh McGowan bought it and changed the name to McGowan's Warehouse. (Courtesy of Charles Horne Collection.)

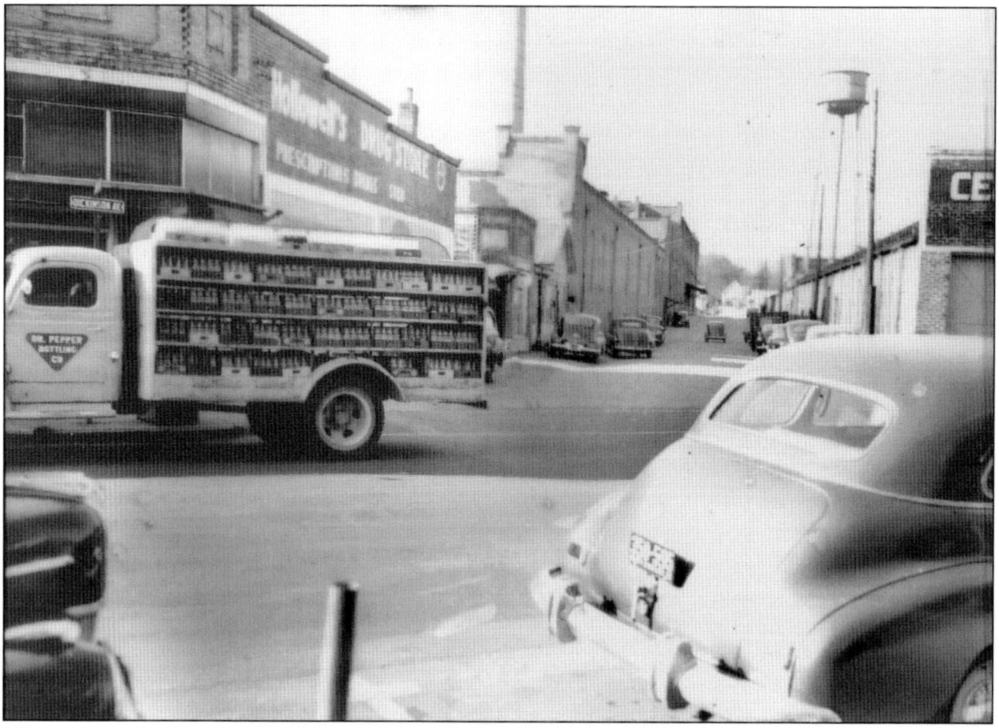

This scene looks down Atlantic Avenue from Dickinson Avenue *c.* 1954. (Courtesy of ECMC.)

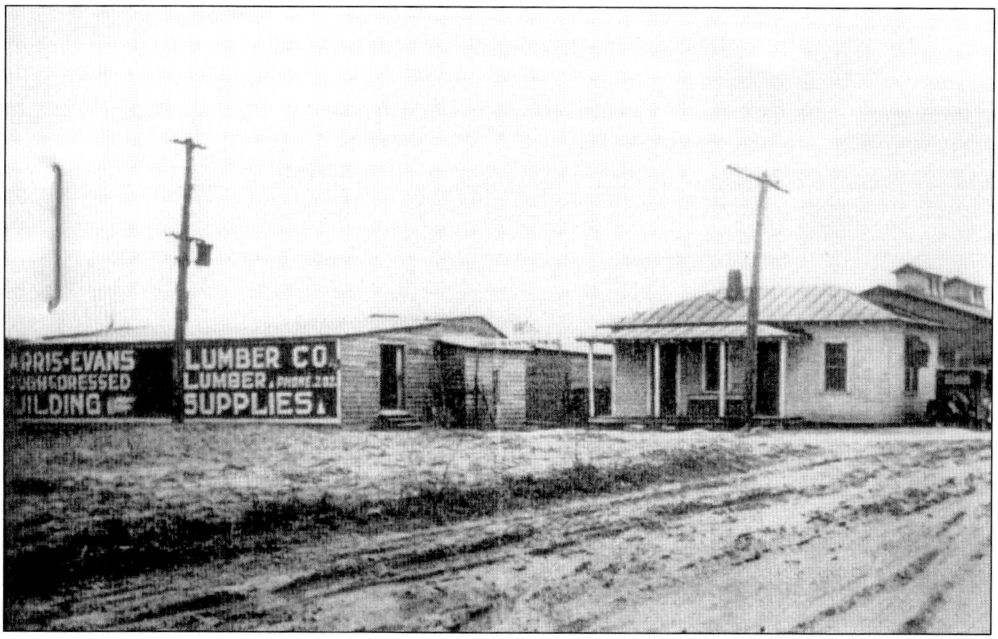

The Garris-Evans Lumber Company, owned by L.B. Garris and G.T. Evans, opened on Ridgeway Street in 1920 in front off the Greenville Oil and Fertilizer Company. In 1948, it was owned by S. Reynolds May and David A. Evans. They later built new facilities on the Fourteenth Street edge of their property. (Courtesy of ECMC.)

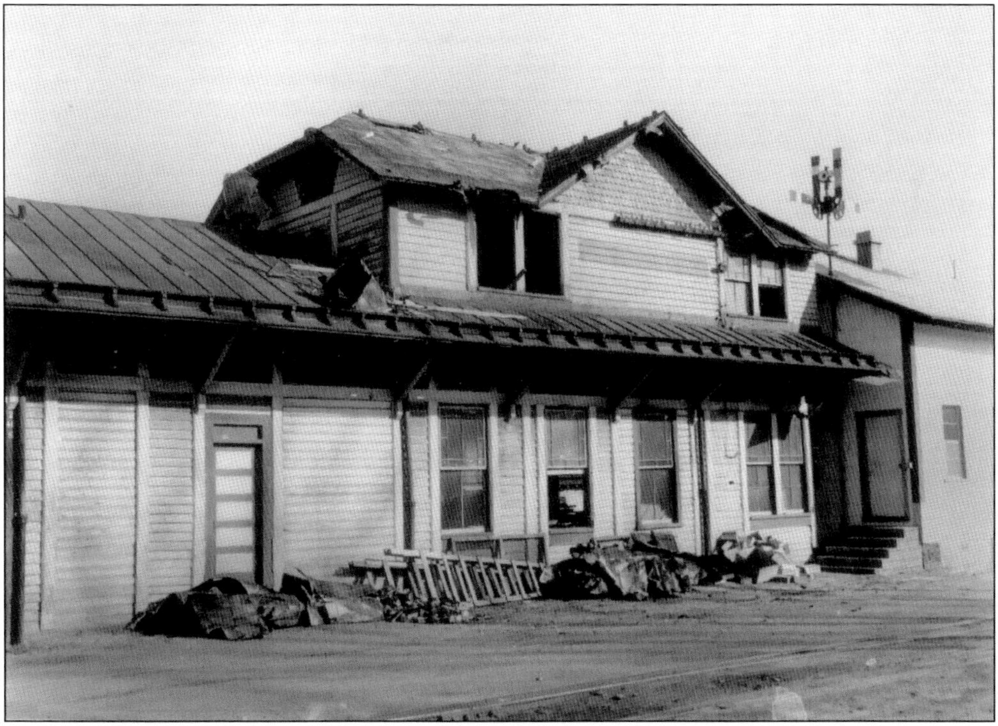

The Old Atlantic Coast Line Railroad passenger station was located near the intersection of Tenth Street and Dickinson Avenue. The town's citizens crowded the station daily to watch the trains arrive and to talk about the day's events. The station was built in 1890, but was moved in 1941 from the intersection when Dickinson Avenue was widened. The last regularly scheduled passenger train came through Greenville on April 26, 1942. The station was torn down in March 1958. (Courtesy of ECMC.)

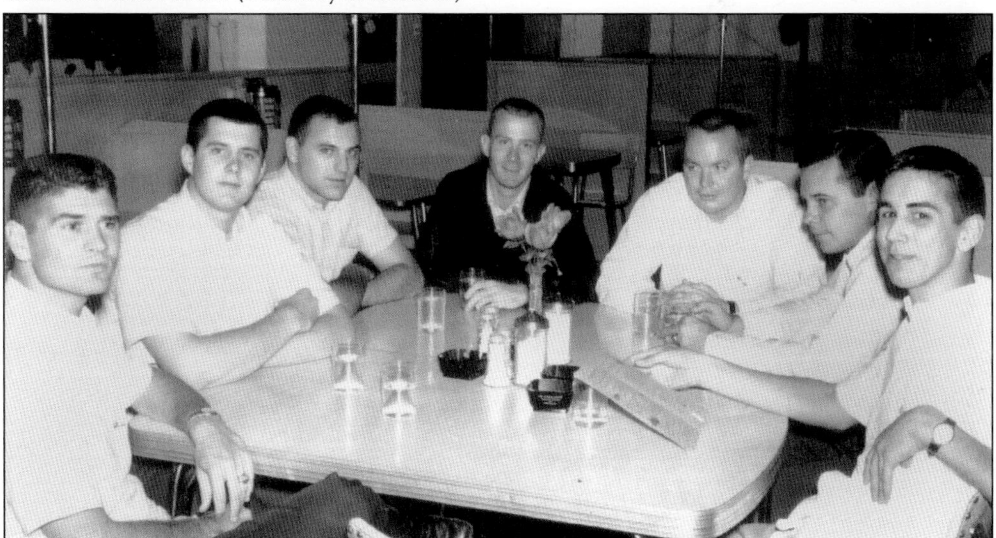

The Carolina Grill, owned by George Saad, was a popular 24-hour eatery located on the corner of Ninth Street and Dickinson Avenue in the "Dogshead" section of Tobacco Town. (Courtesy of George Saad.)

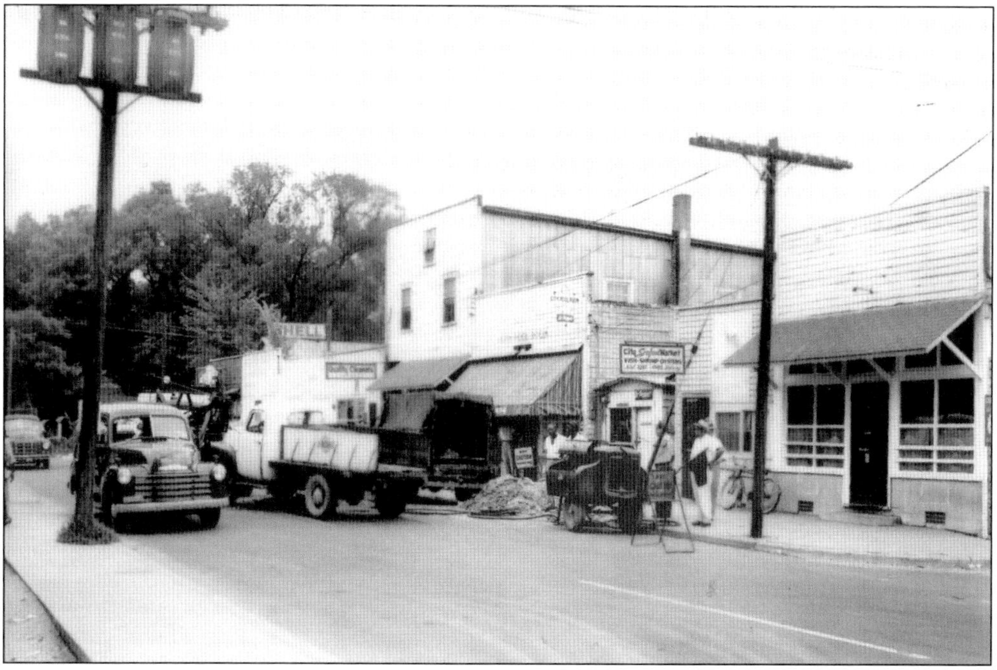

The businesses pictured in the 600 block of Albemarle Avenue in 1954 are, from left to right, Quality Cleaners, run by Karl B. Dickerson and Thomas L. Hannaford; City Pool Room, run by Sylvester Brown; City Seafood Market, run by Robert Puryear and Thomas H. Adams; and the Red Rose Social Club. (Courtesy of ECMC.)

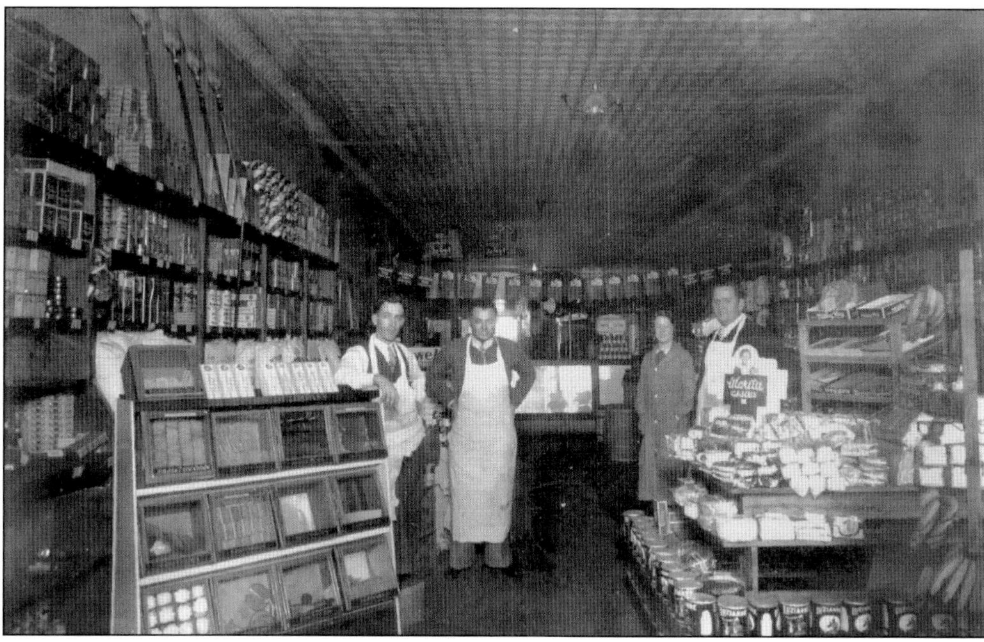

Shown is the interior of City Market in October 1934, located on Dickinson Avenue beside what became the new Hollowell's Drug store. The two store clerks on the left are unidentified, but on the right is owner C.A. Turner and his wife Pearl, who ran the store from 1926 until 1953. (Courtesy of Cecil and Libby Turner.)

Six

People and Places

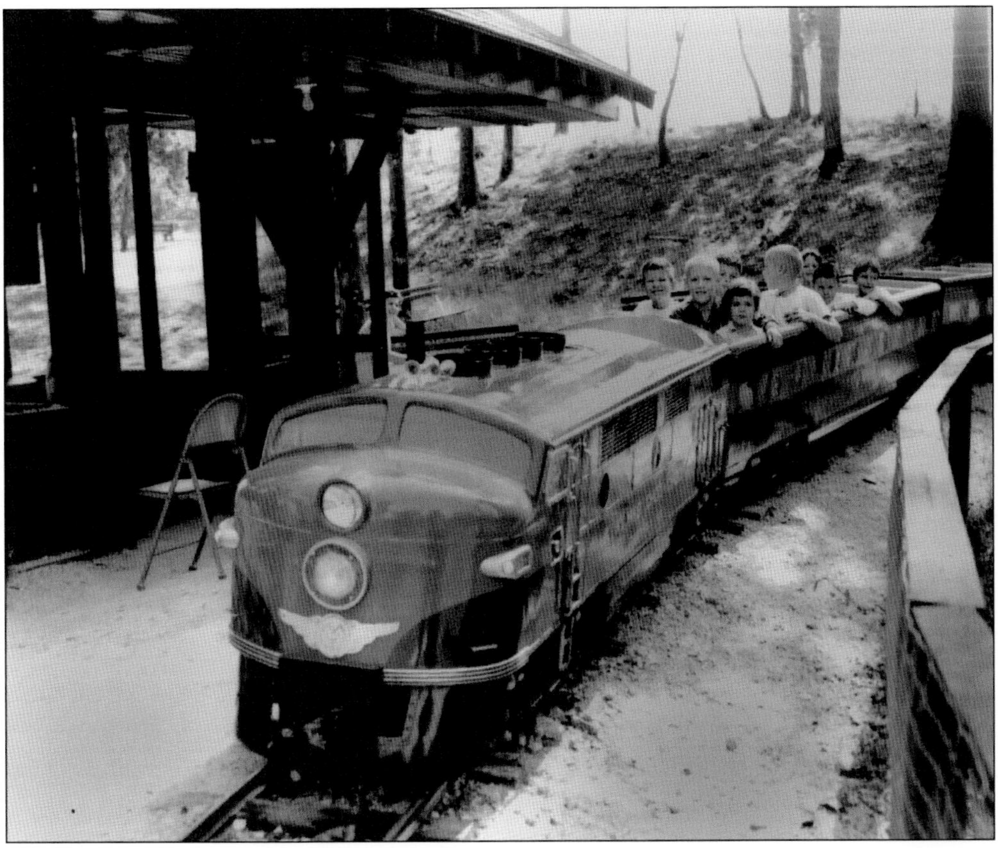

The Kiwanis Club held their "Choo-Choo Kids Day" in September 1956. The train was brought to Greenville by the Kiwanis Club in 1954 and placed at Guy Smith Stadium. In 1955, it was moved to the Kiwanis Park across from Elm Street Park. The train and park were given to the city in 1966. The Kiwanis train stopped running in 1967. (Courtesy of ECMC.)

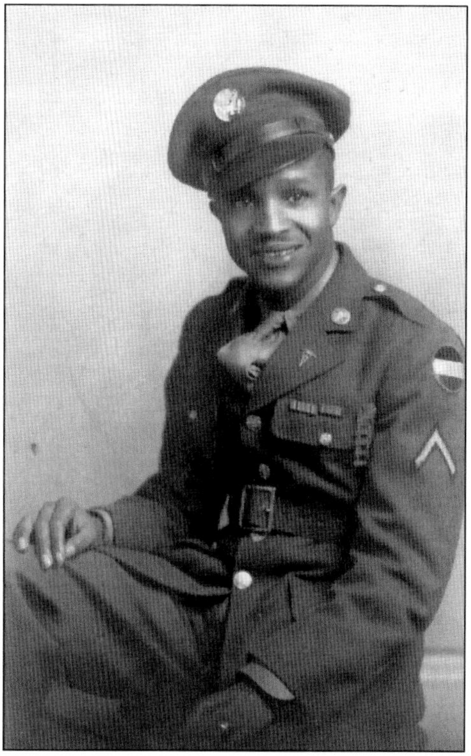

Marion C. Norcott, pictured here *c.* 1942, entered the Army in 1942 and was attached to the Second Army Medical Outfit. After the war, he attended the Mohagany School of Cabinet Making and Upholstering. He later operated an upholstery shop at 611 Tyson Street until 1958. He was custodian to the Recreation Center at the old Armory and for the Greenville City Schools for over 21 years. (Courtesy of Lonnie Norcott.)

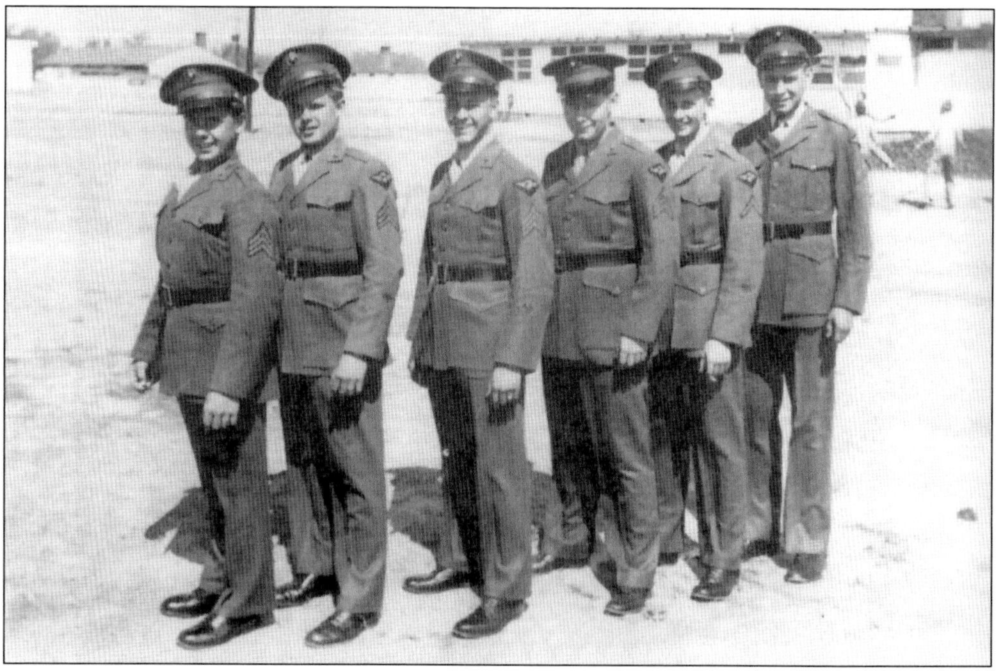

In 1943–1944, a squadron of U.S. Marine pilots, VMSB-343, nicknamed "Gregory's Gorillas," were stationed at the old NYA Center on Elm Street, pictured above. They conducted simulated aircraft carrier landings at the Greenville airport. One of the pilots, Frank Lange, flew his airplane under the Greene Street Bridge. (Courtesy of Ralph Heidenreich.)

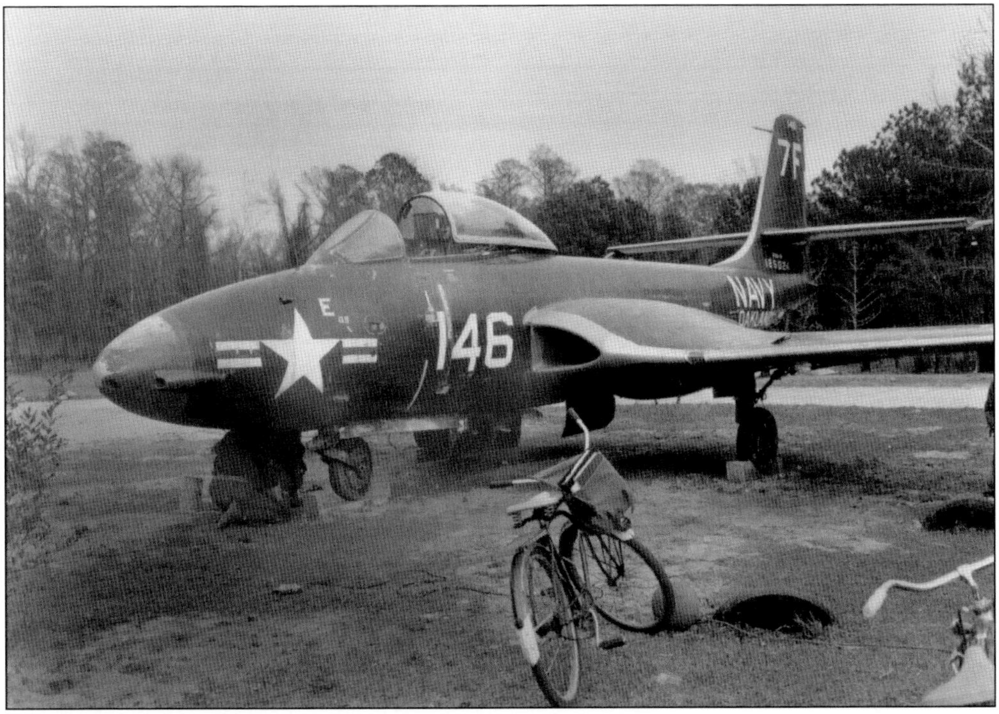

The jet plane *Greenville* is shown at Elm Street Park in 1959. It was donated by Cherry Point Marine Corps Air Station to Greenville Recreation Department along with several others across the state. There was once a World War I tank situated on the courthouse lawn, but it was given away for scrap during World War II. (Courtesy of ECMC.)

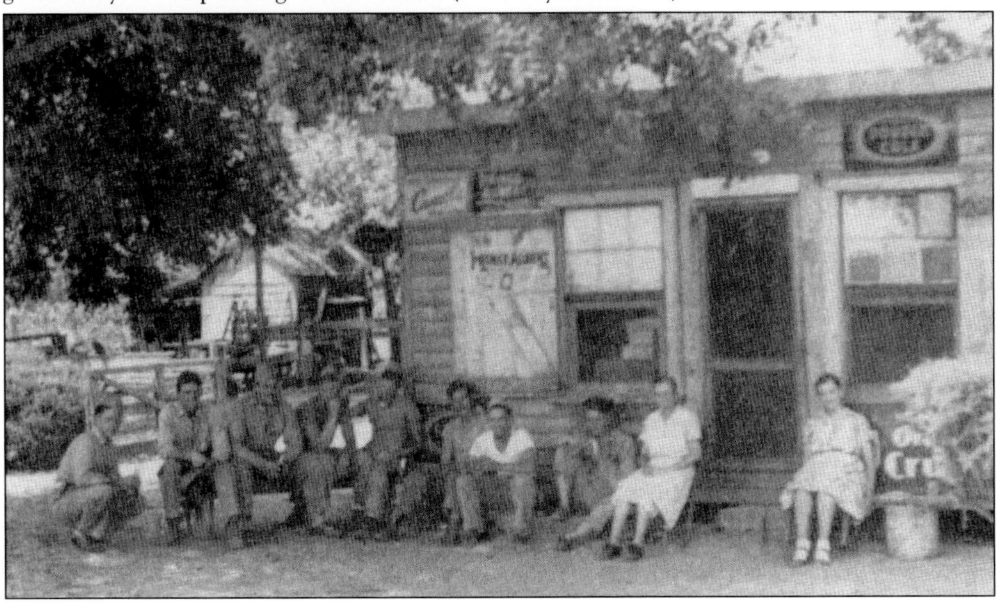

This was the "400 Club," located on Fourteenth Street just outside the fence of the old NYA Center. It was the store of Noah H. Barber and his wife Anna, who sold cigarettes, snacks, and drinks to the servicemen in 1943. The Barbers were like surrogate parents to the Marines and took in their visiting parents. (Courtesy of Ralph Heidenreich.)

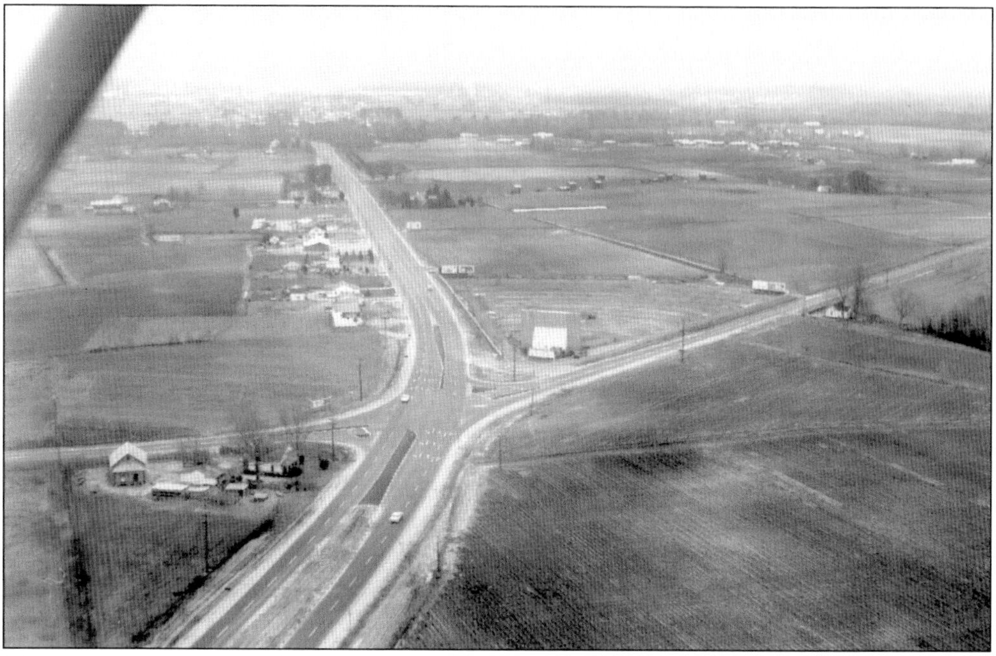

This aerial view shows the intersection of what is now Memorial Drive and Greenville Boulevard in 1960. The old South 11 Drive-In Movie Theatre sits in the center. (Courtesy of ECMC.)

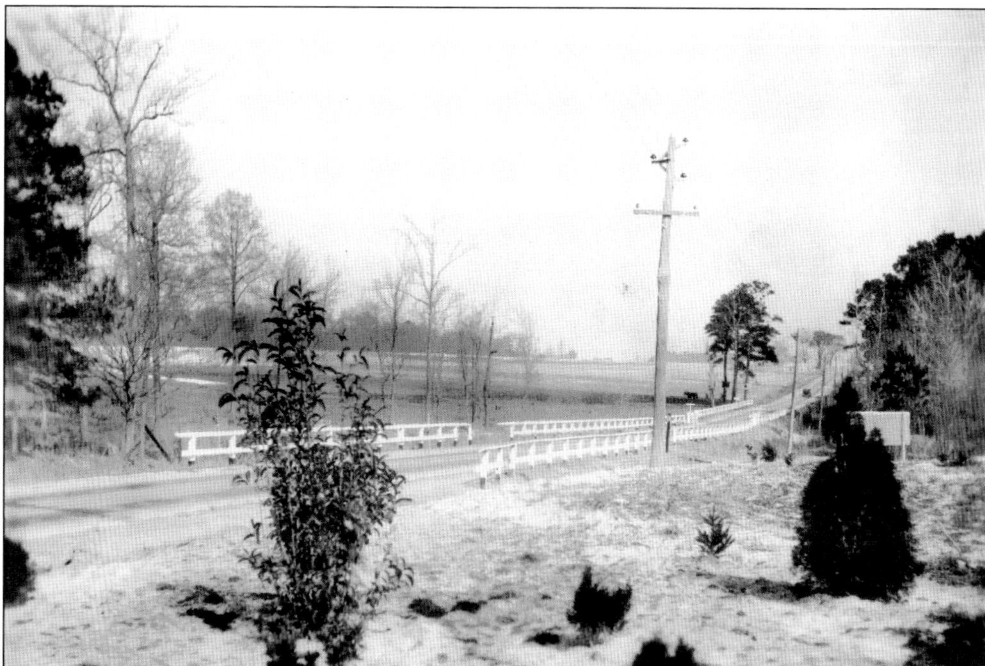

This new sand-clay road was called the Ayden Highway in the 1920s, is now Memorial Drive, and is shown looking north. To the left is what is now Camelot Inn and the former Three Steers Restaurant. (Courtesy of Charles Horne Collection.)

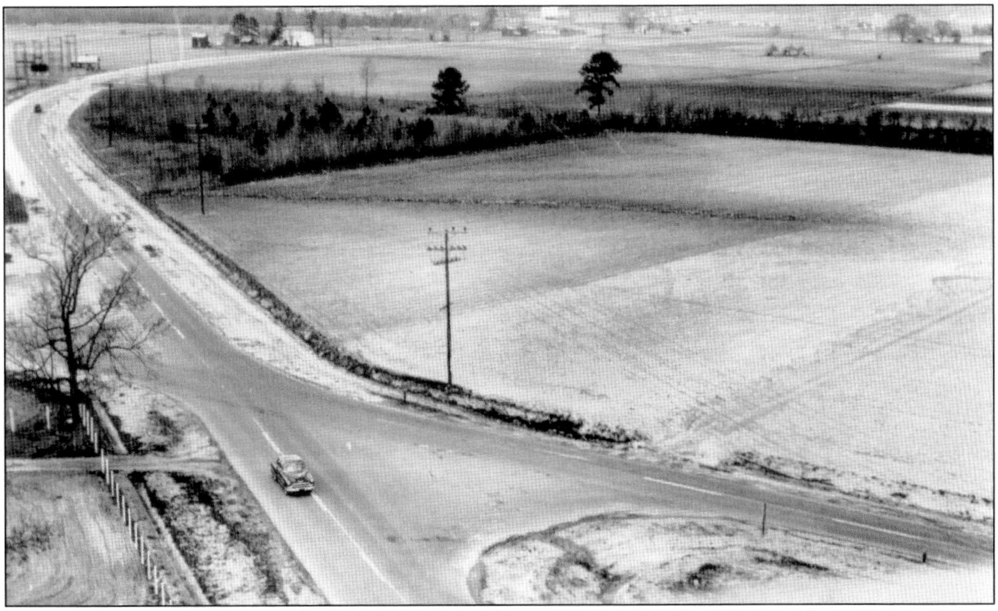

This remarkable 1954 photograph of the intersection of Greenville Boulevard and Evans Street was taken from a fire tower. Now it is one of the busiest commercial districts in town. The white building to the center left is the former English Chapel Church (now the Hilton Hotel). The white square in the center is the former South 11 Drive-In Theatre, then located at the intersection of Greenville Boulevard and Memorial Drive. (Courtesy of ECMC.)

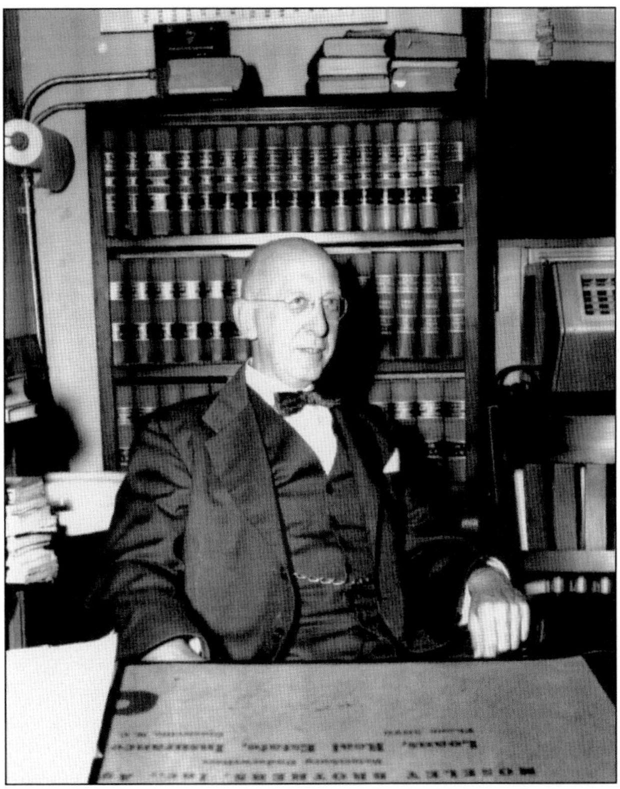

Judge Dink James, a memorable Greenville personality, was the judge of the weekly Pitt County Recorders Court for many years. His first taste of law came in 1907—as a boy he pulled jurors names from a hat and got $1.50 for his services. He went on to law school and was elected judge in 1932. (Courtesy of ECMC.)

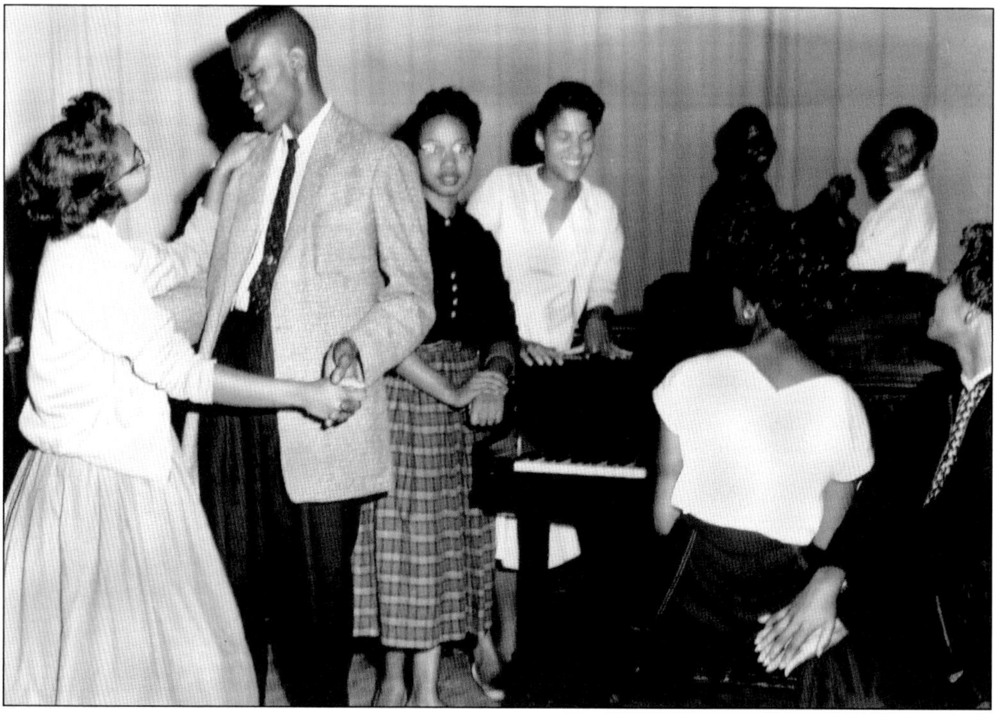

This was the Negro Teenage Club at Eppes School in 1956. This club was designed to furnish wholesome recreation for African-American teenagers and only met on Friday nights during the school year. Dancing was the major activity. (Courtesy of ECMC.)

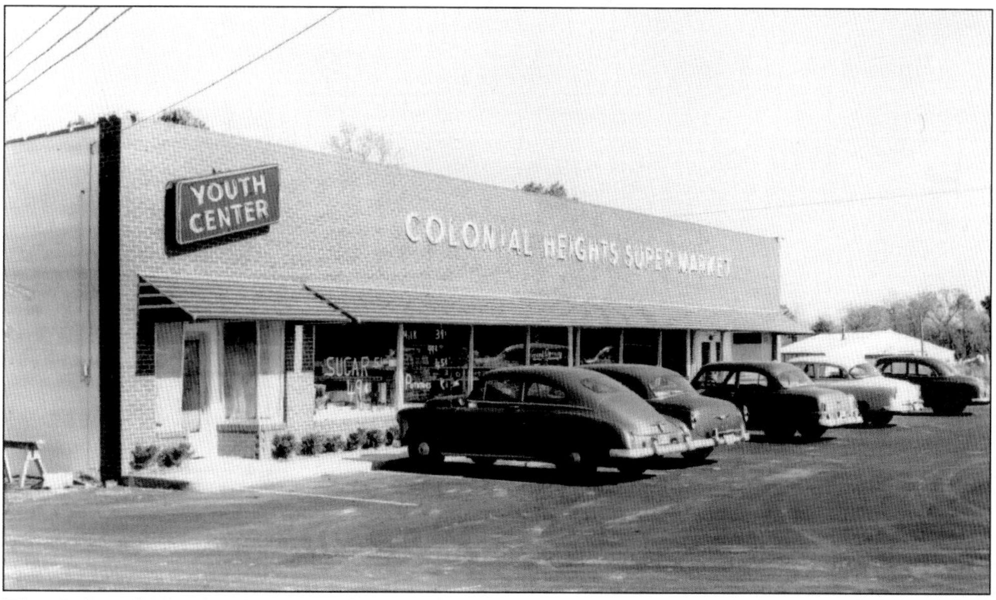

The Colonial Heights Super Market was built on the north side of East Tenth Street in 1954 by L.T. Hardee and Charlie Cox. L.T. Hardee was the manager and Charlie Harris was assistant manager. Also in the building was the Youth Center, a children's clothing store, operated by the wives of the building owners, Mrs. L.T. Hardee and Mrs. Charlie Cox. This was the first store in what was to become the Colonial Heights Shopping Center. (Courtesy of ECMC.)

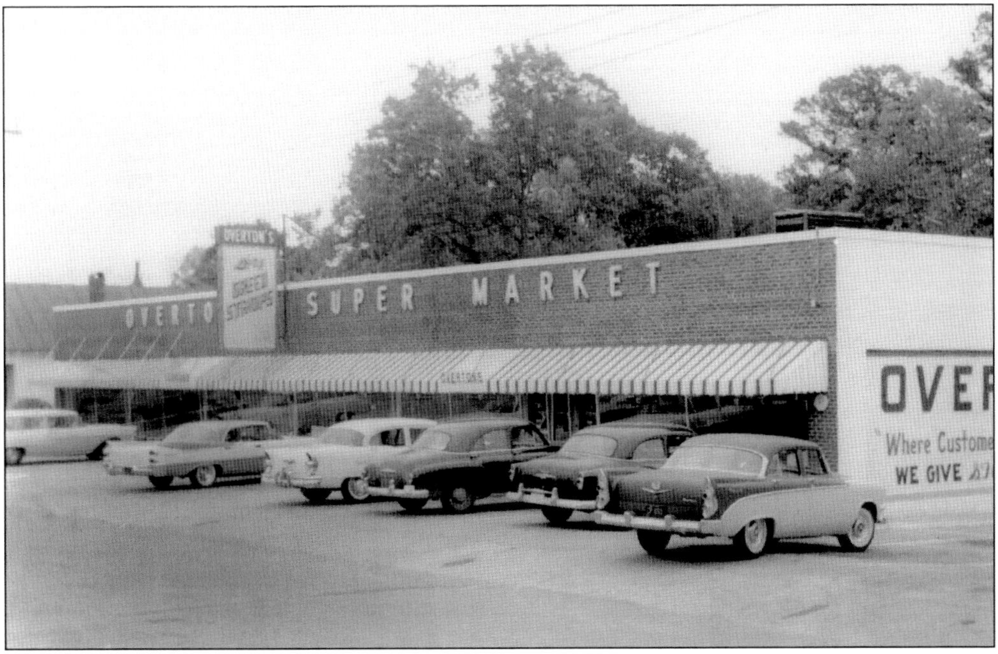

Overton's Supermarket on Jarvis Street is pictured in 1959. Started by Vance Overton in 1946 on the corner of Fourteenth and Evans Streets, the store moved to Jarvis Street in 1948. (Courtesy of ECMC.)

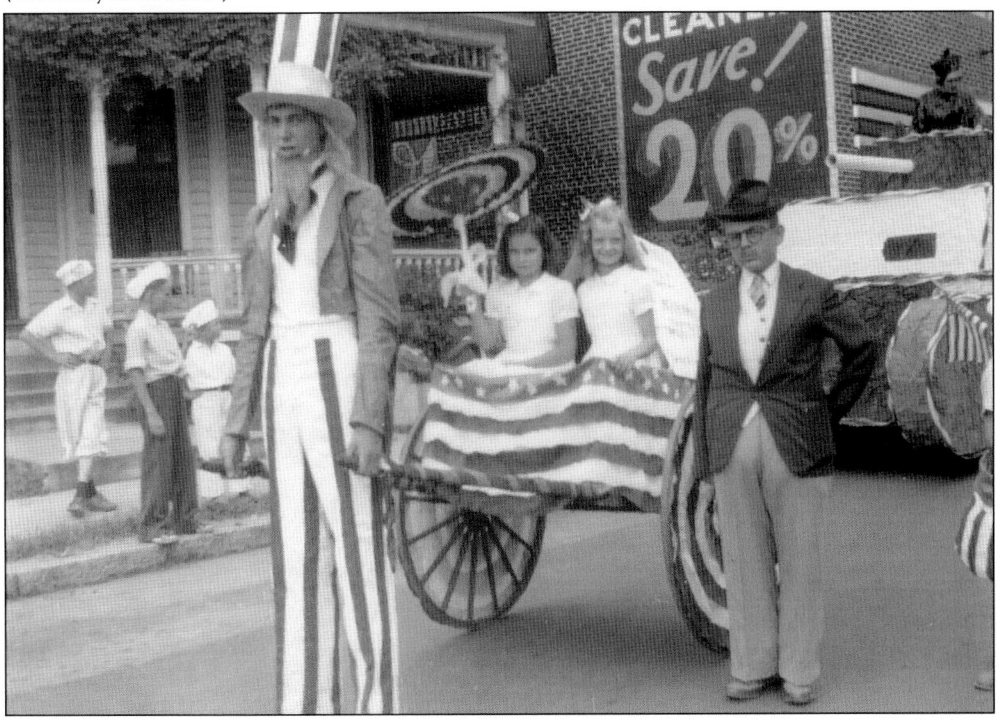

The Victory Day parade was held in Greenville on July 4, 1942. A crowd of 10,000 watched the two-mile parade. Seated in the cart, from left to right, are Virginia Perkins (Sharpe) and Jean Ann King (Sears). (Courtesy of Mrs. Mattie Moye King Bridgers.)

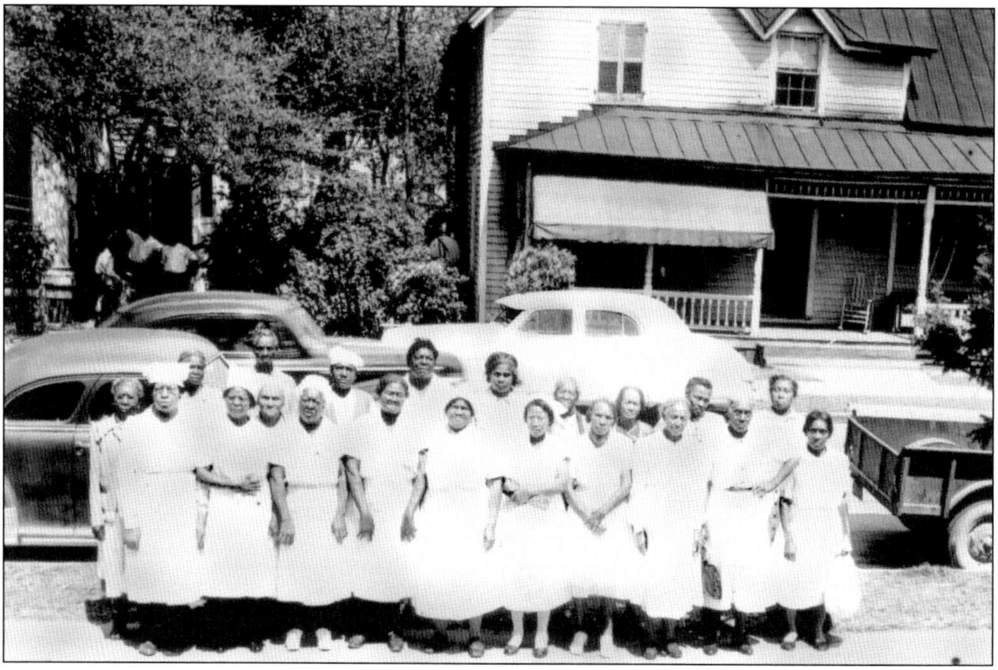

The Negro Midwives Association holds a meeting in 1951. Over 100 midwives existed in Pitt County in the 1920s and only 4 were left in 1968. Requirements included being in good health, being a high school graduate, having good character, and being between ages 21 and 45. Midwives were required to complete a course at the midwife institute, which was usually in Fayetteville. Licenses were renewed every five years. (Courtesy of ECMC.)

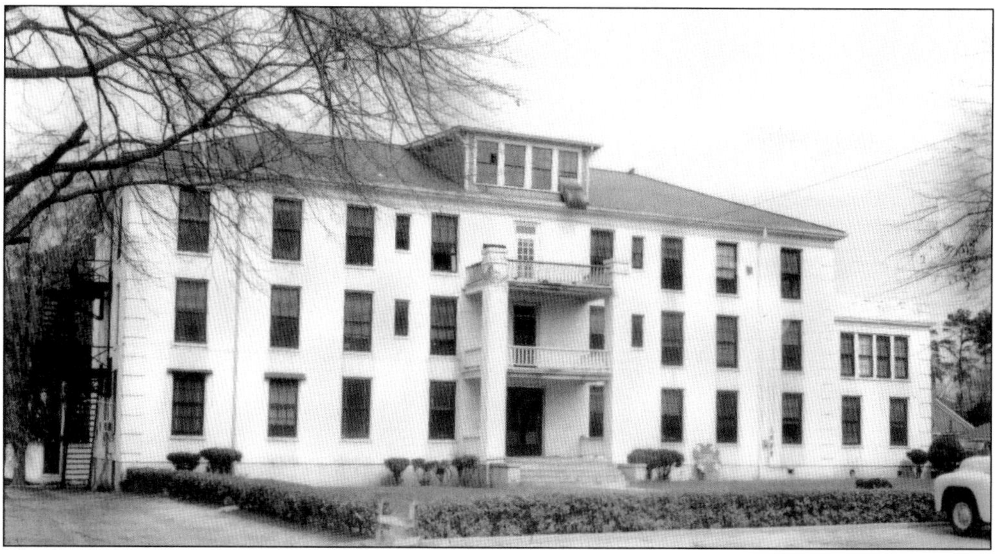

Pitt Community Hospital, located on the corner of Johnston and Woodlawn Streets, was built in 1923–1924 as a private hospital by four doctors—Dr. Charles O'Hagan Laughinghouse, Dr. Karl B. Pace, Dr. William I. Wooten, and Dr. E.T. Dickerson. It opened in 1924 and operated until 1951 when the new Pitt Memorial Hospital opened. St. Frances's Hospital, a black hospital near the corner of Evans and Second Streets, was run by Frances Hopkins in conjunction with Pitt Community. (Courtesy of ECMC.)

Dr. Malene Grant Irons, "the baby doctor," was a native of Gates County, North Carolina. She was a 1935 graduate of East Carolina, and she and her twin sister entered Duke University for further science courses before entering the Medical College of Virginia. She has been in private practice with her husband, Dr. C. Fred Irons, since coming to Greenville in 1946. She has donated hundreds of hours to the community and has garnered many distinguished awards for her service. (Courtesy of ECMC.)

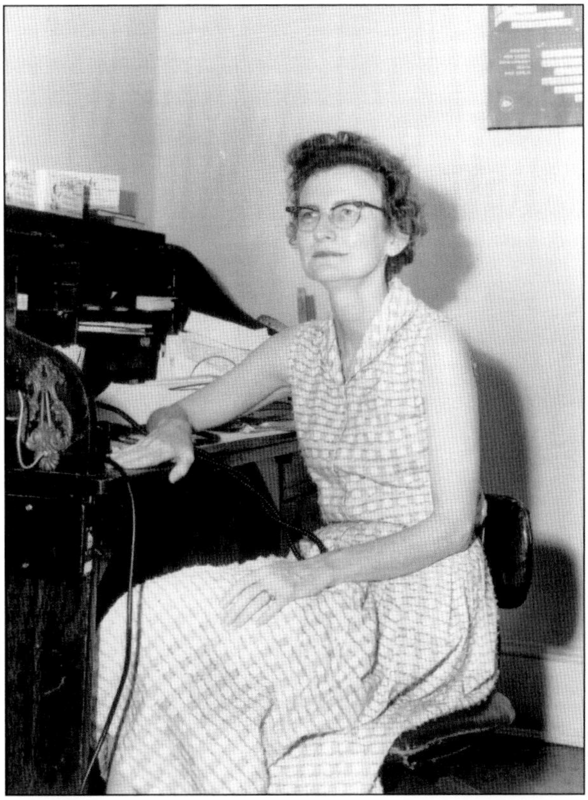

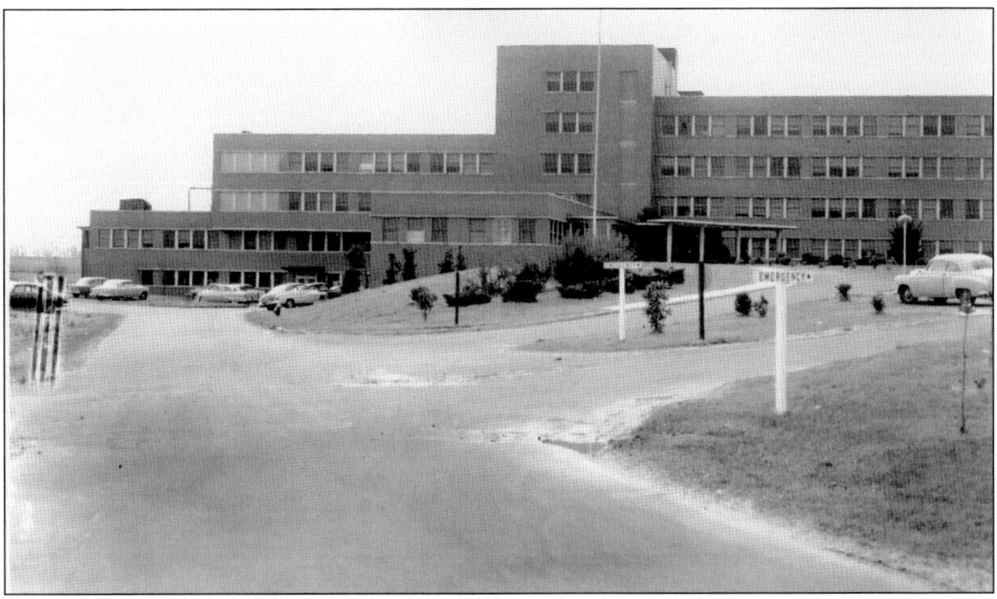

Pitt Memorial Hospital, pictured here in 1960, is on West Fifth Street. It opened in 1951 as a state-of-the-art facility and one of the best-equipped hospitals in the state. Back then, a private room with bath was only $11 a day. The Service League of Greenville heavily supported the hospital and ran a canteen inside it. A new hospital was built next door in 1976. This building now serves as county offices. (Courtesy of ECMC.)

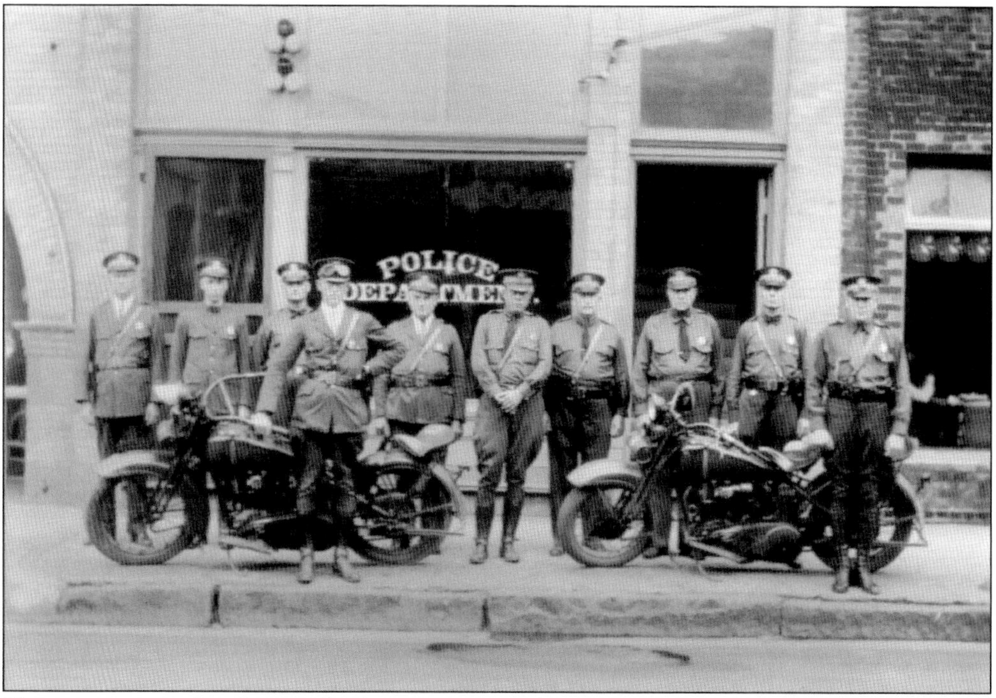

The two motorcycle officers, Chief Lester Jones and J.L. Nobles, and the rest of the Greenville Police Department line up and show off their two motorcycles that they purchased in 1924. They are in front of the old police department near the intersection of Fifth and Cotanche Streets. (Courtesy of Charles Horne Collection.)

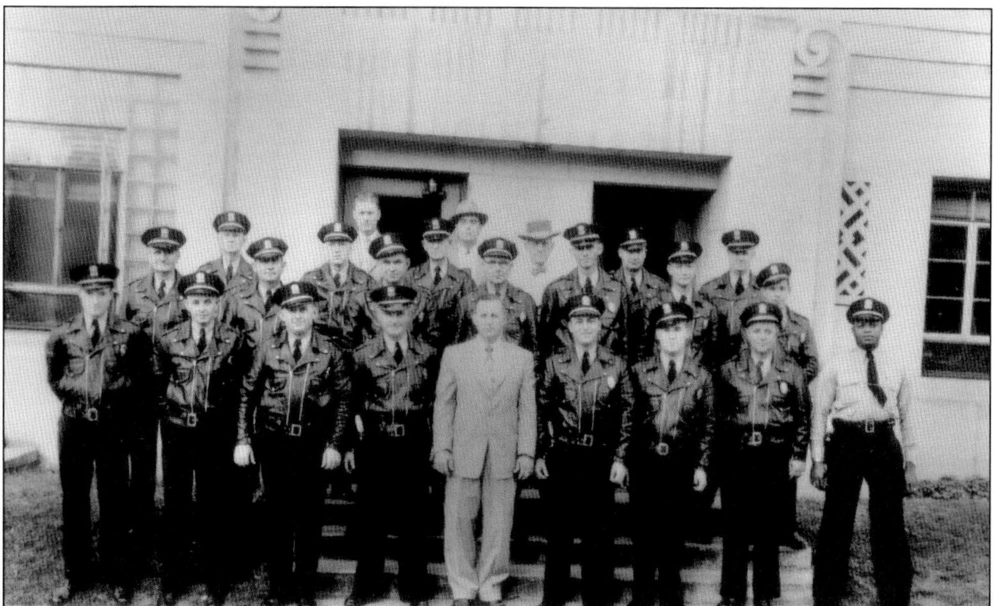

The Greenville Police Department line up in front of city hall in 1951. To the left is Officer Caesar Corbitt Jr., the first black Greenville police officer since the 1800s. Corbitt was a military veteran. (Courtesy of ECMC.)

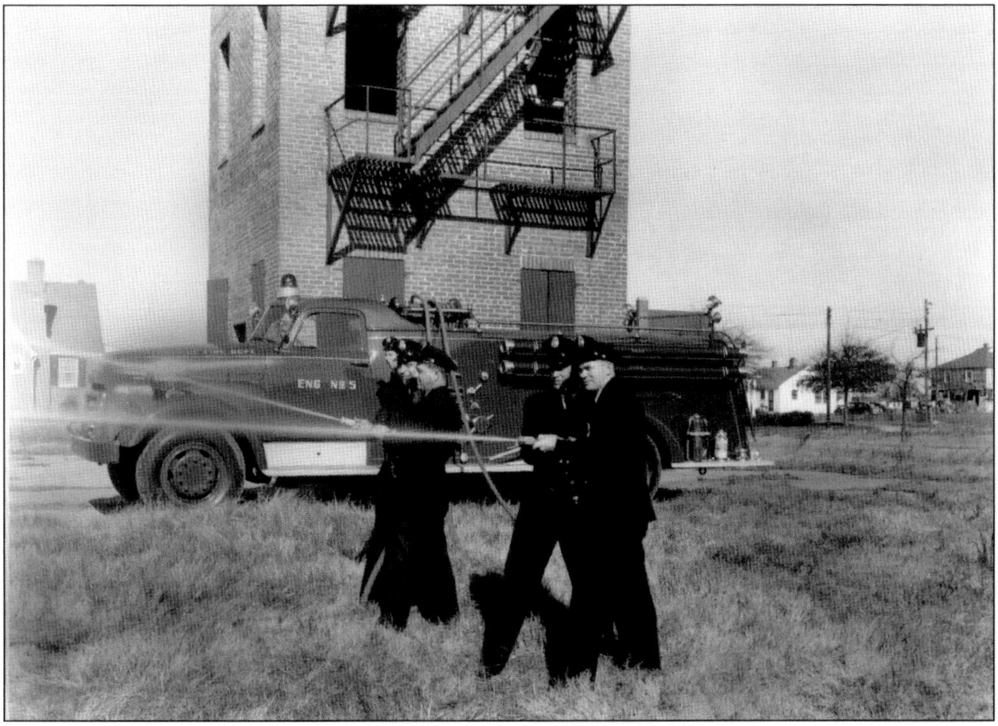

In 1963, J.L. Jones, veteran fireman, became Greenville Fire Chief. He promoted a fire-training program, including classroom and drill tower practice. The drill tower was constructed in 1942 and paid for largely by a $5,000 donation by Mr. and Mrs. M.O. Minges. (Courtesy of ECMC.)

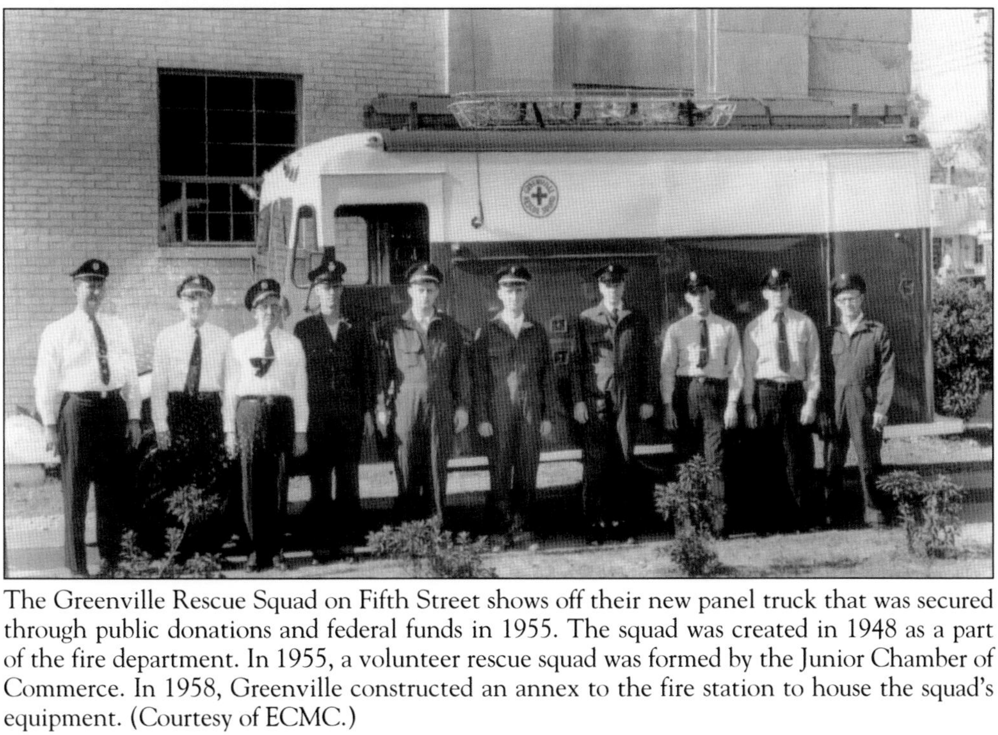

The Greenville Rescue Squad on Fifth Street shows off their new panel truck that was secured through public donations and federal funds in 1955. The squad was created in 1948 as a part of the fire department. In 1955, a volunteer rescue squad was formed by the Junior Chamber of Commerce. In 1958, Greenville constructed an annex to the fire station to house the squad's equipment. (Courtesy of ECMC.)

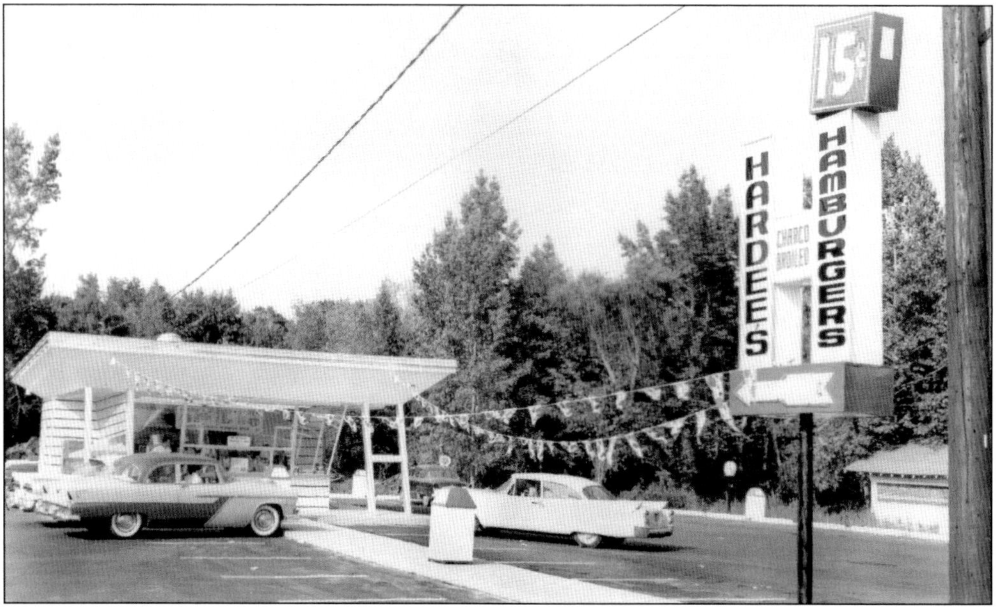

Wilbur Hardee opened the first Hardee's Drive-In Restaurant on Fourteenth Street on September 9, 1960. Two days later, Hurricane Donna hit Greenville. Wilbur Hardee sold off his Hardee's Restaurant to others who created Hardee's Food Systems in Rocky Mount and franchised it across the country. The building was enclosed in 1965 and later became Wilbur's Family Favorites, Chanello's Pizza and Spaghetti House, and finally Med-Center of Eastern North Carolina. The building was torn down in December 1999. (Courtesy of ECMC.)

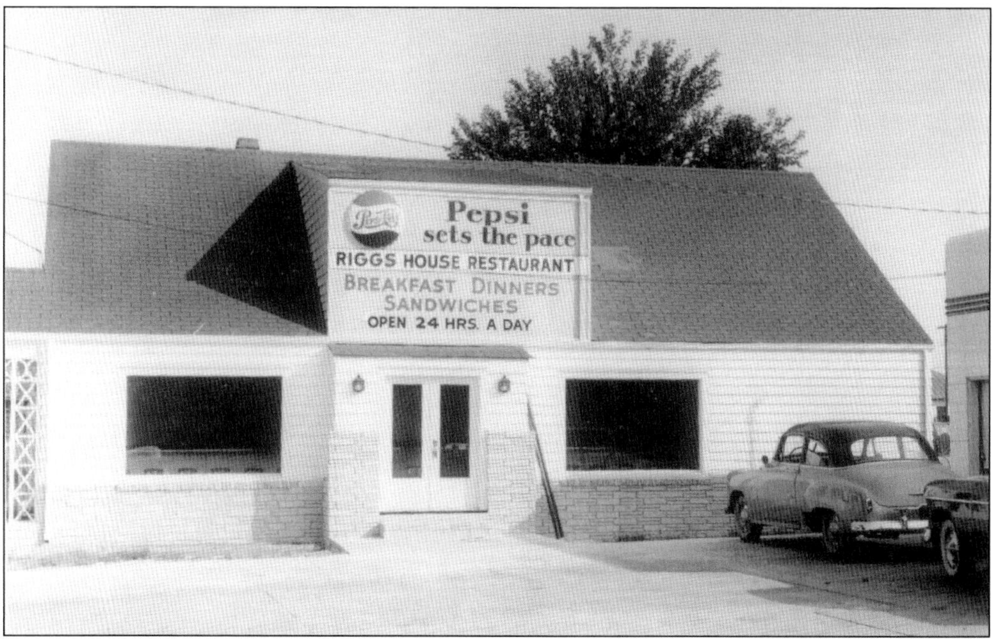

The Riggs House Restaurant, owned by James W. Riggs, was a popular all-night eatery located at 1201 Dickinson Avenue. It opened in August 1958, employed 13 people, and served omelets, a "new thing" in Greenville. The restaurant closed in the mid-1980s and was torn down in June 1987. (Courtesy of ECMC.)

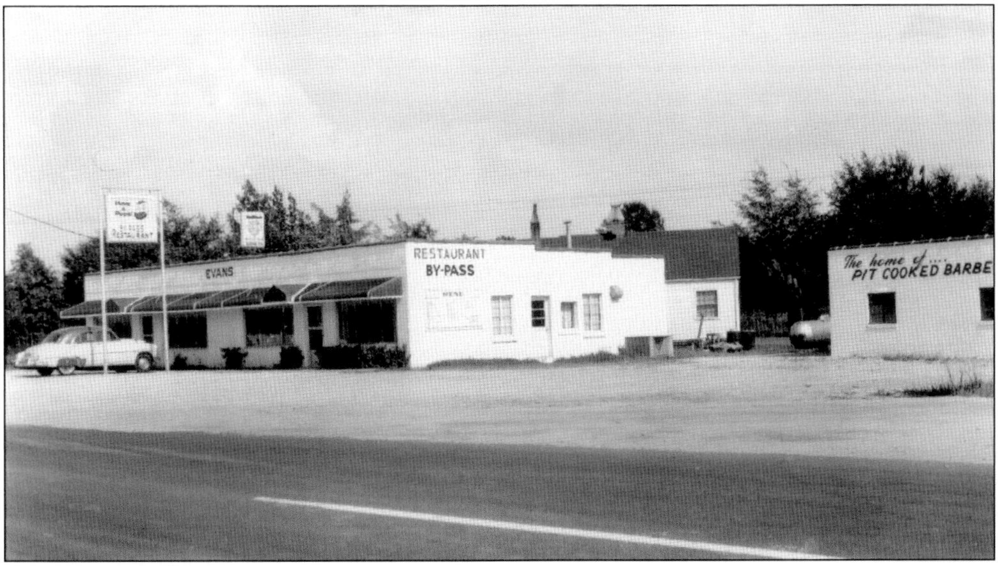

The Bypass Restaurant, located on Greenville Boulevard at Evans Street, opened in September 1960 in a building formerly located across from what is now Circuit City. It was operated by L.C. Smith and J.C. Evans and featured barbecue, barbecued chicken, pork, and steaks of all kinds. (Courtesy of ECMC.)

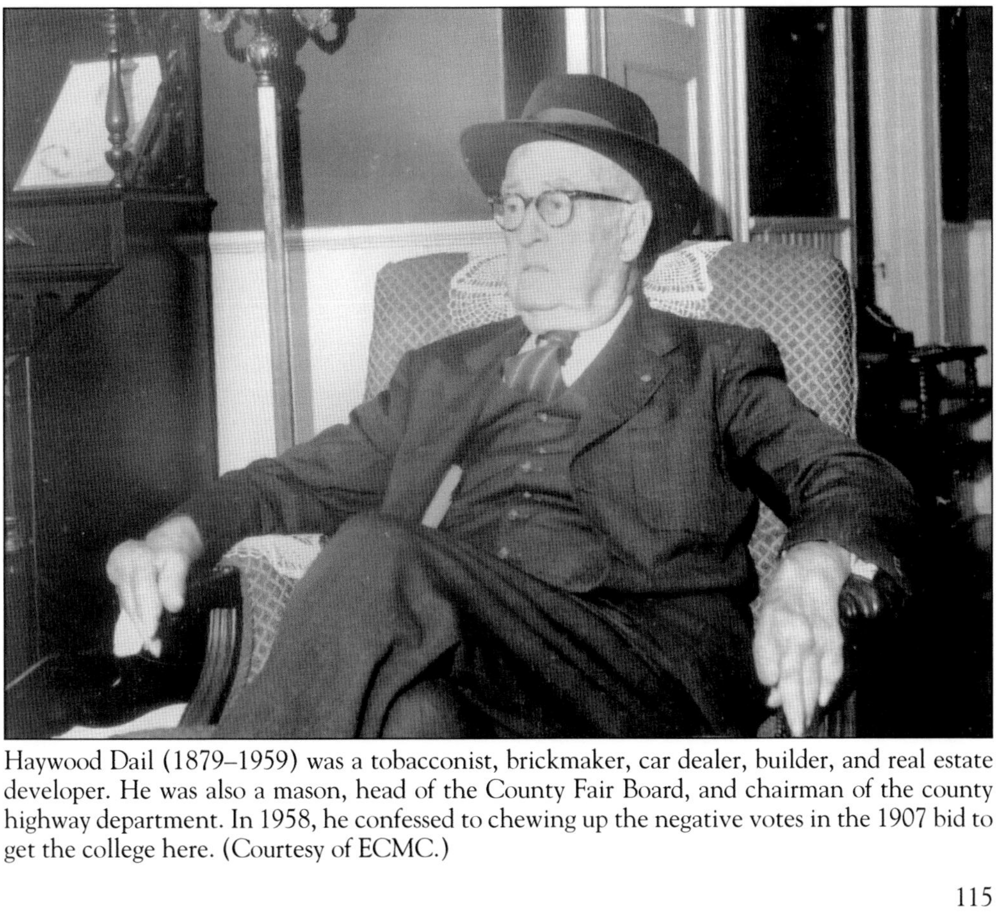

Haywood Dail (1879–1959) was a tobacconist, brickmaker, car dealer, builder, and real estate developer. He was also a mason, head of the County Fair Board, and chairman of the county highway department. In 1958, he confessed to chewing up the negative votes in the 1907 bid to get the college here. (Courtesy of ECMC.)

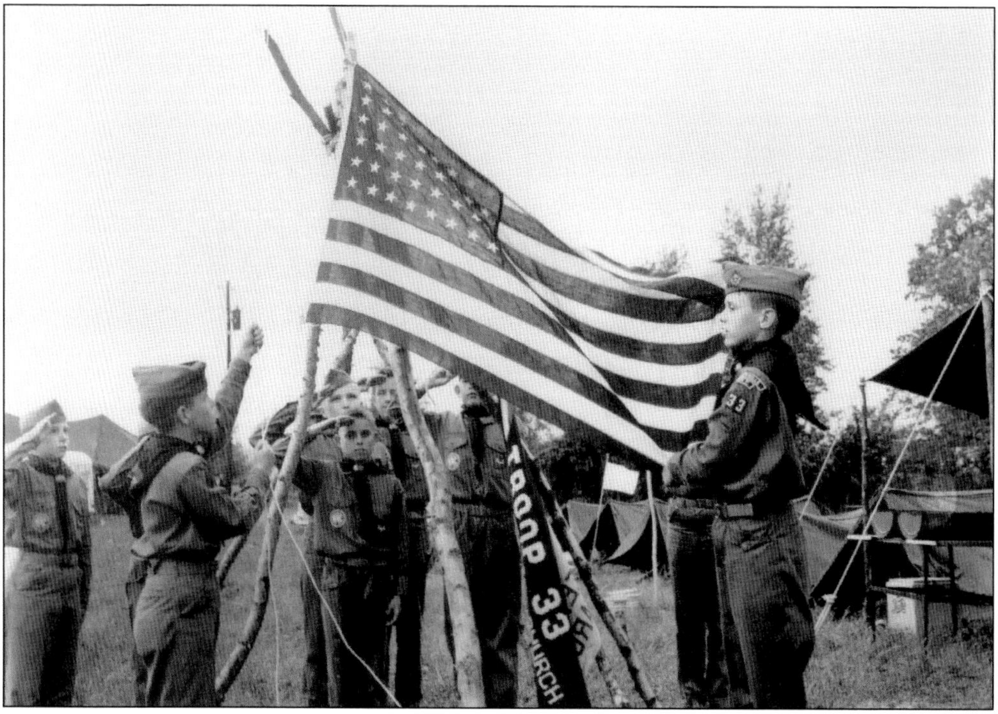

This flag raising took place at the Boy Scouts Annual Camporee near Greenville in 1958. Scouts Charles Boyd and Charles M. Vincent of Troup 33 raise the American Flag as other members of the troop salute. (Courtesy of ECMC.)

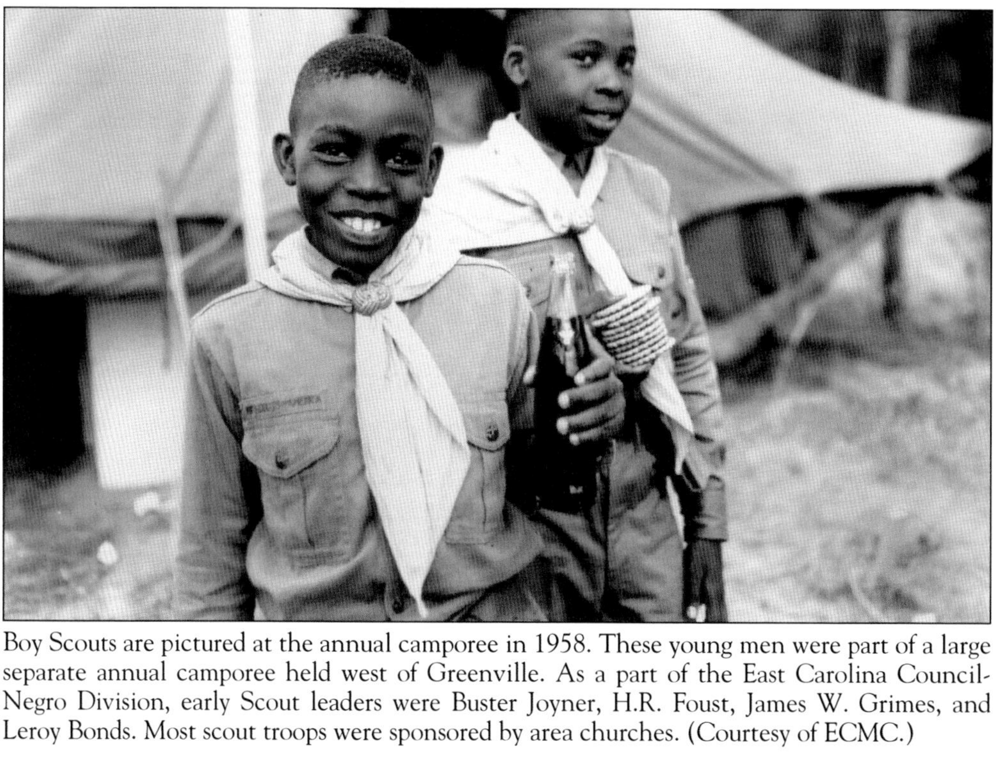

Boy Scouts are pictured at the annual camporee in 1958. These young men were part of a large separate annual camporee held west of Greenville. As a part of the East Carolina Council-Negro Division, early Scout leaders were Buster Joyner, H.R. Foust, James W. Grimes, and Leroy Bonds. Most scout troops were sponsored by area churches. (Courtesy of ECMC.)

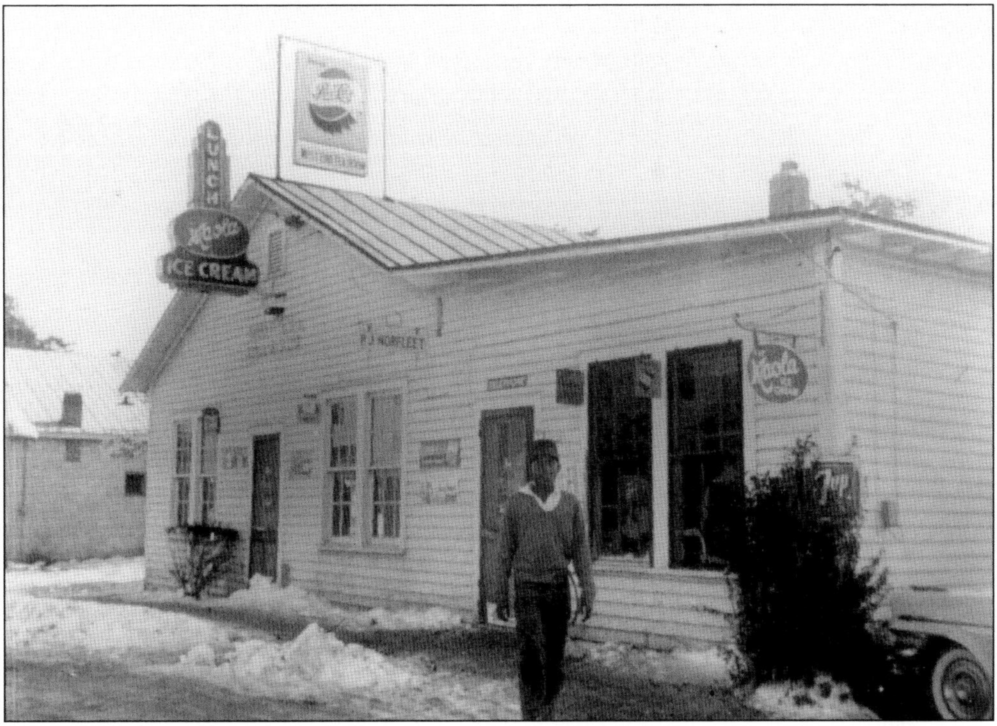

The West End Tea Room on West Fifth Street opened about 1944 by Pasico J. Norfleet as a lunchroom and restaurant. He operated it until about 1971, before it was taken over by his son Roscoe C. Norfleet (owner of Fleetway Cleaners), who closed the restaurant and started a social club known as the Cavalier Club. (Courtesy of Alex Albright.)

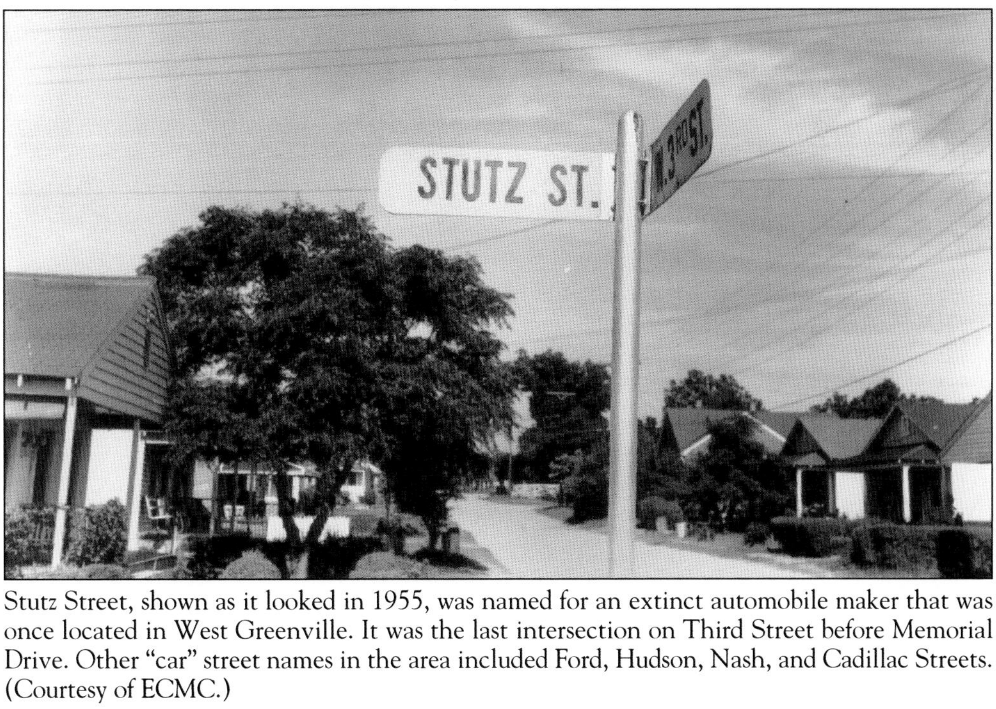

Stutz Street, shown as it looked in 1955, was named for an extinct automobile maker that was once located in West Greenville. It was the last intersection on Third Street before Memorial Drive. Other "car" street names in the area included Ford, Hudson, Nash, and Cadillac Streets. (Courtesy of ECMC.)

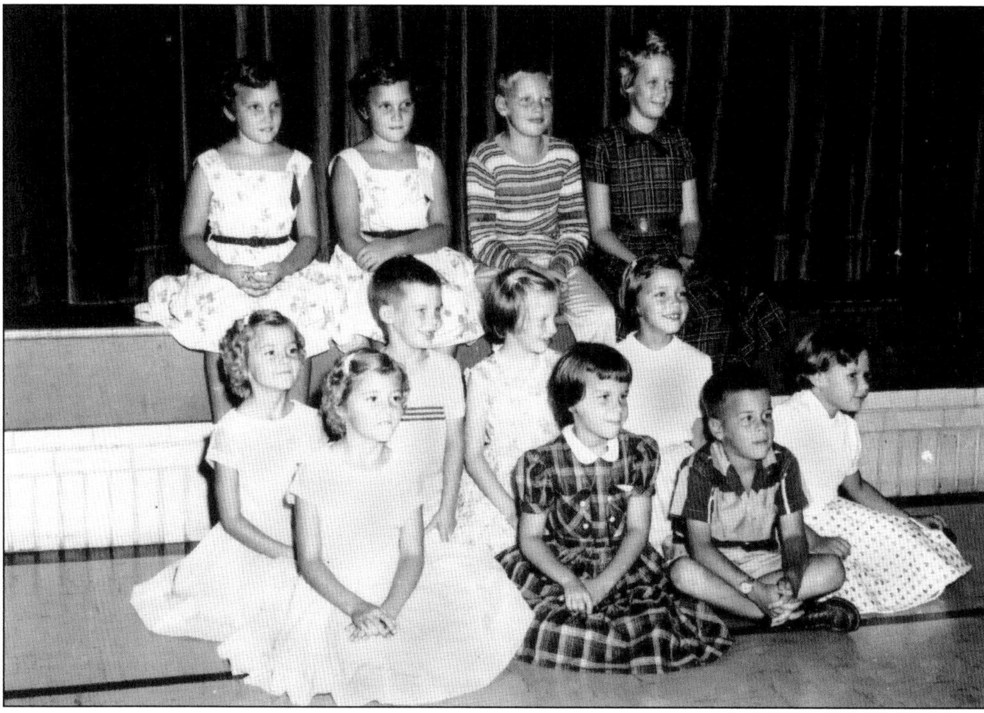

The Elmhurst School twins in 1957 included the following: (top) Carol and Ann Waldrop, daughters of H.T. Waldrop; and Eliza and Johnny Nobles, children of J.E. Nobles; (middle) Mary Anne and Cecil Bilbro, children of W.T. Bilbro; and Barbara and Ann Hardee, daughters of Mrs. Anne Lee Hardee; (bottom) Elaine and Jane Whichard, daughters of W.H. Whichard; and Susan and Edwin Hice, twins of J.D. Hice. (Courtesy of ECMC.)

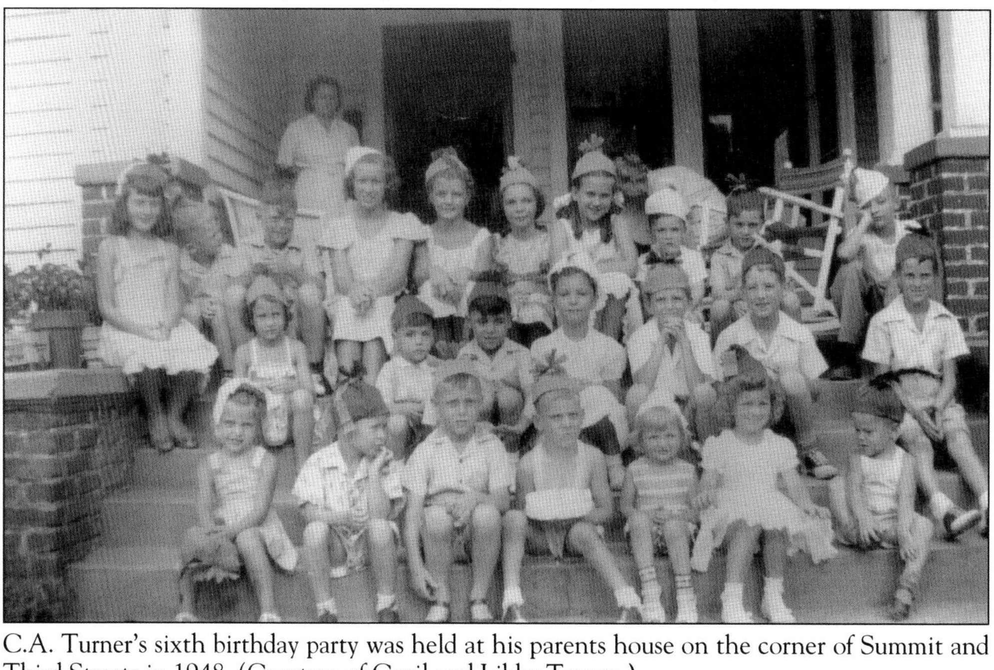

C.A. Turner's sixth birthday party was held at his parents house on the corner of Summit and Third Streets in 1948. (Courtesy of Cecil and Libby Turner.)

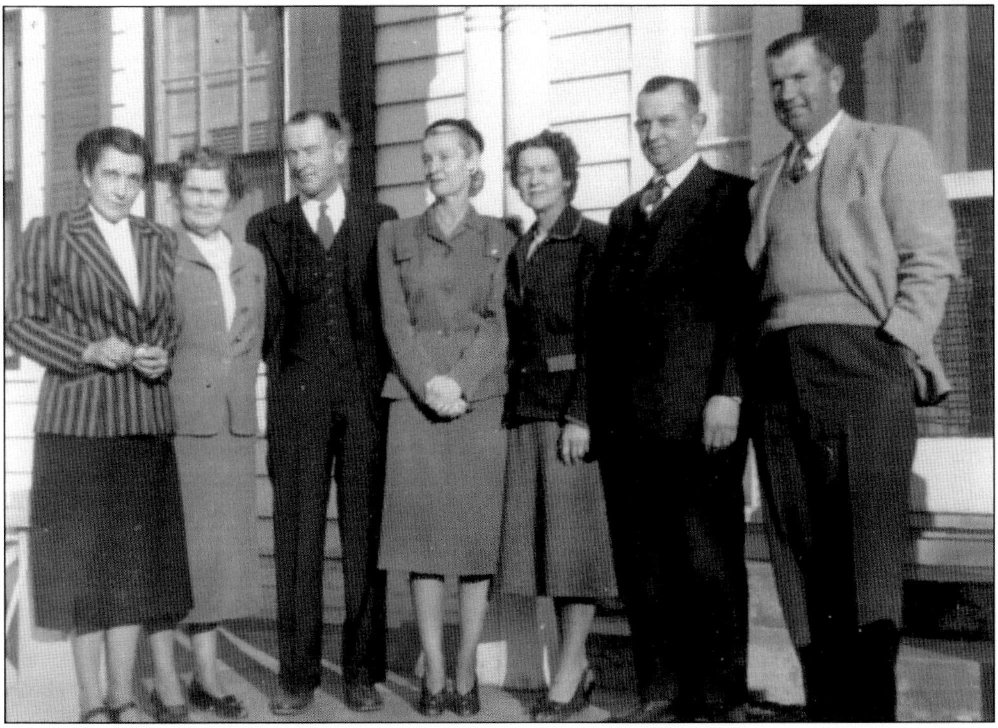

The indomitable King family in 1951, from left to right, are Mattie Moye Gaylord, Amine Moye Galbreath, Richard Warren King Jr., Nancy Elizabeth Hannah, Virginia Dare Perkins, Howard Holton King, and Charles Merrimon King. (Courtesy of Mrs. Mattie Moye King Bridgers.)

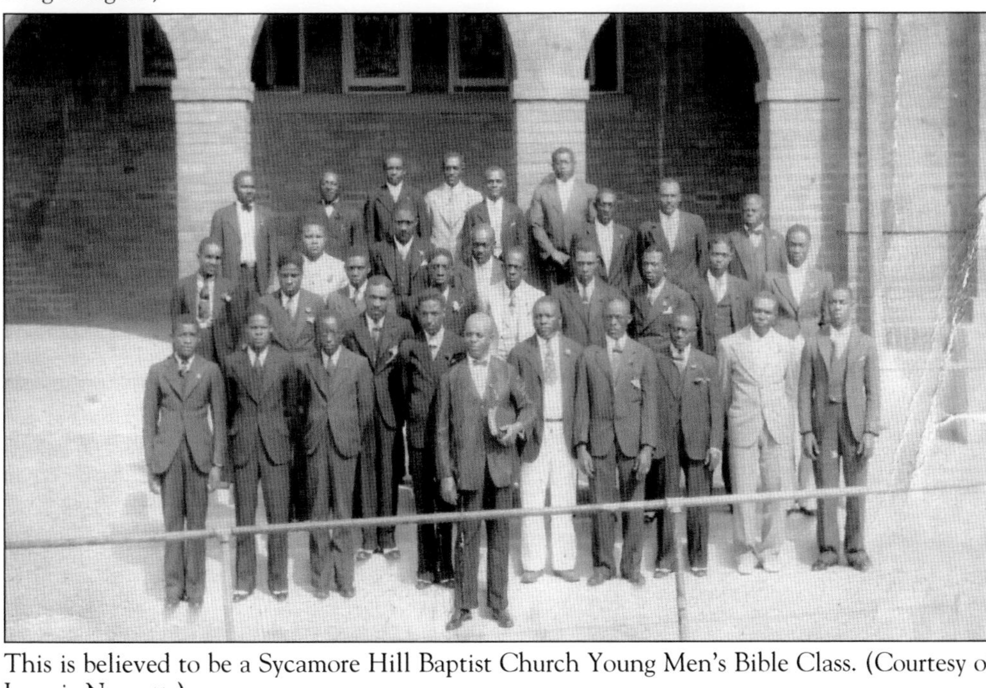

This is believed to be a Sycamore Hill Baptist Church Young Men's Bible Class. (Courtesy of Lonnie Norcott.)

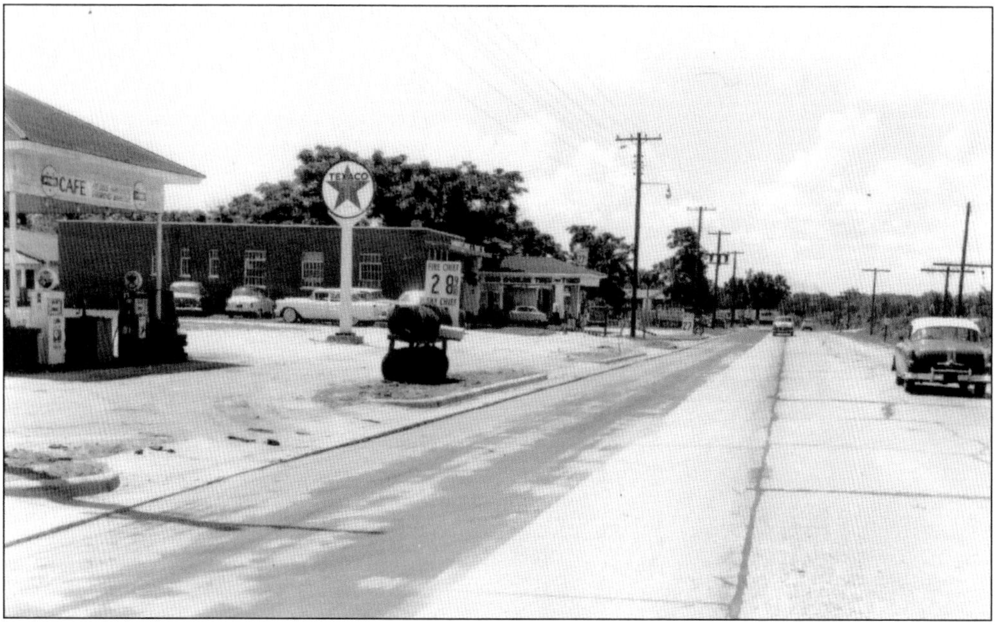

This is a view of North Greene Street looking south in 1955. (Courtesy of ECMC.)

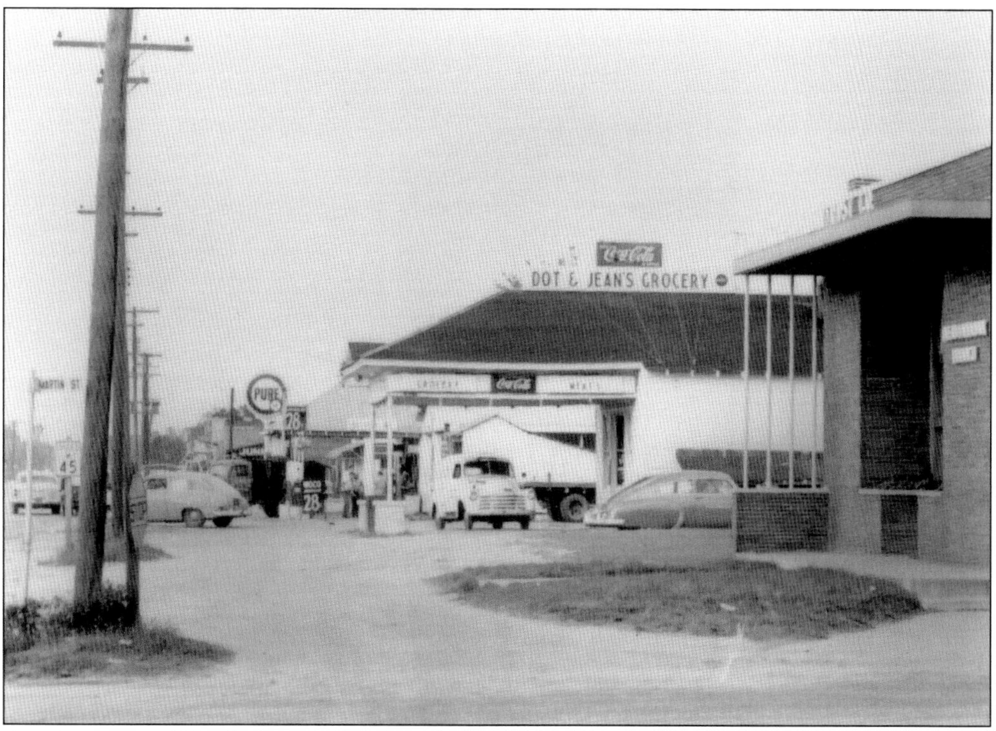

Another view of North Greene Street looks north in 1955. (Courtesy of ECMC.)

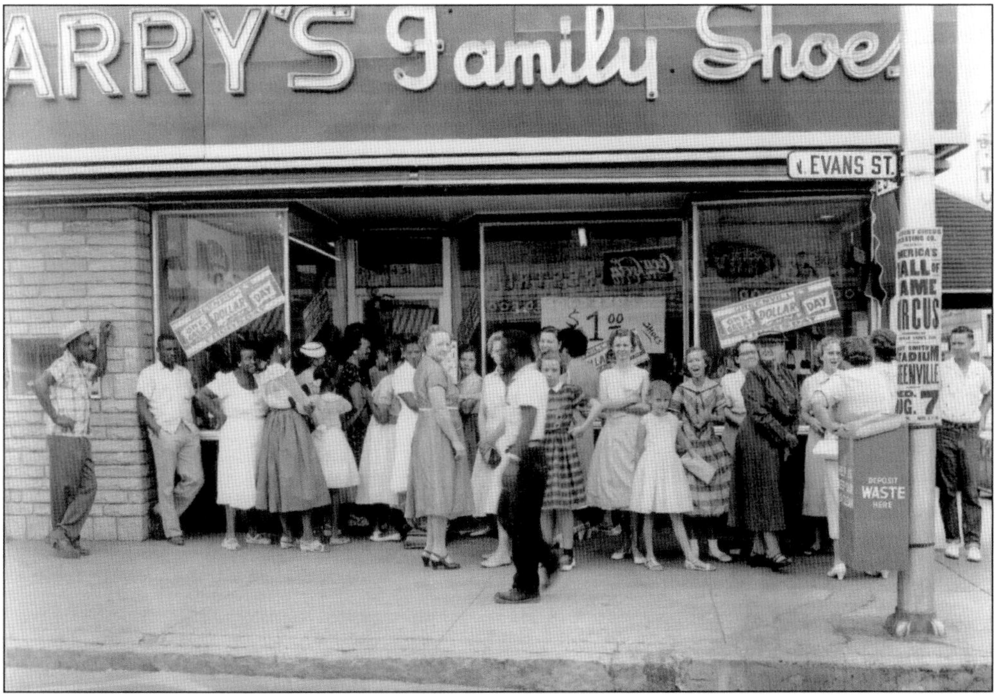

A "Dollar Day" crowd gathers in front of Larry Shoes at 431 Evans Street in 1957. Larry's Shoes was opened in 1955 by Larry L. Averette. It burned down in 1968 and was rebuilt in 1969. In 1964, Larry's offered a free Beatles record with every purchase. (Courtesy of ECMC.)

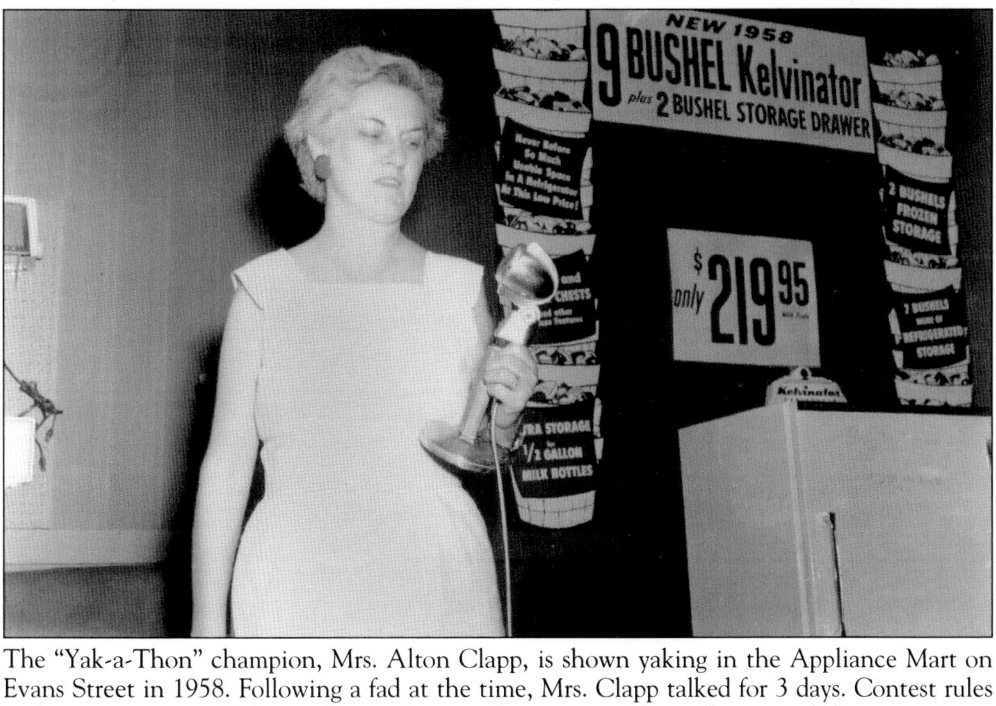

The "Yak-a-Thon" champion, Mrs. Alton Clapp, is shown yaking in the Appliance Mart on Evans Street in 1958. Following a fad at the time, Mrs. Clapp talked for 3 days. Contest rules said participants could do anything as long as they continued to talk, even while eating. Prizes included a refrigerator, television, Hi-Fi, radio, and wrist-watch. (Courtesy of ECMC.)

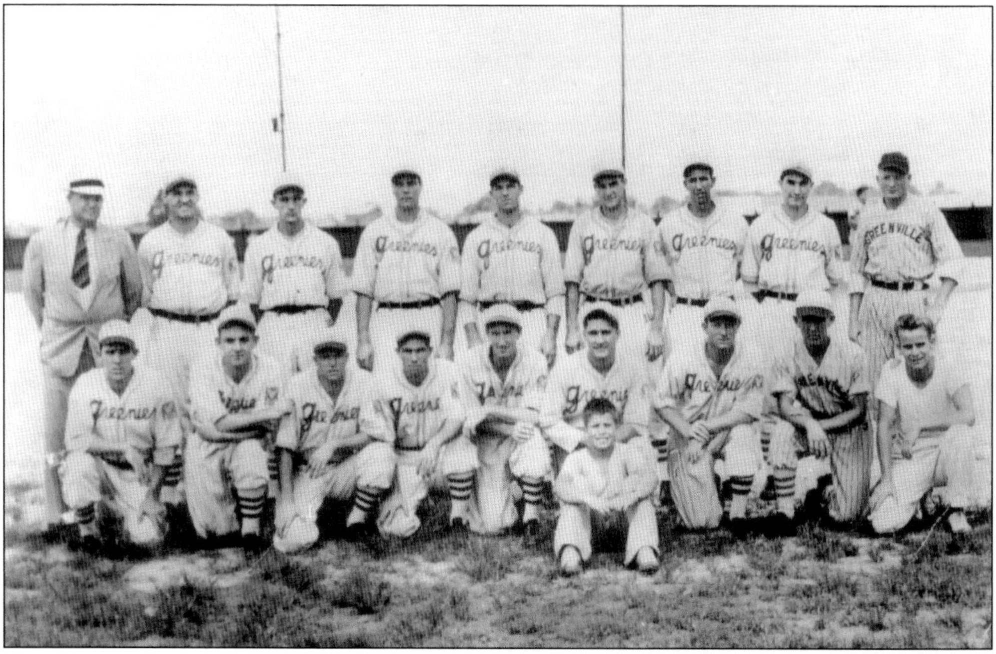

The Greenville Greenies were members of the Coastal Plains League. They were formed in 1934 as a semi-pro baseball club and went to professional baseball in 1937. They disbanded shortly after World War II began, but started again in 1945. They played ball in Guy Smith Stadium, which was built with WPA money in 1939. (Courtesy of ECMC.)

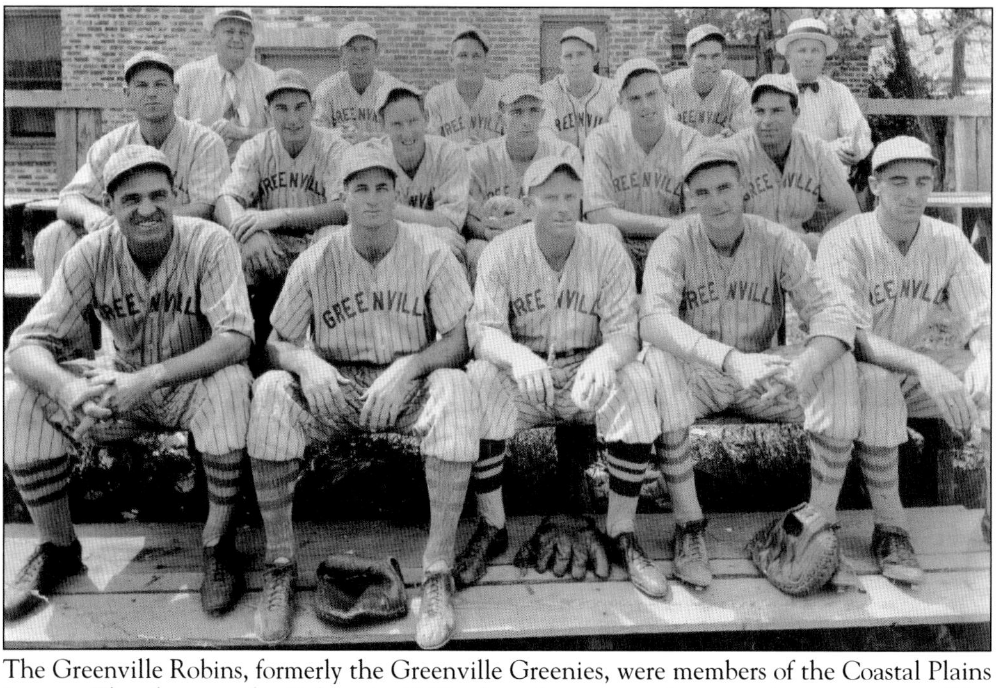

The Greenville Robins, formerly the Greenville Greenies, were members of the Coastal Plains League. They became the Robins in 1950 when they were taken over by new owners. The Robins stayed in a house on West Fifth Street called "Buckingham Palace," an ECTC student and servicemen's home that was run by Mrs. John Horne. (Courtesy of ECMC.)

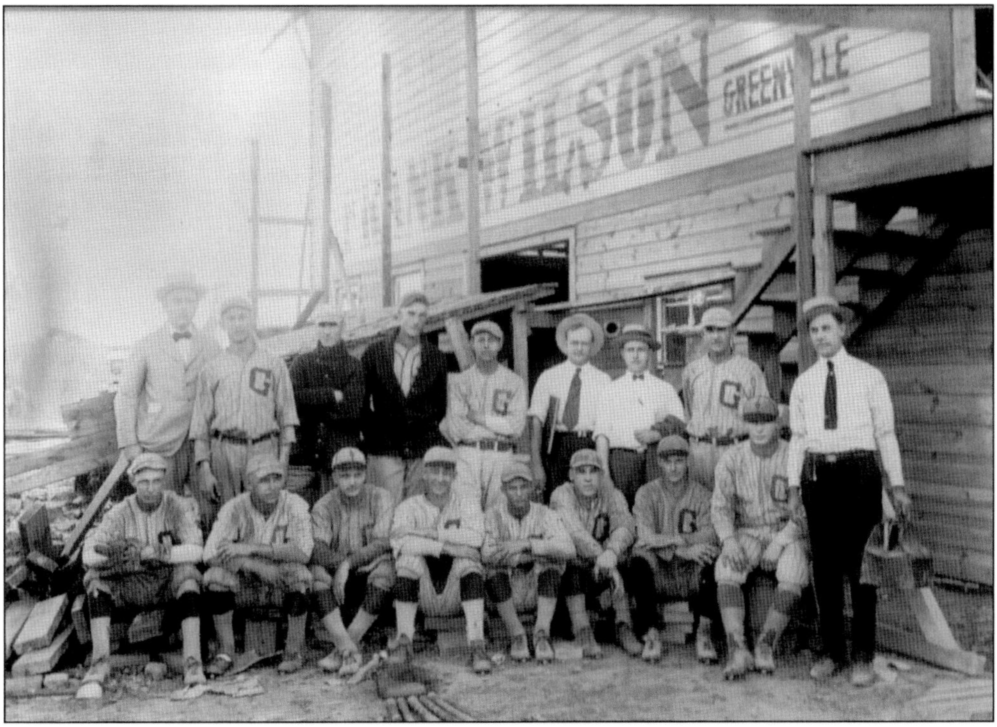

Members of the Greenville Tobacconists, later called the Greenies, pause to be photographed in the 1920s at the old fair grounds (now Guy Smith Stadium). Evangelist Billy Sunday threw out the first ball at the opening game of 1928. (Courtesy of ECMC.)

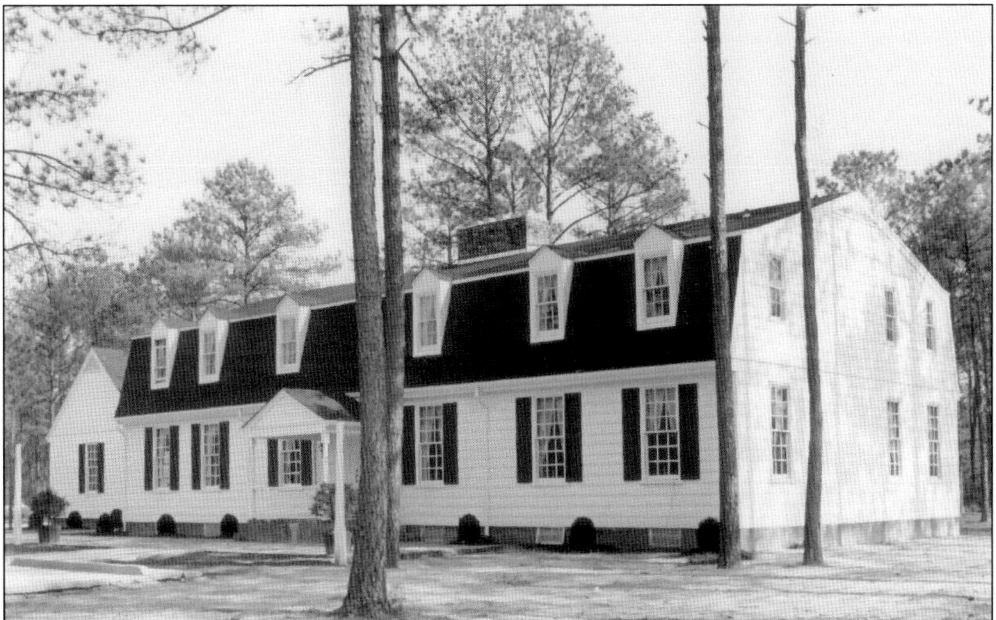

The Candlewick Inn was built in the Williamsburg style in 1964 by Don and Helen Whitehurst. Located four miles from Memorial Drive on Stantonsburg Road, it was destroyed by fire around 1976. (Courtesy of ECMC.)

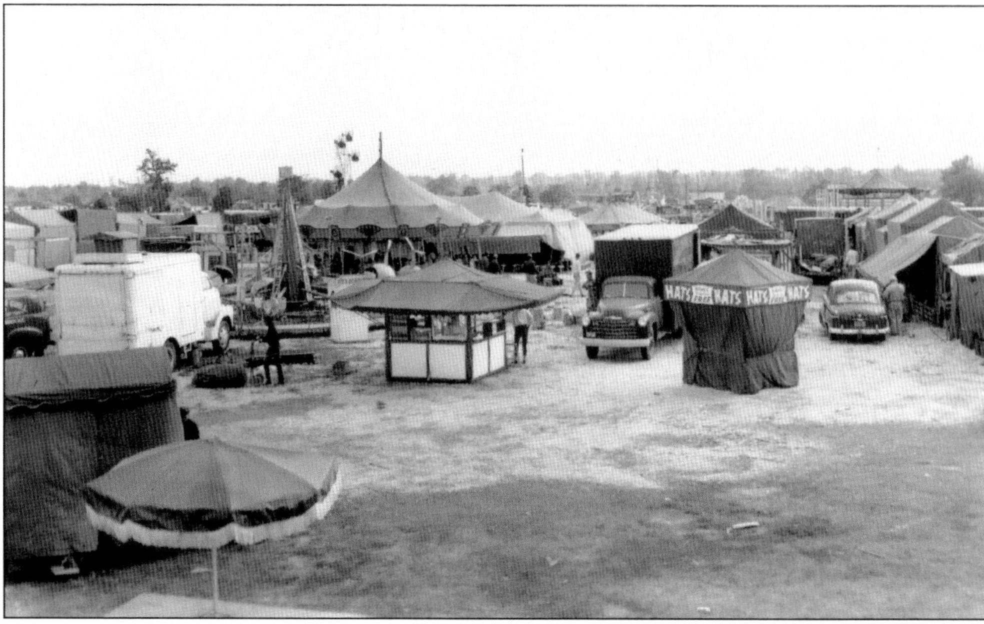

The Pitt County Fair is pictured in 1958. The first fairgrounds were at Guy Smith Stadium, then moved to West Fifth Street by the hospital, then moved to the airport, and in 1978 moved to its present site. (Courtesy of ECMC.)

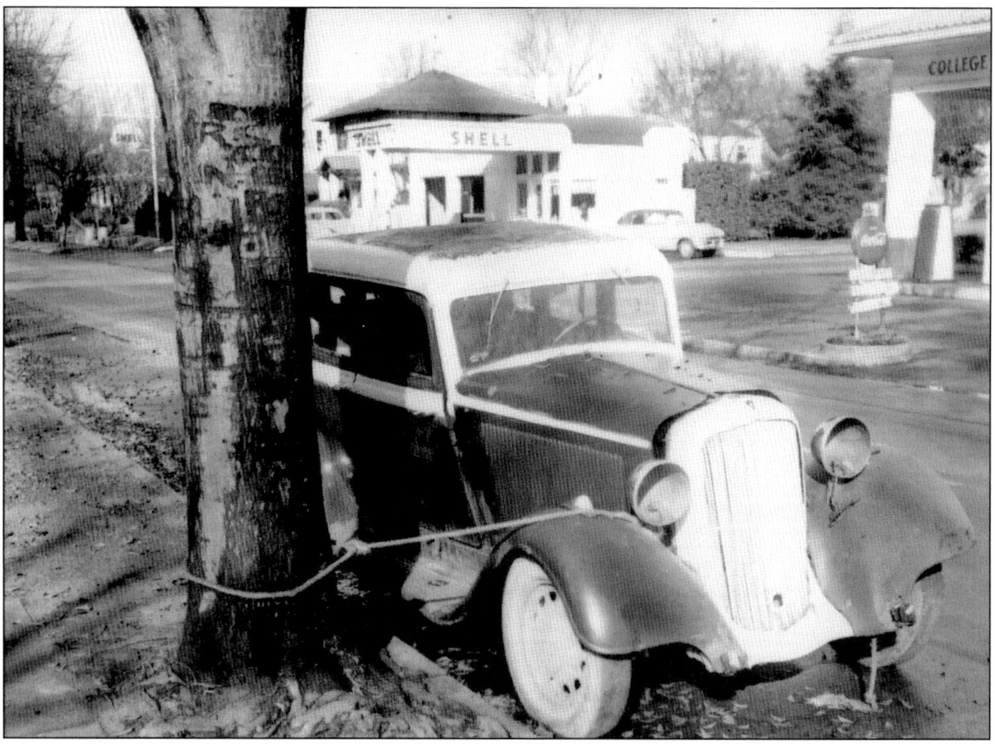

An old car is secured to a tree at Fifth and Harding Streets in 1955. In the background on the left is Clem Garner's Shell Station and on right is the College Esso Station. (Courtesy of ECMC.)

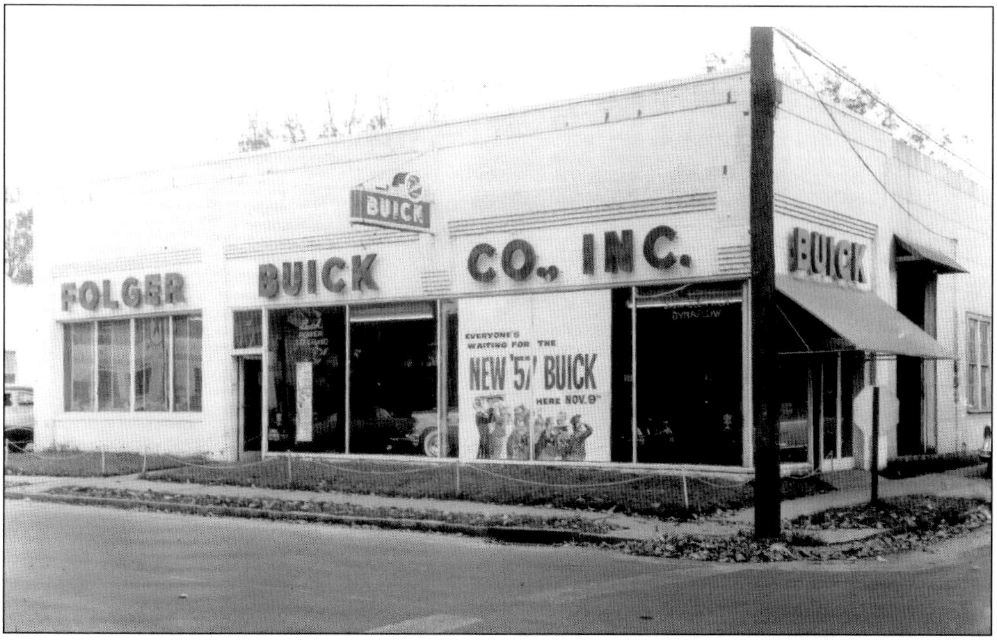

The Folger Buick Company at 117 West Tenth Street was founded in 1936. It was owned by Lee Folger, his wife Eloise Garrett Folger, and son Garrett Folger. Lee Folger was a veteran of World War II. (Courtesy of ECMC.)

Charles M. Eppes and Lawrence Norcott stand in front of the Norcott home on Third Street. Charles Montgomery Eppes (1857–1942) was a native of Halifax County, North Carolina, and came to Greenville in 1903. He served as principal of the Colored Graded and Industrial High School and other schools. Eppes did much to raise the condition in which black people lived in Greenville, especially during the Depression. He was a Mason and a member of York A.M.E. Zion Church; he served on numerous state councils for race and education. A moving spirit in the community, Eppes was also an advocate of industrial education and racial goodwill. (Courtesy of Lonnie Norcott.)

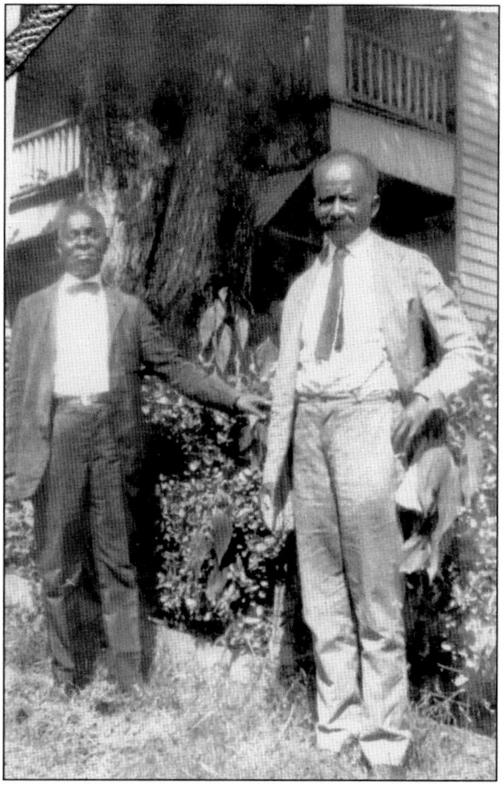

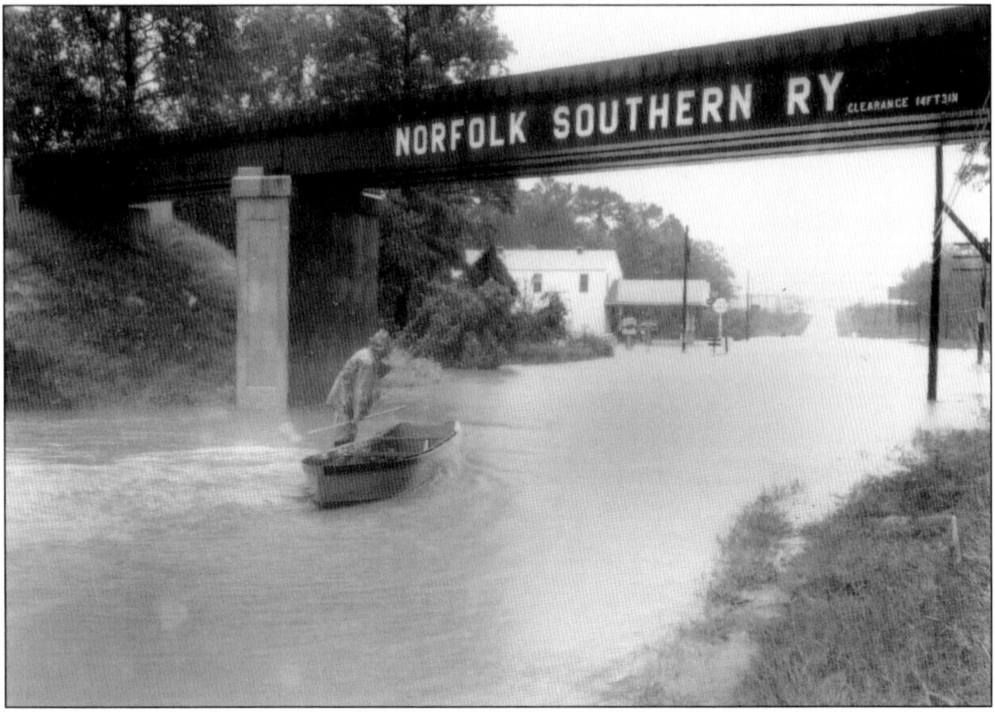

This view shows Green Mill Run flooding Charles Boulevard at the railroad overpass in 1955. The building in the back was the former Wilson's Grocery store, which later became Huey's Seafood Restaurant. (Courtesy of ECMC.)

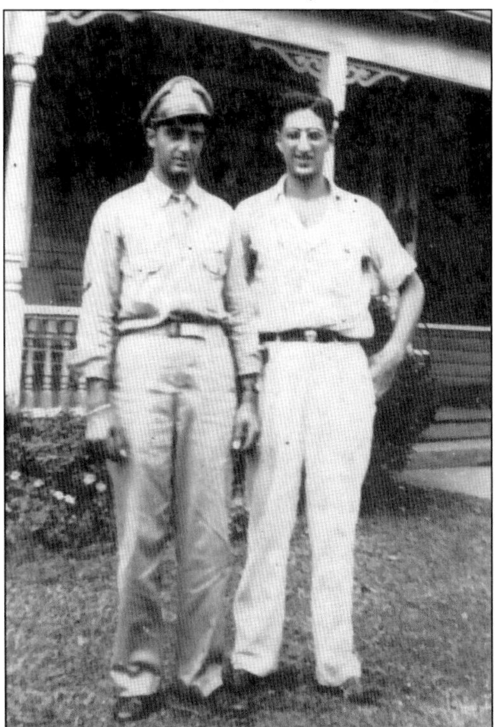

Joe Saad and his brother George Saad stand in front of their parents house on Chestnut Street. Both were veterans of World War II. Joe ran a shoe repair shop on Grand Avenue and elsewhere. George owned the Carolina Grill on Dickinson Avenue and was the Pitt County director for ALSAC, which provided support for St. Jude Children's Research Hospital. (Courtesy of George Saad.)

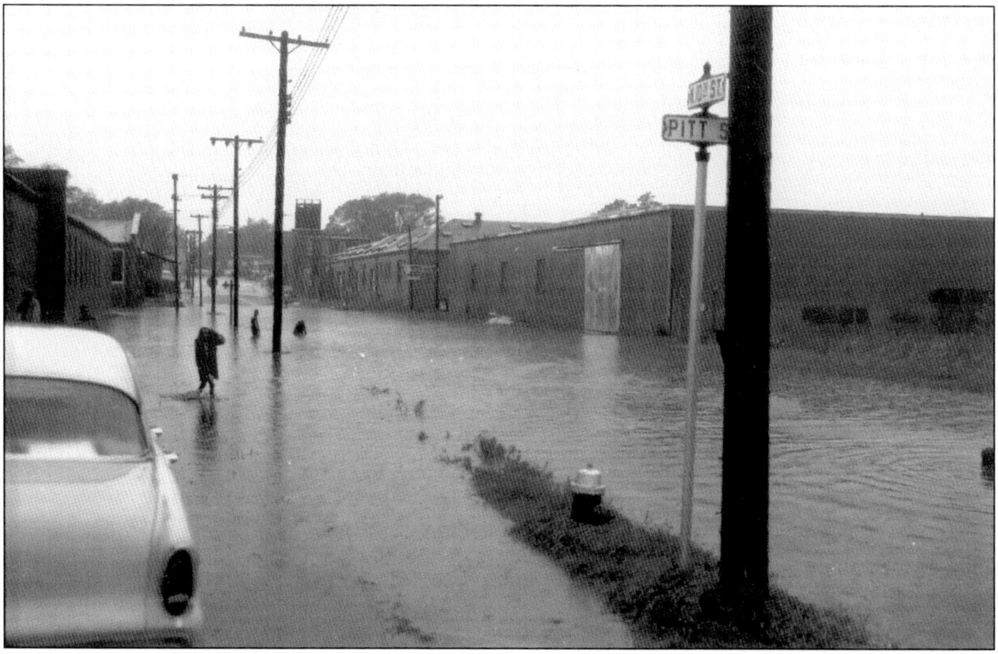

This photograph of Tenth Street looking west from Pitt Street shows flooding in the 1960s. (Courtesy of ECMC.)

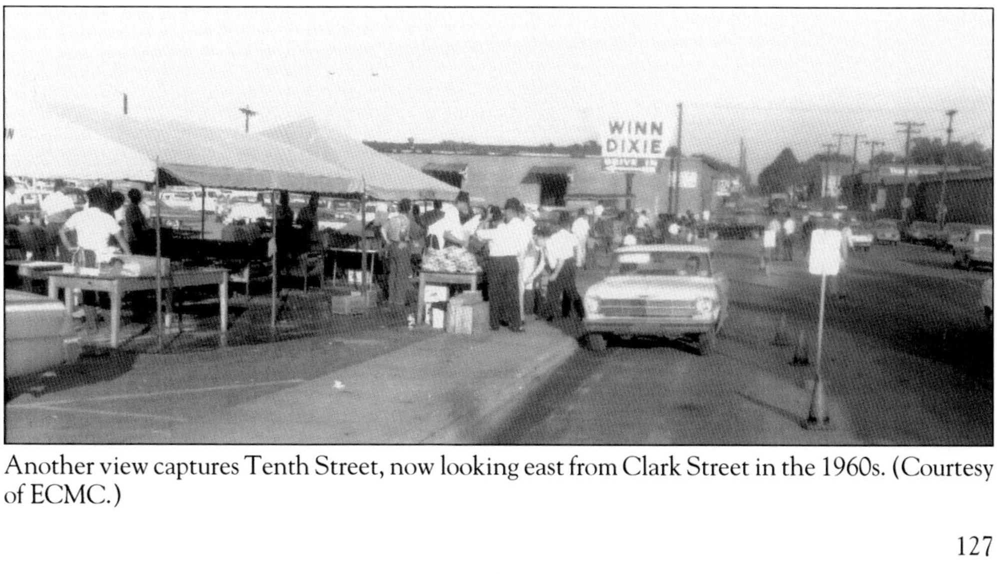

Another view captures Tenth Street, now looking east from Clark Street in the 1960s. (Courtesy of ECMC.)

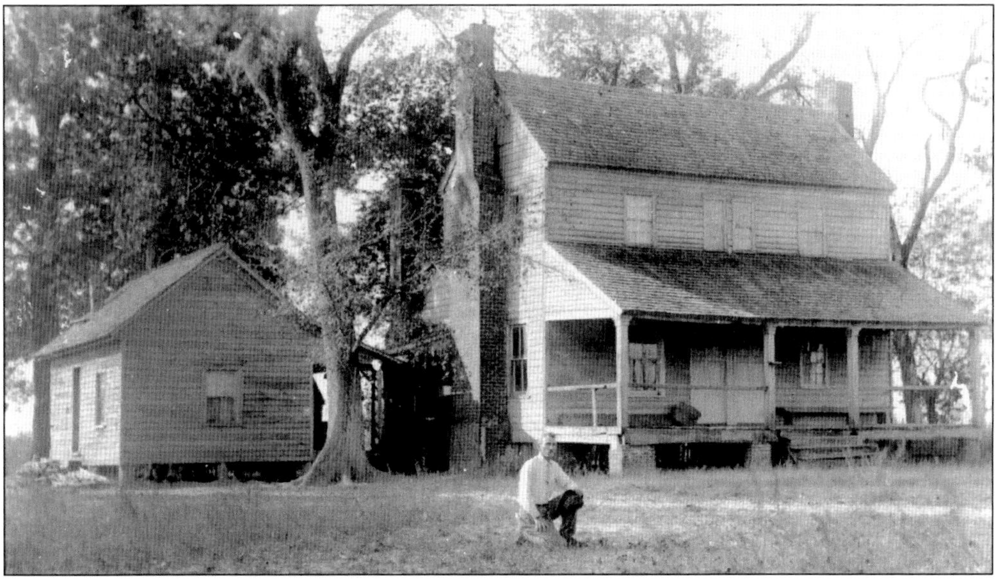

The Amos Evans Plantation was located on Hooker Road and is shown as it appeared in the 1920s. Amos Evans (1823–1888) owned a large tract of land near Greenville and the family cemetery now sits beside the football field at J.H. Rose High School. (Courtesy of Jimmy and Bonnie Evans.)

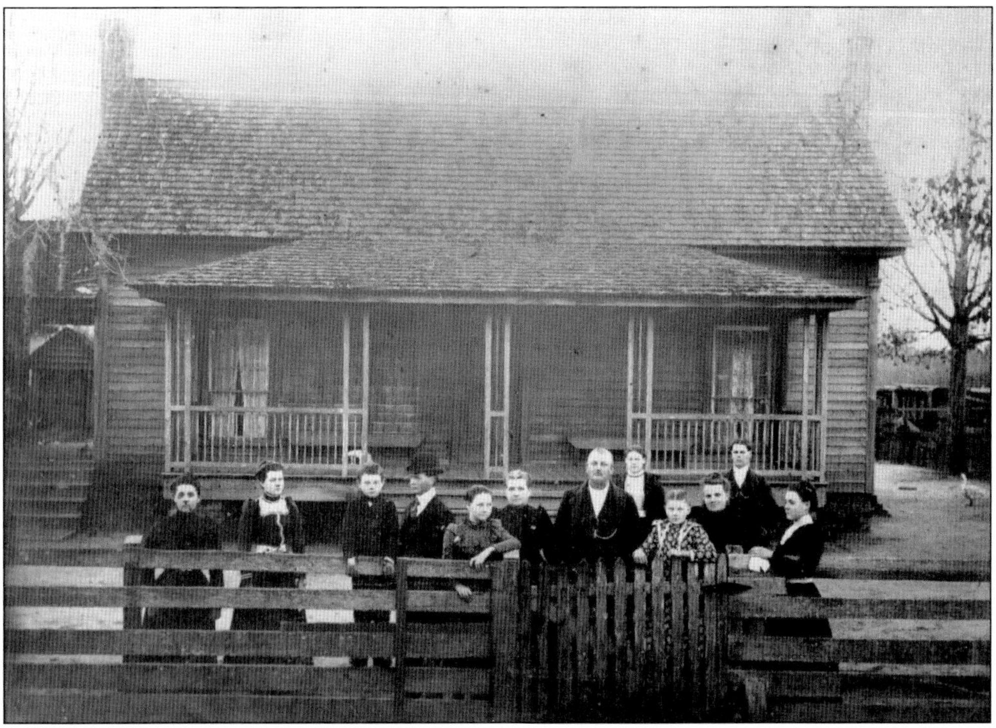

The Noah Forbes Jr. home and family are shown as they appeared in 1900. Now the site of Carolina East Convenience Center, the house was moved to the Allen Road by John F. Moye. Family members pictured, from left to right, are Betty, Bertha, Walter, Edward, Pearl, Martha A.E., Noah, Nora, Neva, Nannie, C. Heber, and Clara Forbes. (Courtesy of John F. Moye.)